FIVE DIALOGUES

(Euthyphro, Apology, Crito, Meno, and Phaedo)

By PLATO

Translated by BENJAMIN JOWETT

Five Dialogues (Euthyphro, Apology, Crito, Meno, and Phaedo)
By Plato
Translated by Benjamin Jowett

Print ISBN 13: 978-1-4209-5162-2
eBook ISBN 13: 978-1-4209-5163-9

Cover Image: A detail of "The Death of Socrates" by Jacques-Louis David, c. 1787.

Please visit *www.digireads.com*

CONTENTS

Euthyphro

INTRODUCTION 5
EUTHYPHRO 9

Apology

INTRODUCTION 24
APOLOGY 33

Crito

INTRODUCTION 53
CRITO 56

Meno

INTRODUCTION 66
ON THE IDEAS OF PLATO 74
MENO 84

Phaedo

INTRODUCTION 114
PHAEDO 143

Euthyphro

INTRODUCTION

In the Meno, Anytus had parted from Socrates with the significant words: 'That in any city, and particularly in the city of Athens, it is easier to do men harm than to do them good;' and Socrates was anticipating another opportunity of talking with him. In the Euthyphro, Socrates is awaiting his trial for impiety. But before the trial begins, Plato would like to put the world on their trial, and convince them of ignorance in that very matter touching which Socrates is accused. An incident which may perhaps really have occurred in the family of Euthyphro, a learned Athenian diviner and soothsayer, furnishes the occasion of the discussion.

This Euthyphro and Socrates are represented as meeting in the porch of the King Archon. (Compare Theaet.) Both have legal business in hand. Socrates is defendant in a suit for impiety which Meletus has brought against him (it is remarked by the way that he is not a likely man himself to have brought a suit against another); and Euthyphro too is plaintiff in an action for murder, which he has brought against his own father. The latter has originated in the following manner:—A poor dependant of the family had slain one of their domestic slaves in Naxos. The guilty person was bound and thrown into a ditch by the command of Euthyphro's father, who sent to the interpreters of religion at Athens to ask what should be done with him. Before the messenger came back the criminal had died from hunger and exposure.

This is the origin of the charge of murder which Euthyphro brings against his father. Socrates is confident that before he could have undertaken the responsibility of such a prosecution, he must have been perfectly informed of the nature of piety and impiety; and as he is going to be tried for impiety himself, he thinks that he cannot do better than learn of Euthyphro (who will be admitted by everybody, including the judges, to be an unimpeachable authority) what piety is, and what is impiety. What then is piety?

Euthyphro, who, in the abundance of his knowledge, is very willing to undertake all the responsibility, replies: That piety is doing as I do, prosecuting your father (if he is guilty) on a charge of murder; doing as the gods do—as Zeus did to Cronos, and Cronos to Uranus.

Socrates has a dislike to these tales of mythology, and he fancies that this dislike of his may be the reason why he is charged with impiety. 'Are they really true?' 'Yes, they are;' and Euthyphro will gladly tell Socrates some more of them. But Socrates would like first of all to have a more satisfactory answer to the question, 'What is piety?'

'Doing as I do, charging a father with murder,' may be a single instance of piety, but can hardly be regarded as a general definition.

Euthyphro replies, that 'Piety is what is dear to the gods, and impiety is what is not dear to them.' But may there not be differences of opinion, as among men, so also among the gods? Especially, about good and evil, which have no fixed rule; and these are precisely the sort of differences which give rise to quarrels. And therefore what may be dear to one god may not be dear to another, and the same action may be both pious and impious; e.g. your chastisement of your father, Euthyphro, may be dear or pleasing to Zeus (who inflicted a similar chastisement on his own father), but not equally pleasing to Cronos or Uranus (who suffered at the hands of their sons).

Euthyphro answers that there is no difference of opinion, either among gods or men, as to the propriety of punishing a murderer. Yes, rejoins Socrates, when they know him to be a murderer; but you are assuming the point at issue. If all the circumstances of the case are considered, are you able to show that your father was guilty of murder, or that all the gods are agreed in approving of our prosecution of him? And must you not allow that what is hated by one god may be liked by another? Waiving this last, however, Socrates proposes to amend the definition, and say that 'what all the gods love is pious, and what they all hate is impious.' To this Euthyphro agrees.

Socrates proceeds to analyze the new form of the definition. He shows that in other cases the act precedes the state; e.g. the act of being carried, loved, etc. precedes the state of being carried, loved, etc., and therefore that which is dear to the gods is dear to the gods because it is first loved of them, not loved of them because it is dear to them. But the pious or holy is loved by the gods because it is pious or holy, which is equivalent to saying, that it is loved by them because it is dear to them. Here then appears to be a contradiction,—Euthyphro has been giving an attribute or accident of piety only, and not the essence. Euthyphro acknowledges himself that his explanations seem to walk away or go round in a circle, like the moving figures of Daedalus, the ancestor of Socrates, who has communicated his art to his descendants.

Socrates, who is desirous of stimulating the indolent intelligence of Euthyphro, raises the question in another manner: 'Is all the pious just?' 'Yes.' 'Is all the just pious?' 'No.' 'Then what part of justice is piety?' Euthyphro replies that piety is that part of justice which 'attends' to the gods, as there is another part of justice which 'attends' to men. But what is the meaning of 'attending' to the gods? The word 'attending,' when applied to dogs, horses, and men, implies that in some way they are made better. But how do pious or holy acts make the gods any better? Euthyphro explains that he means by pious acts, acts of service or ministration. Yes; but the ministrations of the husbandman, the physician, and the builder have an end. To what end do we serve the gods, and what do we help them to accomplish? Euthyphro replies, that all these difficult questions cannot be resolved in a short time; and he would rather say simply that piety is knowing how to please the gods in word and deed, by prayers and sacrifices. In other words, says Socrates, piety is 'a science of asking and giving'— asking what we want and giving what they want; in short, a mode of doing business between gods and men. But although they are the givers of all good, how can we give them any good in return? 'Nay, but we give them honour.' Then we give them not what is beneficial, but what is pleasing or dear to them; and this is the point which has been already disproved.

Socrates, although weary of the subterfuges and evasions of Euthyphro, remains unshaken in his conviction that he must know the nature of piety, or he would never have prosecuted his old father. He is still hoping that he will condescend to instruct him. But Euthyphro is in a hurry and cannot stay. And Socrates' last hope of knowing the nature of piety before he is prosecuted for impiety has disappeared. As in the Euthydemus the irony is carried on to the end.

The Euthyphro is manifestly designed to contrast the real nature of piety and impiety with the popular conceptions of them. But when the popular conceptions of them have been overthrown, Socrates does not offer any definition of his own: as in the Laches and Lysis, he prepares the way for an answer to the question which he has raised; but true to his own character, refuses to answer himself.

Euthyphro is a religionist, and is elsewhere spoken of, if he be the same person, as the author of a philosophy of names, by whose 'prancing steeds' Socrates in the Cratylus is carried away. He has the conceit and self-confidence of a Sophist; no doubt that he is right in prosecuting his father has ever entered into his mind. Like a Sophist too, he is incapable either of framing a general definition or of following the course of an argument. His wrong-headedness, one-sidedness, narrowness, positiveness, are characteristic of his priestly office. His failure to apprehend an argument may be compared to a similar defect which is observable in the rhapsode Ion. But he is not a bad man, and he is friendly to Socrates, whose familiar sign he recognizes with interest. Though unable to follow him he is very willing to be led by him, and eagerly catches at any suggestion which saves him from the trouble of thinking. Moreover he is the enemy of Meletus, who, as he says, is availing himself of the popular dislike to innovations in religion in order to injure Socrates; at the same time he is amusingly confident that he has weapons in his own armoury which would be more than a match for him. He is quite sincere in his prosecution of his father, who has accidentally been guilty of homicide, and is not wholly free from blame. To purge away the crime appears to him in the light of a duty, whoever may be the criminal.

Thus begins the contrast between the religion of the letter, or of the narrow and unenlightened conscience, and the higher notion of religion which Socrates vainly endeavours to elicit from him. 'Piety is doing as I do' is the idea of religion which first occurs to him, and to many others who do not say what they think with equal frankness. For men are not easily persuaded that any other religion is better than their own; or that other nations, e.g. the Greeks in the time of Socrates, were equally serious in their religious beliefs and difficulties. The chief difference between us and them is, that they were slowly learning what we are in process of forgetting. Greek mythology hardly admitted of the distinction between accidental homicide and murder: that the pollution of blood was the same in both cases is also the feeling of the Athenian diviner. He had not as yet learned the lesson, which philosophy was teaching, that Homer and Hesiod, if not banished from the state, or whipped out of the assembly, as Heraclitus more rudely proposed, at any rate were not to be appealed to as authorities in religion; and he is ready to defend his conduct by the examples of the gods. These are the very tales which Socrates cannot abide; and his dislike of them, as he suspects, has branded him with the reputation of impiety. Here is one answer to the question, 'Why Socrates was put to death,' suggested by the way. Another is conveyed in the words, 'The Athenians do not care about any man being thought wise until he begins to make other men wise; and then for some reason or other they are angry:' which may be said to be the rule of popular toleration in most other countries, and not at Athens only. In the course of the argument Socrates remarks that the controversial nature of morals and religion arises out of the difficulty of verifying them. There is no measure or standard to which they can be referred.

The next definition, 'Piety is that which is loved of the gods,' is shipwrecked on a refined distinction between the state and the act, corresponding respectively to the adjective (philon) and the participle (philoumenon), or rather perhaps to the participle and the verb (philoumenon and phileitai). The act is prior to the state (as in Aristotle the energeia precedes the dunamis); and the state of being loved is preceded by the act of being loved. But piety or holiness is preceded by the act of being pious, not by the act of being loved; and therefore piety and the state of being loved are different. Through such subtleties of dialectic Socrates is working his way into a deeper region of thought and feeling. He means to say that the words 'loved of the gods' express an attribute only, and not the essence of piety.

Then follows the third and last definition, 'Piety is a part of justice.' Thus far Socrates has proceeded in placing religion on a moral foundation. He is seeking to realize the harmony of religion and morality, which the great poets Aeschylus, Sophocles, and Pindar had unconsciously anticipated, and which is the universal want of all men.

To this the soothsayer adds the ceremonial element, 'attending upon the gods.' When further interrogated by Socrates as to the nature of this 'attention to the gods,' he replies, that piety is an affair of business, a science of giving and asking, and the like. Socrates points out the anthropomorphism of these notions, (compare Symp.; Republic; Politicus.) But when we expect him to go on and show that the true service of the gods is the service of the spirit and the co-operation with them in all things true and good, he stops short; this was a lesson which the soothsayer could not have been made to understand, and which every one must learn for himself.

There seem to be altogether three aims or interests in this little Dialogue: (1) the dialectical development of the idea of piety; (2) the antithesis of true and false religion, which is carried to a certain extent only; (3) the defence of Socrates.

The subtle connection with the Apology and the Crito; the holding back of the conclusion, as in the Charmides, Lysis, Laches, Protagoras, and other Dialogues; the deep insight into the religious world; the dramatic power and play of the two characters; the inimitable irony, are reasons for believing that the Euthyphro is a genuine Platonic writing. The spirit in which the popular representations of mythology are denounced recalls Republic II. The virtue of piety has been already mentioned as one of five in the Protagoras, but is not reckoned among the four cardinal virtues of Republic IV. The figure of Daedalus has occurred in the Meno; that of Proteus in the Euthydemus and Io. The kingly science has already appeared in the Euthydemus, and will reappear in the Republic and Statesman. But neither from these nor any other indications of similarity or difference, and still less from arguments respecting the suitableness of this little work to aid Socrates at the time of his trial or the reverse, can any evidence of the date be obtained.

EUTHYPHRO

PERSONS OF THE DIALOGUE: Socrates, Euthyphro.

SCENE: The Porch of the King Archon.

EUTHYPHRO: Why have you left the Lyceum, Socrates? and what are you doing in the Porch of the King Archon? Surely you cannot be concerned in a suit before the King, like myself?

SOCRATES: Not in a suit, Euthyphro; impeachment is the word which the Athenians use.

EUTHYPHRO: What! I suppose that some one has been prosecuting you, for I cannot believe that you are the prosecutor of another.

SOCRATES: Certainly not.

EUTHYPHRO: Then some one else has been prosecuting you?

SOCRATES: Yes.

EUTHYPHRO: And who is he?

SOCRATES: A young man who is little known, Euthyphro; and I hardly know him: his name is Meletus, and he is of the deme of Pitthis. Perhaps you may remember his appearance; he has a beak, and long straight hair, and a beard which is ill grown.

EUTHYPHRO: No, I do not remember him, Socrates. But what is the charge which he brings against you?

SOCRATES: What is the charge? Well, a very serious charge, which shows a good deal of character in the young man, and for which he is certainly not to be despised. He says he knows how the youth are corrupted and who are their corruptors. I fancy that he must be a wise man, and seeing that I am the reverse of a wise man, he has found me out, and is going to accuse me of corrupting his young friends. And of this our mother the state is to be the judge. Of all our political men he is the only one who seems to me to begin in the right way, with the cultivation of virtue in youth; like a good husbandman, he makes the young shoots his first care, and clears away us who are the destroyers of them. This is only the first step; he will afterwards attend to the elder branches; and if he goes on as he has begun, he will be a very great public benefactor.

EUTHYPHRO: I hope that he may; but I rather fear, Socrates, that the opposite will turn out to be the truth. My opinion is that in attacking you he is simply aiming a blow at the foundation of the state. But in what way does he say that you corrupt the young?

SOCRATES: He brings a wonderful accusation against me, which at first hearing excites surprise: he says that I am a poet or maker of gods, and that I invent new gods and deny the existence of old ones; this is the ground of his indictment.

EUTHYPHRO: I understand, Socrates; he means to attack you about the familiar sign which occasionally, as you say, comes to you. He thinks that you are a neologian, and he is going to have you up before the court for this. He knows that such a charge is readily received by the world, as I myself know too well; for when I speak in the assembly about divine things, and foretell the future to them, they laugh at me and think me a madman. Yet every word that I say is true. But they are jealous of us all; and we must be brave and go at them.

SOCRATES: Their laughter, friend Euthyphro, is not a matter of much consequence. For a man may be thought wise; but the Athenians, I suspect, do not much trouble themselves about him until he begins to impart his wisdom to others, and then for some reason or other, perhaps, as you say, from jealousy, they are angry.

EUTHYPHRO: I am never likely to try their temper in this way.

SOCRATES: I dare say not, for you are reserved in your behaviour, and seldom impart your wisdom. But I have a benevolent habit of pouring out myself to everybody, and would even pay for a listener, and I am afraid that the Athenians may think me too talkative. Now if, as I was saying, they would only laugh at me, as you say that they laugh at you, the time might pass gaily enough in the court; but perhaps they may be in earnest, and then what the end will be you soothsayers only can predict.

EUTHYPHRO: I dare say that the affair will end in nothing, Socrates, and that you will win your cause; and I think that I shall win my own.

SOCRATES: And what is your suit, Euthyphro? are you the pursuer or the defendant?

EUTHYPHRO: I am the pursuer.

SOCRATES: Of whom?

EUTHYPHRO: You will think me mad when I tell you.

SOCRATES: Why, has the fugitive wings?

EUTHYPHRO: Nay, he is not very volatile at his time of life.

SOCRATES: Who is he?

EUTHYPHRO: My father.

SOCRATES: Your father! my good man?

EUTHYPHRO: Yes.

SOCRATES: And of what is he accused?

EUTHYPHRO: Of murder, Socrates.

SOCRATES: By the powers, Euthyphro! how little does the common herd know of the nature of right and truth. A man must be an extraordinary man, and have made great strides in wisdom, before he could have seen his way to bring such an action.

EUTHYPHRO: Indeed, Socrates, he must.

SOCRATES: I suppose that the man whom your father murdered was one of your relatives—clearly he was; for if he had been a stranger you would never have thought of prosecuting him.

EUTHYPHRO: I am amused, Socrates, at your making a distinction between one who is a relation and one who is not a relation; for surely the pollution is the same in either case, if you knowingly associate with the murderer when you ought to clear yourself and him by proceeding against him. The real question is whether the murdered man has been justly slain. If justly, then your duty is to let the matter alone; but if unjustly, then even if the murderer lives under the same roof with you and eats at the same table, proceed against him. Now the man who is dead was a poor dependant of mine who worked for us as a field labourer on our farm in Naxos, and one day in a fit of drunken passion he got into a quarrel with one of our domestic servants and slew him. My father bound him hand and foot and threw him into a ditch, and then sent to Athens to ask of a diviner what he should do with him. Meanwhile he never attended to him and took no care about him, for he regarded him as a murderer; and thought that no great harm would be done even if he did die. Now this was just what happened. For such was the effect of cold and hunger and chains upon him, that before the messenger returned from the diviner, he was dead. And my father and family are angry with me for taking the part of the murderer and prosecuting my father. They say that he did not kill him, and that if he did, the dead man was but a murderer, and I ought not to take any notice, for that a son is impious who prosecutes a father. Which shows, Socrates, how little they know what the gods think about piety and impiety.

SOCRATES: Good heavens, Euthyphro! and is your knowledge of religion and of things pious and impious so very exact, that, supposing the circumstances to be as you state them, you are not afraid lest you too may be doing an impious thing in bringing an action against your father?

EUTHYPHRO: The best of Euthyphro, and that which distinguishes him, Socrates, from other men, is his exact knowledge of all such matters. What should I be good for without it?

SOCRATES: Rare friend! I think that I cannot do better than be your disciple. Then before the trial with Meletus comes on I shall challenge him, and say that I have always had a great interest in religious questions, and now, as he charges me with rash imaginations and innovations in religion, I have become your disciple. You, Meletus, as I shall say to him, acknowledge Euthyphro to be a great theologian, and sound in his opinions; and if you approve of him you ought to approve of me, and not have me into court; but if you disapprove, you should begin by indicting him who is my teacher, and who will be the ruin, not of the young, but of the old; that is to say, of myself whom he instructs, and of his old father whom he admonishes and chastises. And if Meletus refuses to listen to me, but will go on, and will not shift the indictment from me to you, I cannot do better than repeat this challenge in the court.

EUTHYPHRO: Yes, indeed, Socrates; and if he attempts to indict me I am mistaken if I do not find a flaw in him; the court shall have a great deal more to say to him than to me.

SOCRATES: And I, my dear friend, knowing this, am desirous of becoming your disciple. For I observe that no one appears to notice you—not even this Meletus; but his sharp eyes have found me out at once, and he has indicted me for impiety. And therefore, I adjure you to tell me the nature of piety and impiety, which you said that you knew so well, and of murder, and of other offences against the gods. What are they? Is not piety in every action always the same? and impiety, again—is it not always the opposite of piety, and also the same with itself, having, as impiety, one notion which includes whatever is impious?

EUTHYPHRO: To be sure, Socrates.

SOCRATES: And what is piety, and what is impiety?

EUTHYPHRO: Piety is doing as I am doing; that is to say, prosecuting any one who is guilty of murder, sacrilege, or of any similar crime—whether he be your father or mother, or whoever he may be—that makes no difference; and not to prosecute them is impiety. And please to consider, Socrates, what a notable proof I will give you of the truth of my words, a proof which I have already given to others:—of the principle, I mean, that the impious, whoever he may be, ought not to go unpunished. For do not men regard Zeus as the best and most righteous of the gods?—and yet they admit that he bound his father (Cronos) because he wickedly devoured his sons, and that he too had punished his own father (Uranus) for a similar reason, in a nameless manner. And yet when I proceed against my father, they are angry with me. So inconsistent are they in their way of talking when the gods are concerned, and when I am concerned.

SOCRATES: May not this be the reason, Euthyphro, why I am charged with impiety—that I cannot away with these stories about the gods? and therefore I suppose that people think me wrong. But, as you who are well informed about them approve of them, I cannot do better than assent to your superior wisdom. What else can I say, confessing as I do, that I know nothing about them? Tell me, for the love of Zeus, whether you really believe that they are true.

EUTHYPHRO: Yes, Socrates; and things more wonderful still, of which the world is in ignorance.

SOCRATES: And do you really believe that the gods fought with one another, and had dire quarrels, battles, and the like, as the poets say, and as you may see represented in the works of great artists? The temples are full of them; and notably the robe of Athene, which is carried up to the Acropolis at the great Panathenaea, is embroidered with them. Are all these tales of the gods true, Euthyphro?

EUTHYPHRO: Yes, Socrates; and, as I was saying, I can tell you, if you would like to hear them, many other things about the gods which would quite amaze you.

SOCRATES: I dare say; and you shall tell me them at some other time when I have leisure. But just at present I would rather hear from you a more precise answer, which you have not as yet given, my friend, to the question, What is 'piety'? When asked, you only replied, Doing as you do, charging your father with murder.

EUTHYPHRO: And what I said was true, Socrates.

SOCRATES: No doubt, Euthyphro; but you would admit that there are many other pious acts?

EUTHYPHRO: There are.

SOCRATES: Remember that I did not ask you to give me two or three examples of piety, but to explain the general idea which makes all pious things to be pious. Do you not recollect that there was one idea which made the impious impious, and the pious pious?

EUTHYPHRO: I remember.

SOCRATES: Tell me what is the nature of this idea, and then I shall have a standard to which I may look, and by which I may measure actions, whether yours or those of any one else, and then I shall be able to say that such and such an action is pious, such another impious.

EUTHYPHRO: I will tell you, if you like.

SOCRATES: I should very much like.

EUTHYPHRO: Piety, then, is that which is dear to the gods, and impiety is that which is not dear to them.

SOCRATES: Very good, Euthyphro; you have now given me the sort of answer which I wanted. But whether what you say is true or not I cannot as yet tell, although I make no doubt that you will prove the truth of your words.

EUTHYPHRO: Of course.

SOCRATES: Come, then, and let us examine what we are saying. That thing or person which is dear to the gods is pious, and that thing or person which is hateful to the gods is impious, these two being the extreme opposites of one another. Was not that said?

EUTHYPHRO: It was.

SOCRATES: And well said?

EUTHYPHRO: Yes, Socrates, I thought so; it was certainly said.

SOCRATES: And further, Euthyphro, the gods were admitted to have enmities and hatreds and differences?

EUTHYPHRO: Yes, that was also said.

SOCRATES: And what sort of difference creates enmity and anger? Suppose for example that you and I, my good friend, differ about a number; do differences of this sort make us enemies and set us at variance with one another? Do we not go at once to arithmetic, and put an end to them by a sum?

EUTHYPHRO: True.

SOCRATES: Or suppose that we differ about magnitudes, do we not quickly end the differences by measuring?

EUTHYPHRO: Very true.

SOCRATES: And we end a controversy about heavy and light by resorting to a weighing machine?

EUTHYPHRO: To be sure.

SOCRATES: But what differences are there which cannot be thus decided, and which therefore make us angry and set us at enmity with one another? I dare say the answer does not occur to you at the moment, and therefore I will suggest that these enmities arise when the matters of difference are the just and unjust, good and evil, honourable and dishonourable. Are not these the points about which men differ, and about which when we are unable satisfactorily to decide our differences, you and I and all of us quarrel, when we do quarrel? (Compare Alcib.)

EUTHYPHRO: Yes, Socrates, the nature of the differences about which we quarrel is such as you describe.

SOCRATES: And the quarrels of the gods, noble Euthyphro, when they occur, are of a like nature?

EUTHYPHRO: Certainly they are.

SOCRATES: They have differences of opinion, as you say, about good and evil, just and unjust, honourable and dishonourable: there would have been no quarrels among them, if there had been no such differences—would there now?

EUTHYPHRO: You are quite right.

SOCRATES: Does not every man love that which he deems noble and just and good, and hate the opposite of them?

EUTHYPHRO: Very true.

SOCRATES: But, as you say, people regard the same things, some as just and others as unjust,—about these they dispute; and so there arise wars and fightings among them.

EUTHYPHRO: Very true.

SOCRATES: Then the same things are hated by the gods and loved by the gods, and are both hateful and dear to them?

EUTHYPHRO: True.

SOCRATES: And upon this view the same things, Euthyphro, will be pious and also impious?

EUTHYPHRO: So I should suppose.

SOCRATES: Then, my friend, I remark with surprise that you have not answered the question which I asked. For I certainly did not ask you to tell me what action is both pious and impious: but now it would seem that what is loved by the gods is also hated by them. And therefore, Euthyphro, in thus chastising your father you may very likely be doing what is agreeable to Zeus but disagreeable to Cronos or Uranus, and what is acceptable to Hephaestus but unacceptable to Herè, and there may be other gods who have similar differences of opinion.

EUTHYPHRO: But I believe, Socrates, that all the gods would be agreed as to the propriety of punishing a murderer: there would be no difference of opinion about that.

SOCRATES: Well, but speaking of men, Euthyphro, did you ever hear any one arguing that a murderer or any sort of evil-doer ought to be let off?

EUTHYPHRO: I should rather say that these are the questions which they are always arguing, especially in courts of law: they commit all sorts of crimes, and there is nothing which they will not do or say in their own defence.

SOCRATES: But do they admit their guilt, Euthyphro, and yet say that they ought not to be punished?

EUTHYPHRO: No; they do not.

SOCRATES: Then there are some things which they do not venture to say and do: for they do not venture to argue that the guilty are to be unpunished, but they deny their guilt, do they not?

EUTHYPHRO: Yes.

SOCRATES: Then they do not argue that the evil-doer should not be punished, but they argue about the fact of who the evil-doer is, and what he did and when?

EUTHYPHRO: True.

SOCRATES: And the gods are in the same case, if as you assert they quarrel about just and unjust, and some of them say while others deny that injustice is done among them. For surely neither God nor man will ever venture to say that the doer of injustice is not to be punished?

EUTHYPHRO: That is true, Socrates, in the main.

SOCRATES: But they join issue about the particulars—gods and men alike; and, if they dispute at all, they dispute about some act which is called in question, and which by some is affirmed to be just, by others to be unjust. Is not that true?

EUTHYPHRO: Quite true.

SOCRATES: Well then, my dear friend Euthyphro, do tell me, for my better instruction and information, what proof have you that in the opinion of all the gods a servant who is guilty of murder, and is put in chains by the master of the dead man, and dies because he is put in chains before he who bound him can learn from the interpreters of the gods what he ought to do with him, dies unjustly; and that on behalf of such an one a son ought to proceed against his father and accuse him of murder. How would you show that all the gods absolutely agree in approving of his act? Prove to me that they do, and I will applaud your wisdom as long as I live.

EUTHYPHRO: It will be a difficult task; but I could make the matter very clear indeed to you.

SOCRATES: I understand; you mean to say that I am not so quick of apprehension as the judges: for to them you will be sure to prove that the act is unjust, and hateful to the gods.

EUTHYPHRO: Yes indeed, Socrates; at least if they will listen to me.

SOCRATES: But they will be sure to listen if they find that you are a good speaker. There was a notion that came into my mind while you were speaking; I said to myself: 'Well, and what if Euthyphro does prove to me that all the gods regarded the death of the serf as unjust, how do I know anything more of the nature of piety and impiety? for granting that this action may be hateful to the gods, still piety and impiety are not adequately defined by these distinctions, for that which is hateful to the gods has been shown to be also pleasing and dear to them.' And therefore, Euthyphro, I do not ask you to prove this; I will suppose, if you like, that all the gods condemn and abominate such an action. But I will amend the definition so far as to say that what all the gods hate is impious, and what they love pious or holy; and what some of them love and others hate is both or neither. Shall this be our definition of piety and impiety?

EUTHYPHRO: Why not, Socrates?

SOCRATES: Why not! certainly, as far as I am concerned, Euthyphro, there is no reason why not. But whether this admission will greatly assist you in the task of instructing me as you promised, is a matter for you to consider.

EUTHYPHRO: Yes, I should say that what all the gods love is pious and holy, and the opposite which they all hate, impious.

SOCRATES: Ought we to enquire into the truth of this, Euthyphro, or simply to accept the mere statement on our own authority and that of others? What do you say?

EUTHYPHRO: We should enquire; and I believe that the statement will stand the test of enquiry.

SOCRATES: We shall know better, my good friend, in a little while. The point which I should first wish to understand is whether the pious or holy is beloved by the gods because it is holy, or holy because it is beloved of the gods.

EUTHYPHRO: I do not understand your meaning, Socrates.

SOCRATES: I will endeavour to explain: we speak of carrying and we speak of being carried, of leading and being led, seeing and being seen. You know that in all such cases there is a difference, and you know also in what the difference lies?

EUTHYPHRO: I think that I understand.

SOCRATES: And is not that which is beloved distinct from that which loves?

EUTHYPHRO: Certainly.

SOCRATES: Well; and now tell me, is that which is carried in this state of carrying because it is carried, or for some other reason?

EUTHYPHRO: No; that is the reason.

SOCRATES: And the same is true of what is led and of what is seen?

EUTHYPHRO: True.

SOCRATES: And a thing is not seen because it is visible, but conversely, visible because it is seen; nor is a thing led because it is in the state of being led, or carried because it is in the state of being carried, but the converse of this. And now I think, Euthyphro, that my meaning will be intelligible; and my meaning is, that any state of action or passion implies previous action or passion. It does not become because it is becoming, but it is in a state of becoming because it becomes; neither does it suffer because it is in a state of suffering, but it is in a state of suffering because it suffers. Do you not agree?

EUTHYPHRO: Yes.

SOCRATES: Is not that which is loved in some state either of becoming or suffering?

EUTHYPHRO: Yes.

SOCRATES: And the same holds as in the previous instances; the state of being loved follows the act of being loved, and not the act the state.

EUTHYPHRO: Certainly.

SOCRATES: And what do you say of piety, Euthyphro: is not piety, according to your definition, loved by all the gods?

EUTHYPHRO: Yes.

SOCRATES: Because it is pious or holy, or for some other reason?

EUTHYPHRO: No, that is the reason.

SOCRATES: It is loved because it is holy, not holy because it is loved?

EUTHYPHRO: Yes.

SOCRATES: And that which is dear to the gods is loved by them, and is in a state to be loved of them because it is loved of them?

EUTHYPHRO: Certainly.

SOCRATES: Then that which is dear to the gods, Euthyphro, is not holy, nor is that which is holy loved of God, as you affirm; but they are two different things.

EUTHYPHRO: How do you mean, Socrates?

SOCRATES: I mean to say that the holy has been acknowledged by us to be loved of God because it is holy, not to be holy because it is loved.

EUTHYPHRO: Yes.

SOCRATES: But that which is dear to the gods is dear to them because it is loved by them, not loved by them because it is dear to them.

EUTHYPHRO: True.

SOCRATES: But, friend Euthyphro, if that which is holy is the same with that which is dear to God, and is loved because it is holy, then that which is dear to God would have been loved as being dear to God; but if that which is dear to God is dear to him because loved by him, then that which is holy would have been holy because loved by him. But now you see that the reverse is the case, and that they are quite different from one another. For one (theophiles) is of a kind to be loved cause it is loved, and the other (osion) is loved because it is of a kind to be loved. Thus you appear to me, Euthyphro, when I ask you what is the essence of holiness, to offer an attribute only, and not the essence—the attribute of being loved by all the gods. But you still refuse to explain to me the nature of holiness. And therefore, if you please, I will ask you not to hide your treasure, but to tell me once more what holiness or piety really is, whether dear to the gods or not (for that is a matter about which we will not quarrel); and what is impiety?

EUTHYPHRO: I really do not know, Socrates, how to express what I mean. For somehow or other our arguments, on whatever ground we rest them, seem to turn round and walk away from us.

SOCRATES: Your words, Euthyphro, are like the handiwork of my ancestor Daedalus; and if I were the sayer or propounder of them, you might say that my arguments walk away and will not remain fixed where they are placed because I am a descendant of his. But now, since these notions are your own, you must find some other gibe, for they certainly, as you yourself allow, show an inclination to be on the move.

EUTHYPHRO: Nay, Socrates, I shall still say that you are the Daedalus who sets arguments in motion; not I, certainly, but you make them move or go round, for they would never have stirred, as far as I am concerned.

SOCRATES: Then I must be a greater than Daedalus: for whereas he only made his own inventions to move, I move those of other people as well. And the beauty of it is, that I would rather not. For I would give the wisdom of Daedalus, and the wealth of Tantalus, to be able to detain them and keep them fixed. But enough of this. As I perceive that you are lazy, I will myself endeavour to show you how you might instruct me in the nature of piety; and I hope that you will not grudge your labour. Tell me, then—Is not that which is pious necessarily just?

EUTHYPHRO: Yes.

SOCRATES: And is, then, all which is just pious? or, is that which is pious all just, but that which is just, only in part and not all, pious?

EUTHYPHRO: I do not understand you, Socrates.

SOCRATES: And yet I know that you are as much wiser than I am, as you are younger. But, as I was saying, revered friend, the abundance of your wisdom makes you lazy. Please to exert yourself, for there is no real difficulty in understanding me. What I mean I may explain by an illustration of what I do not mean. The poet (Stasinus) sings—

'Of Zeus, the author and creator of all these things,
You will not tell: for where there is fear there is also reverence.'

Now I disagree with this poet. Shall I tell you in what respect?

EUTHYPHRO: By all means.

SOCRATES: I should not say that where there is fear there is also reverence; for I am sure that many persons fear poverty and disease, and the like evils, but I do not perceive that they reverence the objects of their fear.

EUTHYPHRO: Very true.

SOCRATES: But where reverence is, there is fear; for he who has a feeling of reverence and shame about the commission of any action, fears and is afraid of an ill reputation.

EUTHYPHRO: No doubt.

SOCRATES: Then we are wrong in saying that where there is fear there is also reverence; and we should say, where there is reverence there is also fear. But there is not always reverence where there is fear; for fear is a more extended notion, and reverence is a part of fear, just as the odd is a part of number, and number is a more extended notion than the odd. I suppose that you follow me now?

EUTHYPHRO: Quite well.

SOCRATES: That was the sort of question which I meant to raise when I asked whether the just is always the pious, or the pious always the just; and whether there may not be justice where there is not piety; for justice is the more extended notion of which piety is only a part. Do you dissent?

EUTHYPHRO: No, I think that you are quite right.

SOCRATES: Then, if piety is a part of justice, I suppose that we should enquire what part? If you had pursued the enquiry in the previous cases; for instance, if you had asked me what is an even number, and what part of number the even is, I should have had no difficulty in replying, a number which represents a figure having two equal sides. Do you not agree?

EUTHYPHRO: Yes, I quite agree.

SOCRATES: In like manner, I want you to tell me what part of justice is piety or holiness, that I may be able to tell Meletus not to do me injustice, or indict me for impiety, as I am now adequately instructed by you in the nature of piety or holiness, and their opposites.

EUTHYPHRO: Piety or holiness, Socrates, appears to me to be that part of justice which attends to the gods, as there is the other part of justice which attends to men.

SOCRATES: That is good, Euthyphro; yet still there is a little point about which I should like to have further information, What is the meaning of 'attention'? For attention can hardly be used in the same sense when applied to the gods as when applied to other things. For instance, horses are said to require attention, and not every person is able to attend to them, but only a person skilled in horsemanship. Is it not so?

EUTHYPHRO: Certainly.

SOCRATES: I should suppose that the art of horsemanship is the art of attending to horses?

EUTHYPHRO: Yes.

SOCRATES: Nor is every one qualified to attend to dogs, but only the huntsman?

EUTHYPHRO: True.

SOCRATES: And I should also conceive that the art of the huntsman is the art of attending to dogs?

EUTHYPHRO: Yes.

SOCRATES: As the art of the oxherd is the art of attending to oxen?

EUTHYPHRO: Very true.

SOCRATES: In like manner holiness or piety is the art of attending to the gods?—that would be your meaning, Euthyphro?

EUTHYPHRO: Yes.

SOCRATES: And is not attention always designed for the good or benefit of that to which the attention is given? As in the case of horses, you may observe that when attended to by the horseman's art they are benefited and improved, are they not?

EUTHYPHRO: True.

SOCRATES: As the dogs are benefited by the huntsman's art, and the oxen by the art of the oxherd, and all other things are tended or attended for their good and not for their hurt?

EUTHYPHRO: Certainly, not for their hurt.

SOCRATES: But for their good?

EUTHYPHRO: Of course.

SOCRATES: And does piety or holiness, which has been defined to be the art of attending to the gods, benefit or improve them? Would you say that when you do a holy act you make any of the gods better?

EUTHYPHRO: No, no; that was certainly not what I meant.

SOCRATES: And I, Euthyphro, never supposed that you did. I asked you the question about the nature of the attention, because I thought that you did not.

EUTHYPHRO: You do me justice, Socrates; that is not the sort of attention which I mean.

SOCRATES: Good: but I must still ask what is this attention to the gods which is called piety?

EUTHYPHRO: It is such, Socrates, as servants show to their masters.

SOCRATES: I understand—a sort of ministration to the gods.

EUTHYPHRO: Exactly.

SOCRATES: Medicine is also a sort of ministration or service, having in view the attainment of some object—would you not say of health?

EUTHYPHRO: I should.

SOCRATES: Again, there is an art which ministers to the ship-builder with a view to the attainment of some result?

EUTHYPHRO: Yes, Socrates, with a view to the building of a ship.

SOCRATES: As there is an art which ministers to the house-builder with a view to the building of a house?

EUTHYPHRO: Yes.

SOCRATES: And now tell me, my good friend, about the art which ministers to the gods: what work does that help to accomplish? For you must surely know if, as you say, you are of all men living the one who is best instructed in religion.

EUTHYPHRO: And I speak the truth, Socrates.

SOCRATES: Tell me then, oh tell me—what is that fair work which the gods do by the help of our ministrations?

EUTHYPHRO: Many and fair, Socrates, are the works which they do.

SOCRATES: Why, my friend, and so are those of a general. But the chief of them is easily told. Would you not say that victory in war is the chief of them?

EUTHYPHRO: Certainly.

SOCRATES: Many and fair, too, are the works of the husbandman, if I am not mistaken; but his chief work is the production of food from the earth?

EUTHYPHRO: Exactly.

SOCRATES: And of the many and fair things done by the gods, which is the chief or principal one?

EUTHYPHRO: I have told you already, Socrates, that to learn all these things accurately will be very tiresome. Let me simply say that piety or holiness is learning how to please the gods in word and deed, by prayers and sacrifices. Such piety is the salvation of families and states, just as the impious, which is unpleasing to the gods, is their ruin and destruction.

SOCRATES: I think that you could have answered in much fewer words the chief question which I asked, Euthyphro, if you had chosen. But I see plainly that you are not disposed to instruct me—clearly not: else why, when we reached the point, did you turn aside? Had you only answered me I should have truly learned of you by this time the nature of piety. Now, as the asker of a question is necessarily dependent on the answerer, whither he leads I must follow; and can only ask again, what is the pious, and what is piety? Do you mean that they are a sort of science of praying and sacrificing?

EUTHYPHRO: Yes, I do.

SOCRATES: And sacrificing is giving to the gods, and prayer is asking of the gods?

EUTHYPHRO: Yes, Socrates.

SOCRATES: Upon this view, then, piety is a science of asking and giving?

EUTHYPHRO: You understand me capitally, Socrates.

SOCRATES: Yes, my friend; the reason is that I am a votary of your science, and give my mind to it, and therefore nothing which you say will be thrown away upon me. Please then to tell me, what is the nature of this service to the gods? Do you mean that we prefer requests and give gifts to them?

EUTHYPHRO: Yes, I do.

SOCRATES: Is not the right way of asking to ask of them what we want?

EUTHYPHRO: Certainly.

SOCRATES: And the right way of giving is to give to them in return what they want of us. There would be no meaning in an art which gives to any one that which he does not want.

EUTHYPHRO: Very true, Socrates.

SOCRATES: Then piety, Euthyphro, is an art which gods and men have of doing business with one another?

EUTHYPHRO: That is an expression which you may use, if you like.

SOCRATES: But I have no particular liking for anything but the truth. I wish, however, that you would tell me what benefit accrues to the gods from our gifts. There is no doubt about what they give to us; for there is no good thing which they do not give; but how we can give any good thing to them in return is far from being equally clear. If they give everything and we give nothing, that must be an affair of business in which we have very greatly the advantage of them.

EUTHYPHRO: And do you imagine, Socrates, that any benefit accrues to the gods from our gifts?

SOCRATES: But if not, Euthyphro, what is the meaning of gifts which are conferred by us upon the gods?

EUTHYPHRO: What else, but tributes of honour; and, as I was just now saying, what pleases them?

SOCRATES: Piety, then, is pleasing to the gods, but not beneficial or dear to them?

EUTHYPHRO: I should say that nothing could be dearer.

SOCRATES: Then once more the assertion is repeated that piety is dear to the gods?

EUTHYPHRO: Certainly.

SOCRATES: And when you say this, can you wonder at your words not standing firm, but walking away? Will you accuse me of being the Daedalus who makes them walk away, not perceiving that there is another and far greater artist than Daedalus who makes them go round in a circle, and he is yourself; for the argument, as you will perceive, comes round to the same point. Were we not saying that the holy or pious was not the same with that which is loved of the gods? Have you forgotten?

EUTHYPHRO: I quite remember.

SOCRATES: And are you not saying that what is loved of the gods is holy; and is not this the same as what is dear to them—do you see?

EUTHYPHRO: True.

SOCRATES: Then either we were wrong in our former assertion; or, if we were right then, we are wrong now.

EUTHYPHRO: One of the two must be true.

SOCRATES: Then we must begin again and ask, What is piety? That is an enquiry which I shall never be weary of pursuing as far as in me lies; and I entreat you not to scorn me, but to apply your mind to the utmost, and tell me the truth. For, if any man knows, you are he; and therefore I must detain you, like Proteus, until you tell. If you had not certainly known the nature of piety and impiety, I am confident that you would never, on behalf of a serf, have charged your aged father with murder. You would not have run such a risk of doing wrong in the sight of the gods, and you would have had too much respect for the opinions of men. I am sure, therefore, that you know the nature of piety and impiety. Speak out then, my dear Euthyphro, and do not hide your knowledge.

EUTHYPHRO: Another time, Socrates; for I am in a hurry, and must go now.

SOCRATES: Alas! my companion, and will you leave me in despair? I was hoping that you would instruct me in the nature of piety and impiety; and then I might have cleared myself of Meletus and his indictment. I would have told him that I had been enlightened by Euthyphro, and had given up rash innovations and speculations, in which I indulged only through ignorance, and that now I am about to lead a better life.

Apology

INTRODUCTION

In what relation the Apology of Plato stands to the real defence of Socrates, there are no means of determining. It certainly agrees in tone and character with the description of Xenophon, who says in the Memorabilia that Socrates might have been acquitted 'if in any moderate degree he would have conciliated the favour of the dicasts;' and who informs us in another passage, on the testimony of Hermogenes, the friend of Socrates, that he had no wish to live; and that the divine sign refused to allow him to prepare a defence, and also that Socrates himself declared this to be unnecessary, on the ground that all his life long he had been preparing against that hour. For the speech breathes throughout a spirit of defiance, ('*ut non supplex aut reus sed magister aut dominus videretur esse judicum*' (Cic. de Orat.); and the loose and desultory style is an imitation of the 'accustomed manner' in which Socrates spoke in 'the agora and among the tables of the money-changers.' The allusion in the Crito may, perhaps, be adduced as a further evidence of the literal accuracy of some parts. But in the main it must be regarded as the ideal of Socrates, according to Plato's conception of him, appearing in the greatest and most public scene of his life, and in the height of his triumph, when he is weakest, and yet his mastery over mankind is greatest, and his habitual irony acquires a new meaning and a sort of tragic pathos in the face of death. The facts of his life are summed up, and the features of his character are brought out as if by accident in the course of the defence. The conversational manner, the seeming want of arrangement, the ironical simplicity, are found to result in a perfect work of art, which is the portrait of Socrates.

Yet some of the topics may have been actually used by Socrates; and the recollection of his very words may have rung in the ears of his disciple. The Apology of Plato may be compared generally with those speeches of Thucydides in which he has embodied his conception of the lofty character and policy of the great Pericles, and which at the same time furnish a commentary on the situation of affairs from the point of view of the historian. So in the Apology there is an ideal rather than a literal truth; much is said which was not said, and is only Plato's view of the situation. Plato was not, like Xenophon, a chronicler of facts; he does not appear in any of his writings to have aimed at literal accuracy. He is not therefore to be supplemented from the Memorabilia and Symposium of Xenophon, who belongs to an entirely different class of writers. The Apology of Plato is not the report of what Socrates said, but an elaborate composition, quite as much so in fact as one of the Dialogues. And we may perhaps even indulge in the fancy that the actual defence of Socrates was as much greater than the Platonic defence as the master was greater than the disciple. But in any case, some of the words used by him must have been remembered, and some of the facts recorded must have actually occurred. It is significant that Plato is said to have been present at the defence (Apol.), as he is also said to have been absent at the last scene in the Phaedo. Is it fanciful to suppose that he meant to give the stamp of authenticity to the one and not to the other?—especially when we consider that these two passages are the only ones in which Plato makes mention of himself. The circumstance that Plato was to be one of his sureties for the payment of the fine which he proposed has the appearance of truth. More suspicious is the statement that Socrates received the first impulse to his favourite calling of cross-examining the world from the Oracle of Delphi; for he must already have been famous before Chaerephon went to consult the Oracle (Riddell), and the story is of a kind which is very likely to have been invented. On the whole we arrive at the conclusion that the Apology is true to the character of Socrates, but we cannot show that any single sentence in it was actually spoken by him. It breathes the spirit of Socrates, but has been cast anew in the mould of Plato.

There is not much in the other Dialogues which can be compared with the Apology. The same recollection of his master may have been present to the mind of Plato when depicting the sufferings of the Just in the Republic. The Crito may also be regarded as a sort of appendage to the Apology, in which Socrates, who has defied the judges, is nevertheless represented as scrupulously obedient to the laws. The idealization of the sufferer is carried still further in the Gorgias, in which the thesis is maintained, that 'to suffer is better than to do evil;' and the art of rhetoric is described as only useful for the purpose of self-accusation. The parallelisms which occur in the so-called Apology of Xenophon are not worth noticing, because the writing in which they are contained is manifestly spurious. The statements of the Memorabilia respecting the trial and death of Socrates agree generally with Plato; but they have lost the flavour of Socratic irony in the narrative of Xenophon.

The Apology or Platonic defence of Socrates is divided into three parts: 1st. The defence properly so called; 2nd. The shorter address in mitigation of the penalty; 3rd. The last words of prophetic rebuke and exhortation.

The first part commences with an apology for his colloquial style; he is, as he has always been, the enemy of rhetoric, and knows of no rhetoric but truth; he will not falsify his character by making a speech. Then he proceeds to divide his accusers into two classes; first, there is the nameless accuser—public opinion. All the world from their earliest years had heard that he was a corrupter of youth, and had seen him caricatured in the Clouds of Aristophanes. Secondly, there are the professed accusers, who are but the mouth-piece of the others. The accusations of both might be summed up in a formula. The first say, 'Socrates is an evil-doer and a curious person, searching into things under the earth and above the heaven; and making the worse appear the better cause, and teaching all this to others.' The second, 'Socrates is an evil-doer and corrupter of the youth, who does not receive the gods whom the state receives, but introduces other new divinities.' These last words appear to have been the actual indictment (compare Xen. Mem.); and the previous formula, which is a summary of public opinion, assumes the same legal style.

The answer begins by clearing up a confusion. In the representations of the Comic poets, and in the opinion of the multitude, he had been identified with the teachers of physical science and with the Sophists. But this was an error. For both of them he professes a respect in the open court, which contrasts with his manner of speaking about them in other places. (Compare for Anaxagoras, Phaedo, Laws; for the Sophists, Meno, Republic, Tim., Theaet., Soph., etc.) But at the same time he shows that he is not one of them. Of natural philosophy he knows nothing; not that he despises such pursuits, but the fact is that he is ignorant of them, and never says a word about them. Nor is he paid for giving instruction—that is another mistaken notion:—he has nothing to teach. But he commends Evenus for teaching virtue at such a 'moderate' rate as five minae. Something of the 'accustomed irony,' which may perhaps be expected to sleep in the ear of the multitude, is lurking here.

He then goes on to explain the reason why he is in such an evil name. That had arisen out of a peculiar mission which he had taken upon himself. The enthusiastic Chaerephon (probably in anticipation of the answer which he received) had gone to Delphi and asked the oracle if there was any man wiser than Socrates; and the answer was, that there was no man wiser. What could be the meaning of this—that he who knew nothing, and knew that he knew nothing, should be declared by the oracle to be the wisest of men? Reflecting upon the answer, he determined to refute it by finding 'a wiser;' and first he went to the politicians, and then to the poets, and then to the craftsmen, but always with the same result—he found that they knew nothing, or hardly anything more than himself; and that the little advantage which in some cases they possessed was more than counter-balanced by their conceit of knowledge. He knew nothing, and knew that he knew nothing: they knew little or nothing, and imagined that they knew all things. Thus he had passed his life as a sort of missionary in detecting the pretended wisdom of mankind; and this occupation had quite absorbed him and taken him away both from public and private affairs. Young men of the richer sort had made a pastime of the same pursuit, 'which was not unamusing.' And hence bitter enmities had arisen; the professors of knowledge had revenged themselves by calling him a villainous corrupter of youth, and by repeating the commonplaces about atheism and materialism and sophistry, which are the stock-accusations against all philosophers when there is nothing else to be said of them.

The second accusation he meets by interrogating Meletus, who is present and can be interrogated. 'If he is the corrupter, who is the improver of the citizens?' (Compare Meno.) 'All men everywhere.' But how absurd, how contrary to analogy is this! How inconceivable too, that he should make the citizens worse when he has to live with them. This surely cannot be intentional; and if unintentional, he ought to have been instructed by Meletus, and not accused in the court.

But there is another part of the indictment which says that he teaches men not to receive the gods whom the city receives, and has other new gods. 'Is that the way in which he is supposed to corrupt the youth?' 'Yes, it is.' 'Has he only new gods, or none at all?' 'None at all.' 'What, not even the sun and moon?' 'No; why, he says that the sun is a stone, and the moon earth.' That, replies Socrates, is the old confusion about Anaxagoras; the Athenian people are not so ignorant as to attribute to the influence of Socrates notions which have found their way into the drama, and may be learned at the theatre. Socrates undertakes to show that Meletus (rather unjustifiably) has been compounding a riddle in this part of the indictment: 'There are no gods, but Socrates believes in the existence of the sons of gods, which is absurd.'

Leaving Meletus, who has had enough words spent upon him, he returns to the original accusation. The question may be asked, Why will he persist in following a profession which leads him to death? Why?— because he must remain at his post where the god has placed him, as he remained at Potidaea, and Amphipolis, and Delium, where the generals placed him. Besides, he is not so overwise as to imagine that he knows whether death is a good or an evil; and he is certain that desertion of his duty is an evil. Anytus is quite right in saying that they should never have indicted him if they meant to let him go. For he will certainly obey God rather than man; and will continue to preach to all men of all ages the necessity of virtue and improvement; and if they refuse to listen to him he will still persevere and reprove them. This is his way of corrupting the youth, which he will not cease to follow in obedience to the god, even if a thousand deaths await him.

He is desirous that they should let him live—not for his own sake, but for theirs; because he is their heaven-sent friend (and they will never have such another), or, as he may be ludicrously described, he is the gadfly who stirs the generous steed into motion. Why then has he never taken part in public affairs? Because the familiar divine voice has hindered him; if he had been a public man, and had fought for the right, as he would certainly have fought against the many, he would not have lived, and could therefore have done no good. Twice in public matters he has risked his life for the sake of justice—once at the trial of the generals; and again in resistance to the tyrannical commands of the Thirty.

But, though not a public man, he has passed his days in instructing the citizens without fee or reward—this was his mission. Whether his disciples have turned out well or ill, he cannot justly be charged with the result, for he never promised to teach them anything. They might come if they liked, and they might stay away if they liked: and they did come, because they found an amusement in hearing the pretenders to wisdom detected. If they have been corrupted, their elder relatives (if not themselves) might surely come into court and witness against him, and there is an opportunity still for them to appear. But their fathers and brothers all appear in court (including 'this' Plato), to witness on his behalf; and if their relatives are corrupted, at least they are uncorrupted; 'and they are my witnesses. For they know that I am speaking the truth, and that Meletus is lying.'

This is about all that he has to say. He will not entreat the judges to spare his life; neither will he present a spectacle of weeping children, although he, too, is not made of 'rock or oak.' Some of the judges themselves may have complied with this practice on similar occasions, and he trusts that they will not be angry with him for not following their example. But he feels that such conduct brings discredit on the name of Athens: he feels too, that the judge has sworn not to give away justice; and he cannot be guilty of the impiety of asking the judge to break his oath, when he is himself being tried for impiety.

As he expected, and probably intended, he is convicted. And now the tone of the speech, instead of being more conciliatory, becomes more lofty and commanding. Anytus proposes death as the penalty: and what counter- proposition shall he make? He, the benefactor of the Athenian people, whose whole life has been spent in doing them good, should at least have the Olympic victor's reward of maintenance in the Prytaneum. Or why should he propose any counter-penalty when he does not know whether death, which Anytus proposes, is a good or an evil? And he is certain that imprisonment is an evil, exile is an evil. Loss of money might be an evil, but then he has none to give; perhaps he can make up a mina. Let that be the penalty, or, if his friends wish, thirty minae; for which they will be excellent securities.

(He is condemned to death.)

He is an old man already, and the Athenians will gain nothing but disgrace by depriving him of a few years of life. Perhaps he could have escaped, if he had chosen to throw down his arms and entreat for his life. But he does not at all repent of the manner of his defence; he would rather die in his own fashion than live in theirs. For the penalty of unrighteousness is swifter than death; that penalty has already overtaken his accusers as death will soon overtake him.

And now, as one who is about to die, he will prophesy to them. They have put him to death in order to escape the necessity of giving an account of their lives. But his death 'will be the seed' of many disciples who will convince them of their evil ways, and will come forth to reprove them in harsher terms, because they are younger and more inconsiderate.

He would like to say a few words, while there is time, to those who would have acquitted him. He wishes them to know that the divine sign never interrupted him in the course of his defence; the reason of which, as he conjectures, is that the death to which he is going is a good and not an evil. For either death is a long sleep, the best of sleeps, or a journey to another world in which the souls of the dead are gathered together, and in which there may be a hope of seeing the heroes of old—in which, too, there are just judges; and as all are immortal, there can be no fear of any one suffering death for his opinions.

Nothing evil can happen to the good man either in life or death, and his own death has been permitted by the gods, because it was better for him to depart; and therefore he forgives his judges because they have done him no harm, although they never meant to do him any good.

He has a last request to make to them—that they will trouble his sons as he has troubled them, if they appear to prefer riches to virtue, or to think themselves something when they are nothing.

'Few persons will be found to wish that Socrates should have defended himself otherwise,'—if, as we must add, his defence was that with which Plato has provided him. But leaving this question, which does not admit of a precise solution, we may go on to ask what was the impression which Plato in the Apology intended to give of the character and conduct of his master in the last great scene? Did he intend to represent him (1) as employing sophistries; (2) as designedly irritating the judges? Or are these sophistries to be regarded as belonging to the age in which he lived and to his personal character, and this apparent haughtiness as flowing from the natural elevation of his position?

For example, when he says that it is absurd to suppose that one man is the corrupter and all the rest of the world the improvers of the youth; or, when he argues that he never could have corrupted the men with whom he had to live; or, when he proves his belief in the gods because he believes in the sons of gods, is he serious or jesting? It may be observed that these sophisms all occur in his cross-examination of Meletus, who is easily foiled and mastered in the hands of the great dialectician. Perhaps he regarded these answers as good enough for his accuser, of whom he makes very light. Also there is a touch of irony in them, which takes them out of the category of sophistry. (Compare Euthyph.)

That the manner in which he defends himself about the lives of his disciples is not satisfactory, can hardly be denied. Fresh in the memory of the Athenians, and detestable as they deserved to be to the newly restored democracy, were the names of Alcibiades, Critias, Charmides. It is obviously not a sufficient answer that Socrates had never professed to teach them anything, and is therefore not justly chargeable with their crimes. Yet the defence, when taken out of this ironical form, is doubtless sound: that his teaching had nothing to do with their evil lives. Here, then, the sophistry is rather in form than in substance, though we might desire that to such a serious charge Socrates had given a more serious answer.

Truly characteristic of Socrates is another point in his answer, which may also be regarded as sophistical. He says that 'if he has corrupted the youth, he must have corrupted them involuntarily.' But if, as Socrates argues, all evil is involuntary, then all criminals ought to be admonished and not punished. In these words the Socratic doctrine of the involuntariness of evil is clearly intended to be conveyed. Here again, as in the former instance, the defence of Socrates is untrue practically, but may be true in some ideal or transcendental sense. The commonplace reply, that if he had been guilty of corrupting the youth their relations would surely have witnessed against him, with which he concludes this part of his defence, is more satisfactory.

Again, when Socrates argues that he must believe in the gods because he believes in the sons of gods, we must remember that this is a refutation not of the original indictment, which is consistent enough—'Socrates does not receive the gods whom the city receives, and has other new divinities'—but of the interpretation put upon the words by Meletus, who has affirmed that he is a downright atheist. To this Socrates fairly answers, in accordance with the ideas of the time, that a downright atheist cannot believe in the sons of gods or in divine things. The notion that demons or lesser divinities are the sons of gods is not to be regarded as ironical or sceptical. He is arguing 'ad hominem' according to the notions of mythology current in his age. Yet he abstains from saying that he believed in the gods whom the State approved. He does not defend himself, as Xenophon has defended him, by appealing to his practice of religion. Probably he neither wholly believed, nor disbelieved, in the existence of the popular gods; he had no means of knowing about them. According to Plato (compare Phaedo; Symp.), as well as Xenophon (Memor.), he was punctual in the performance of the least religious duties; and he must have believed in his own oracular sign, of which he seemed to have an internal witness. But the existence of Apollo or Zeus, or the other gods whom the State approves, would have appeared to him both uncertain and unimportant in comparison of the duty of self-examination, and of those principles of truth and right which he deemed to be the foundation of religion. (Compare Phaedr.; Euthyph.; Republic.)

The second question, whether Plato meant to represent Socrates as braving or irritating his judges, must also be answered in the negative. His irony, his superiority, his audacity, 'regarding not the person of man,' necessarily flow out of the loftiness of his situation. He is not acting a part upon a great occasion, but he is what he has been all his life long, 'a king of men.' He would rather not appear insolent, if he could avoid it (*ouch os authadizomenos touto lego*). Neither is he desirous of hastening his own end, for life and death are simply indifferent to him. But such a defence as would be acceptable to his judges and might procure an acquittal, it is not in his nature to make. He will not say or do anything that might pervert the course of justice; he cannot have his tongue bound even 'in the throat of death.' With his accusers he will only fence and play, as he had fenced with other 'improvers of youth,' answering the Sophist according to his sophistry all his life long. He is serious when he is speaking of his own mission, which seems to distinguish him from all other reformers of mankind, and originates in an accident. The dedication of himself to the improvement of his fellow-citizens is not so remarkable as the ironical spirit in which he goes about doing good only in vindication of the credit of the oracle, and in the vain hope of finding a wiser man than himself. Yet this singular and almost accidental character of his mission agrees with the divine sign which, according to our notions, is equally accidental and irrational, and is nevertheless accepted by him as the guiding principle of his life. Socrates is nowhere represented to us as a freethinker or sceptic. There is no reason to doubt his sincerity when he speculates on the possibility of seeing and knowing the heroes of the Trojan war in another world. On the other hand, his hope of immortality is uncertain;—he also conceives of death as a long sleep (in this respect differing from the Phaedo), and at last falls back on resignation to the divine will, and the certainty that no evil can happen to the good man either in life or death. His absolute truthfulness seems to hinder him from asserting positively more than this; and he makes no attempt to veil his ignorance in mythology and figures of speech. The gentleness of the first part of the speech contrasts with the aggravated, almost threatening, tone of the conclusion. He characteristically remarks that he will not speak as a rhetorician, that is to say, he will not make a regular defence such as Lysias or one of the orators might have composed for him, or, according to some accounts, did compose for him. But he first procures himself a hearing by conciliatory words. He does not attack the Sophists; for they were open to the same charges as himself; they were equally ridiculed by the Comic poets, and almost equally hateful to Anytus and Meletus. Yet incidentally the antagonism between Socrates and the Sophists is allowed to appear. He is poor and they are rich; his profession that he teaches nothing is opposed to their readiness to teach all things; his talking in the marketplace to their private instructions; his tarry-at-home life to their wandering from city to city. The tone which he assumes towards them is one of real friendliness, but also of concealed irony. Towards Anaxagoras, who had disappointed him in his hopes of learning about mind and nature, he shows a less kindly feeling, which is also the feeling of Plato in other passages (Laws). But Anaxagoras had been dead thirty years, and was beyond the reach of persecution.

It has been remarked that the prophecy of a new generation of teachers who would rebuke and exhort the Athenian people in harsher and more violent terms was, as far as we know, never fulfilled. No inference can be drawn from this circumstance as to the probability of the words attributed to him having been actually uttered. They express the aspiration of the first martyr of philosophy, that he would leave behind him many followers, accompanied by the not unnatural feeling that they would be fiercer and more inconsiderate in their words when emancipated from his control.

The above remarks must be understood as applying with any

degree of certainty to the Platonic Socrates only. For, although these or similar words may have been spoken by Socrates himself, we cannot exclude the possibility, that like so much else, e.g. the wisdom of Critias, the poem of Solon, the virtues of Charmides, they may have been due only to the imagination of Plato. The arguments of those who maintain that the Apology was composed during the process, resting on no evidence, do not require a serious refutation. Nor are the reasonings of Schleiermacher, who argues that the Platonic defence is an exact or nearly exact reproduction of the words of Socrates, partly because Plato would not have been guilty of the impiety of altering them, and also because many points of the defence might have been improved and strengthened, at all more conclusive. (See English Translation.) What effect the death of Socrates produced on the mind of Plato, we cannot certainly determine; nor can we say how he would or must have written under the circumstances. We observe that the enmity of Aristophanes to Socrates does not prevent Plato from introducing them together in the Symposium engaged in friendly intercourse. Nor is there any trace in the Dialogues of an attempt to make Anytus or Meletus personally odious in the eyes of the Athenian public.

APOLOGY

How you, O Athenians, have been affected by my accusers, I cannot tell; but I know that they almost made me forget who I was—so persuasively did they speak; and yet they have hardly uttered a word of truth. But of the many falsehoods told by them, there was one which quite amazed me;—I mean when they said that you should be upon your guard and not allow yourselves to be deceived by the force of my eloquence. To say this, when they were certain to be detected as soon as I opened my lips and proved myself to be anything but a great speaker, did indeed appear to me most shameless—unless by the force of eloquence they mean the force of truth; for is such is their meaning, I admit that I am eloquent. But in how different a way from theirs! Well, as I was saying, they have scarcely spoken the truth at all; but from me you shall hear the whole truth: not, however, delivered after their manner in a set oration duly ornamented with words and phrases. No, by heaven! but I shall use the words and arguments which occur to me at the moment; for I am confident in the justice of my cause (Or, I am certain that I am right in taking this course.): at my time of life I ought not to be appearing before you, O men of Athens, in the character of a juvenile orator—let no one expect it of me. And I must beg of you to grant me a favour:—If I defend myself in my accustomed manner, and you hear me using the words which I have been in the habit of using in the agora, at the tables of the money-changers, or anywhere else, I would ask you not to be surprised, and not to interrupt me on this account. For I am more than seventy years of age, and appearing now for the first time in a court of law, I am quite a stranger to the language of the place; and therefore I would have you regard me as if I were really a stranger, whom you would excuse if he spoke in his native tongue, and after the fashion of his country:—Am I making an unfair request of you? Never mind the manner, which may or may not be good; but think only of the truth of my words, and give heed to that: let the speaker speak truly and the judge decide justly.

And first, I have to reply to the older charges and to my first accusers, and then I will go on to the later ones. For of old I have had many accusers, who have accused me falsely to you during many years; and I am more afraid of them than of Anytus and his associates, who are dangerous, too, in their own way. But far more dangerous are the others, who began when you were children, and took possession of your minds with their falsehoods, telling of one Socrates, a wise man, who speculated about the heaven above, and searched into the earth beneath, and made the worse appear the better cause. The disseminators of this tale are the accusers whom I dread; for their hearers are apt to fancy that such enquirers do not believe in the existence of the gods. And they are many, and their charges against me are of ancient date, and they were made by them in the days when you were more impressible than you are now—in childhood, or it may have been in youth—and the cause when heard went by default, for there was none to answer. And hardest of all, I do not know and cannot tell the names of my accusers; unless in the chance case of a Comic poet. All who from envy and malice have persuaded you—some of them having first convinced themselves—all this class of men are most difficult to deal with; for I cannot have them up here, and cross-examine them, and therefore I must simply fight with shadows in my own defence, and argue when there is no one who answers. I will ask you then to assume with me, as I was saying, that my opponents are of two kinds; one recent, the other ancient: and I hope that you will see the propriety of my answering the latter first, for these accusations you heard long before the others, and much oftener.

Well, then, I must make my defence, and endeavour to clear away in a short time, a slander which has lasted a long time. May I succeed, if to succeed be for my good and yours, or likely to avail me in my cause! The task is not an easy one; I quite understand the nature of it. And so leaving the event with God, in obedience to the law I will now make my defence.

I will begin at the beginning, and ask what is the accusation which has given rise to the slander of me, and in fact has encouraged Meletus to proof this charge against me. Well, what do the slanderers say? They shall be my prosecutors, and I will sum up their words in an affidavit: 'Socrates is an evil-doer, and a curious person, who searches into things under the earth and in heaven, and he makes the worse appear the better cause; and he teaches the aforesaid doctrines to others.' Such is the nature of the accusation: it is just what you have yourselves seen in the comedy of Aristophanes (Aristoph., Clouds.), who has introduced a man whom he calls Socrates, going about and saying that he walks in air, and talking a deal of nonsense concerning matters of which I do not pretend to know either much or little—not that I mean to speak disparagingly of any one who is a student of natural philosophy. I should be very sorry if Meletus could bring so grave a charge against me. But the simple truth is, O Athenians, that I have nothing to do with physical speculations. Very many of those here present are witnesses to the truth of this, and to them I appeal. Speak then, you who have heard me, and tell your neighbours whether any of you have ever known me hold forth in few words or in many upon such matters... You hear their answer. And from what they say of this part of the charge you will be able to judge of the truth of the rest.

As little foundation is there for the report that I am a teacher, and take money; this accusation has no more truth in it than the other. Although, if a man were really able to instruct mankind, to receive money for giving instruction would, in my opinion, be an honour to him. There is Gorgias of Leontium, and Prodicus of Ceos, and Hippias of Elis, who go the round of the cities, and are able to persuade the young men to leave their own citizens by whom they might be taught for nothing, and come to them whom they not only pay, but are thankful if they may be allowed to pay them. There is at this time a Parian philosopher residing in Athens, of whom I have heard; and I came to hear of him in this way:—I came across a man who has spent a world of money on the Sophists, Callias, the son of Hipponicus, and knowing that he had sons, I asked him: 'Callias,' I said, 'if your two sons were foals or calves, there would be no difficulty in finding some one to put over them; we should hire a trainer of horses, or a farmer probably, who would improve and perfect them in their own proper virtue and excellence; but as they are human beings, whom are you thinking of placing over them? Is there any one who understands human and political virtue? You must have thought about the matter, for you have sons; is there any one?' 'There is,' he said. 'Who is he?' said I; 'and of what country? and what does he charge?' 'Evenus the Parian,' he replied; 'he is the man, and his charge is five minae.' Happy is Evenus, I said to myself, if he really has this wisdom, and teaches at such a moderate charge. Had I the same, I should have been very proud and conceited; but the truth is that I have no knowledge of the kind.

I dare say, Athenians, that some one among you will reply, 'Yes, Socrates, but what is the origin of these accusations which are brought against you; there must have been something strange which you have been doing? All these rumours and this talk about you would never have arisen if you had been like other men: tell us, then, what is the cause of them, for we should be sorry to judge hastily of you.' Now I regard this as a fair challenge, and I will endeavour to explain to you the reason why I am called wise and have such an evil fame. Please to attend then. And although some of you may think that I am joking, I declare that I will tell you the entire truth. Men of Athens, this reputation of mine has come of a certain sort of wisdom which I possess. If you ask me what kind of wisdom, I reply, wisdom such as may perhaps be attained by man, for to that extent I am inclined to believe that I am wise; whereas the persons of whom I was speaking have a superhuman wisdom which I may fail to describe, because I have it not myself; and he who says that I have, speaks falsely, and is taking away my character. And here, O men of Athens, I must beg you not to interrupt me, even if I seem to say something extravagant. For the word which I will speak is not mine. I will refer you to a witness who is worthy of credit; that witness shall be the God of Delphi—he will tell you about my wisdom, if I have any, and of what sort it is. You must have known Chaerephon; he was early a friend of mine, and also a friend of yours, for he shared in the recent exile of the people, and returned with you. Well, Chaerephon, as you know, was very impetuous in all his doings, and he went to Delphi and boldly asked the oracle to tell him whether—as I was saying, I must beg you not to interrupt—he asked the oracle to tell him whether anyone was wiser than I was, and the Pythian prophetess answered, that there was no man wiser. Chaerephon is dead himself; but his brother, who is in court, will confirm the truth of what I am saying.

Why do I mention this? Because I am going to explain to you why I have such an evil name. When I heard the answer, I said to myself, What can the god mean? and what is the interpretation of his riddle? for I know that I have no wisdom, small or great. What then can he mean when he says that I am the wisest of men? And yet he is a god, and cannot lie; that would be against his nature. After long consideration, I thought of a method of trying the question. I reflected that if I could only find a man wiser than myself, then I might go to the god with a refutation in my hand. I should say to him, 'Here is a man who is wiser than I am; but you said that I was the wisest.' Accordingly I went to one who had the reputation of wisdom, and observed him—his name I need not mention; he was a politician whom I selected for examination—and the result was as follows: When I began to talk with him, I could not help thinking that he was not really wise, although he was thought wise by many, and still wiser by himself; and thereupon I tried to explain to him that he thought himself wise, but was not really wise; and the consequence was that he hated me, and his enmity was shared by several who were present and heard me. So I left him, saying to myself, as I went away: Well, although I do not suppose that either of us knows anything really beautiful and good, I am better off than he is,—for he knows nothing, and thinks that he knows; I neither know nor think that I know. In this latter particular, then, I seem to have slightly the advantage of him. Then I went to another who had still higher pretensions to wisdom, and my conclusion was exactly the same. Whereupon I made another enemy of him, and of many others besides him.

Then I went to one man after another, being not unconscious of the enmity which I provoked, and I lamented and feared this: but necessity was laid upon me,—the word of God, I thought, ought to be considered first. And I said to myself, Go I must to all who appear to know, and find out the meaning of the oracle. And I swear to you, Athenians, by the dog I swear!—for I must tell you the truth—the result of my mission was just this: I found that the men most in repute were all but the most foolish; and that others less esteemed were really wiser and better. I will tell you the tale of my wanderings and of the 'Herculean' labours, as I may call them, which I endured only to find at last the oracle irrefutable. After the politicians, I went to the poets; tragic, dithyrambic, and all sorts. And there, I said to myself, you will be instantly detected; now you will find out that you are more ignorant than they are. Accordingly, I took them some of the most elaborate passages in their own writings, and asked what was the meaning of them—thinking that they would teach me something. Will you believe me? I am almost ashamed to confess the truth, but I must say that there is hardly a person present who would not have talked better about their poetry than they did themselves. Then I knew that not by wisdom do poets write poetry, but by a sort of genius and inspiration; they are like diviners or soothsayers who also say many fine things, but do not understand the meaning of them. The poets appeared to me to be much in the same case; and I further observed that upon the strength of their poetry they believed themselves to be the wisest of men in other things in which they were not wise. So I departed, conceiving myself to be superior to them for the same reason that I was superior to the politicians.

At last I went to the artisans. I was conscious that I knew nothing at all, as I may say, and I was sure that they knew many fine things; and here I was not mistaken, for they did know many things of which I was ignorant, and in this they certainly were wiser than I was. But I observed that even the good artisans fell into the same error as the poets;—because they were good workmen they thought that they also knew all sorts of high matters, and this defect in them overshadowed their wisdom; and therefore I asked myself on behalf of the oracle, whether I would like to be as I was, neither having their knowledge nor their ignorance, or like them in both; and I made answer to myself and to the oracle that I was better off as I was.

This inquisition has led to my having many enemies of the worst and most dangerous kind, and has given occasion also to many calumnies. And I am called wise, for my hearers always imagine that I myself possess the wisdom which I find wanting in others: but the truth is, O men of Athens, that God only is wise; and by his answer he intends to show that the wisdom of men is worth little or nothing; he is not speaking of Socrates, he is only using my name by way of illustration, as if he said, He, O men, is the wisest, who, like Socrates, knows that his wisdom is in truth worth nothing. And so I go about the world, obedient to the god, and search and make enquiry into the wisdom of any one, whether citizen or stranger, who appears to be wise; and if he is not wise, then in vindication of the oracle I show him that he is not wise; and my occupation quite absorbs me, and I have no time to give either to any public matter of interest or to any concern of my own, but I am in utter poverty by reason of my devotion to the god.

There is another thing:—young men of the richer classes, who have not much to do, come about me of their own accord; they like to hear the pretenders examined, and they often imitate me, and proceed to examine others; there are plenty of persons, as they quickly discover, who think that they know something, but really know little or nothing; and then those who are examined by them instead of being angry with themselves are angry with me: This confounded Socrates, they say; this villainous misleader of youth!—and then if somebody asks them, Why, what evil does he practise or teach? they do not know, and cannot tell; but in order that they may not appear to be at a loss, they repeat the ready-made charges which are used against all philosophers about teaching things up in the clouds and under the earth, and having no gods, and making the worse appear the better cause; for they do not like to confess that their pretence of knowledge has been detected—which is the truth; and as they are numerous and ambitious and energetic, and are drawn up in battle array and have persuasive tongues, they have filled your ears with their loud and inveterate calumnies. And this is the reason why my three accusers, Meletus and Anytus and Lycon, have set upon me; Meletus, who has a quarrel with me on behalf of the poets; Anytus, on behalf of the craftsmen and politicians; Lycon, on behalf of the rhetoricians: and as I said at the beginning, I cannot expect to get rid of such a mass of calumny all in a moment. And this, O men of Athens, is the truth and the whole truth; I have concealed nothing, I have dissembled nothing. And yet, I know that my plainness of speech makes them hate me, and what is their hatred but a proof that I am speaking the truth?—Hence has arisen the prejudice against me; and this is the reason of it, as you will find out either in this or in any future enquiry.

I have said enough in my defence against the first class of my accusers; I turn to the second class. They are headed by Meletus, that good man and true lover of his country, as he calls himself. Against these, too, I must try to make a defence:—Let their affidavit be read: it contains something of this kind: It says that Socrates is a doer of evil, who corrupts the youth; and who does not believe in the gods of the state, but has other new divinities of his own. Such is the charge; and now let us examine the particular counts. He says that I am a doer of evil, and corrupt the youth; but I say, O men of Athens, that Meletus is a doer of evil, in that he pretends to be in earnest when he is only in jest, and is so eager to bring men to trial from a pretended zeal and interest about matters in which he really never had the smallest interest. And the truth of this I will endeavour to prove to you.

Come hither, Meletus, and let me ask a question of you. You think a great deal about the improvement of youth?

Yes, I do.

Tell the judges, then, who is their improver; for you must know, as you have taken the pains to discover their corrupter, and are citing and accusing me before them. Speak, then, and tell the judges who their improver is.—Observe, Meletus, that you are silent, and have nothing to say. But is not this rather disgraceful, and a very considerable proof of what I was saying, that you have no interest in the matter? Speak up, friend, and tell us who their improver is.

The laws.

But that, my good sir, is not my meaning. I want to know who the person is, who, in the first place, knows the laws.

The judges, Socrates, who are present in court.

What, do you mean to say, Meletus, that they are able to instruct and improve youth?

Certainly they are.

What, all of them, or some only and not others?

All of them.

By the goddess Here, that is good news! There are plenty of improvers, then. And what do you say of the audience,—do they improve them?

Yes, they do.

And the senators?

Yes, the senators improve them.

But perhaps the members of the assembly corrupt them?—or do they too improve them?

They improve them.

Then every Athenian improves and elevates them; all with the exception of myself; and I alone am their corrupter? Is that what you affirm?

That is what I stoutly affirm.

I am very unfortunate if you are right. But suppose I ask you a question: How about horses? Does one man do them harm and all the world good? Is not the exact opposite the truth? One man is able to do them good, or at least not many;—the trainer of horses, that is to say, does them good, and others who have to do with them rather injure them? Is not that true, Meletus, of horses, or of any other animals? Most assuredly it is; whether you and Anytus say yes or no. Happy indeed would be the condition of youth if they had one corrupter only, and all the rest of the world were their improvers. But you, Meletus, have sufficiently shown that you never had a thought about the young: your carelessness is seen in your not caring about the very things which you bring against me.

And now, Meletus, I will ask you another question—by Zeus I will: Which is better, to live among bad citizens, or among good ones? Answer, friend, I say; the question is one which may be easily answered. Do not the good do their neighbours good, and the bad do them evil?

Certainly.

And is there anyone who would rather be injured than benefited by those who live with him? Answer, my good friend, the law requires you to answer—does any one like to be injured?

Certainly not.

And when you accuse me of corrupting and deteriorating the youth, do you allege that I corrupt them intentionally or unintentionally?

Intentionally, I say.

But you have just admitted that the good do their neighbours good, and the evil do them evil. Now, is that a truth which your superior wisdom has recognized thus early in life, and am I, at my age, in such darkness and ignorance as not to know that if a man with whom I have to live is corrupted by me, I am very likely to be harmed by him; and yet I corrupt him, and intentionally, too—so you say, although neither I nor any other human being is ever likely to be convinced by you. But either I do not corrupt them, or I corrupt them unintentionally; and on either view of the case you lie. If my offence is unintentional, the law has no cognizance of unintentional offences: you ought to have taken me privately, and warned and admonished me; for if I had been better advised, I should have left off doing what I only did unintentionally— no doubt I should; but you would have nothing to say to me and refused to teach me. And now you bring me up in this court, which is a place not of instruction, but of punishment.

It will be very clear to you, Athenians, as I was saying, that Meletus has no care at all, great or small, about the matter. But still I should like to know, Meletus, in what I am affirmed to corrupt the young. I suppose you mean, as I infer from your indictment, that I teach them not to acknowledge the gods which the state acknowledges, but some other new divinities or spiritual agencies in their stead. These are the lessons by which I corrupt the youth, as you say.

Yes, that I say emphatically.

Then, by the gods, Meletus, of whom we are speaking, tell me and the court, in somewhat plainer terms, what you mean! for I do not as yet understand whether you affirm that I teach other men to acknowledge some gods, and therefore that I do believe in gods, and am not an entire atheist—this you do not lay to my charge,—but only you say that they are not the same gods which the city recognizes—the charge is that they are different gods. Or, do you mean that I am an atheist simply, and a teacher of atheism?

I mean the latter—that you are a complete atheist.

What an extraordinary statement! Why do you think so, Meletus? Do you mean that I do not believe in the godhead of the sun or moon, like other men?

I assure you, judges, that he does not: for he says that the sun is stone, and the moon earth.

Friend Meletus, you think that you are accusing Anaxagoras: and you have but a bad opinion of the judges, if you fancy them illiterate to such a degree as not to know that these doctrines are found in the books of Anaxagoras the Clazomenian, which are full of them. And so, forsooth, the youth are said to be taught them by Socrates, when there are not unfrequently exhibitions of them at the theatre (Probably in allusion to Aristophanes who caricatured, and to Euripides who borrowed the notions of Anaxagoras, as well as to other dramatic poets.) (price of admission one drachma at the most); and they might pay their money, and laugh at Socrates if he pretends to father these extraordinary views. And so, Meletus, you really think that I do not believe in any god?

I swear by Zeus that you believe absolutely in none at all.

Nobody will believe you, Meletus, and I am pretty sure that you do not believe yourself. I cannot help thinking, men of Athens, that Meletus is reckless and impudent, and that he has written this indictment in a spirit of mere wantonness and youthful bravado. Has he not compounded a riddle, thinking to try me? He said to himself:—I shall see whether the wise Socrates will discover my facetious contradiction, or whether I shall be able to deceive him and the rest of them. For he certainly does appear to me to contradict himself in the indictment as much as if he said that Socrates is guilty of not believing in the gods, and yet of believing in them—but this is not like a person who is in earnest.

I should like you, O men of Athens, to join me in examining what I conceive to be his inconsistency; and do you, Meletus, answer. And I must remind the audience of my request that they would not make a disturbance if I speak in my accustomed manner:

Did ever man, Meletus, believe in the existence of human things, and not of human beings?... I wish, men of Athens, that he would answer, and not be always trying to get up an interruption. Did ever any man believe in horsemanship, and not in horses? or in flute-playing, and not in flute- players? No, my friend; I will answer to you and to the court, as you refuse to answer for yourself. There is no man who ever did. But now please to answer the next question: Can a man believe in spiritual and divine agencies, and not in spirits or demigods?

He cannot.

How lucky I am to have extracted that answer, by the assistance of the court! But then you swear in the indictment that I teach and believe in divine or spiritual agencies (new or old, no matter for that); at any rate, I believe in spiritual agencies,—so you say and swear in the affidavit; and yet if I believe in divine beings, how can I help believing in spirits or demigods;—must I not? To be sure I must; and therefore I may assume that your silence gives consent. Now what are spirits or demigods? Are they not either gods or the sons of gods?

Certainly they are.

But this is what I call the facetious riddle invented by you: the demigods or spirits are gods, and you say first that I do not believe in gods, and then again that I do believe in gods; that is, if I believe in demigods. For if the demigods are the illegitimate sons of gods, whether by the nymphs or by any other mothers, of whom they are said to be the sons—what human being will ever believe that there are no gods if they are the sons of gods? You might as well affirm the existence of mules, and deny that of horses and asses. Such nonsense, Meletus, could only have been intended by you to make trial of me. You have put this into the indictment because you had nothing real of which to accuse me. But no one who has a particle of understanding will ever be convinced by you that the same men can believe in divine and superhuman things, and yet not believe that there are gods and demigods and heroes.

I have said enough in answer to the charge of Meletus: any elaborate defence is unnecessary, but I know only too well how many are the enmities which I have incurred, and this is what will be my destruction if I am destroyed;—not Meletus, nor yet Anytus, but the envy and detraction of the world, which has been the death of many good men, and will probably be the death of many more; there is no danger of my being the last of them.

Some one will say: And are you not ashamed, Socrates, of a course of life which is likely to bring you to an untimely end? To him I may fairly answer: There you are mistaken: a man who is good for anything ought not to calculate the chance of living or dying; he ought only to consider whether in doing anything he is doing right or wrong—acting the part of a good man or of a bad. Whereas, upon your view, the heroes who fell at Troy were not good for much, and the son of Thetis above all, who altogether despised danger in comparison with disgrace; and when he was so eager to slay Hector, his goddess mother said to him, that if he avenged his companion Patroclus, and slew Hector, he would die himself—'Fate,' she said, in these or the like words, 'waits for you next after Hector;' he, receiving this warning, utterly despised danger and death, and instead of fearing them, feared rather to live in dishonour, and not to avenge his friend. 'Let me die forthwith,' he replies, 'and be avenged of my enemy, rather than abide here by the beaked ships, a laughing-stock and a burden of the earth.' Had Achilles any thought of death and danger? For wherever a man's place is, whether the place which he has chosen or that in which he has been placed by a commander, there he ought to remain in the hour of danger; he should not think of death or of anything but of disgrace. And this, O men of Athens, is a true saying.

Strange, indeed, would be my conduct, O men of Athens, if I who, when I was ordered by the generals whom you chose to command me at Potidaea and Amphipolis and Delium, remained where they placed me, like any other man, facing death—if now, when, as I conceive and imagine, God orders me to fulfil the philosopher's mission of searching into myself and other men, I were to desert my post through fear of death, or any other fear; that would indeed be strange, and I might justly be arraigned in court for denying the existence of the gods, if I disobeyed the oracle because I was afraid of death, fancying that I was wise when I was not wise. For the fear of death is indeed the pretence of wisdom, and not real wisdom, being a pretence of knowing the unknown; and no one knows whether death, which men in their fear apprehend to be the greatest evil, may not be the greatest good. Is not this ignorance of a disgraceful sort, the ignorance which is the conceit that a man knows what he does not know? And in this respect only I believe myself to differ from men in general, and may perhaps claim to be wiser than they are:—that whereas I know but little of the world below, I do not suppose that I know: but I do know that injustice and disobedience to a better, whether God or man, is evil and dishonourable, and I will never fear or avoid a possible good rather than a certain evil. And therefore if you let me go now, and are not convinced by Anytus, who said that since I had been prosecuted I must be put to death; (or if not that I ought never to have been prosecuted at all); and that if I escape now, your sons will all be utterly ruined by listening to my words—if you say to me, Socrates, this time we will not mind Anytus, and you shall be let off, but upon one condition, that you are not to enquire and speculate in this way any more, and that if you are caught doing so again you shall die;—if this was the condition on which you let me go, I should reply: Men of Athens, I honour and love you; but I shall obey God rather than you, and while I have life and strength I shall never cease from the practice and teaching of philosophy, exhorting any one whom I meet and saying to him after my manner: You, my friend,—a citizen of the great and mighty and wise city of Athens,—are you not ashamed of heaping up the greatest amount of money and honour and reputation, and caring so little about wisdom and truth and the greatest improvement of the soul, which you never regard or heed at all? And if the person with whom I am arguing, says: Yes, but I do care; then I do not leave him or let him go at once; but I proceed to interrogate and examine and cross-examine him, and if I think that he has no virtue in him, but only says that he has, I reproach him with undervaluing the greater, and overvaluing the less. And I shall repeat the same words to every one whom I meet, young and old, citizen and alien, but especially to the citizens, inasmuch as they are my brethren. For know that this is the command of God; and I believe that no greater good has ever happened in the state than my service to the God. For I do nothing but go about persuading you all, old and young alike, not to take thought for your persons or your properties, but first and chiefly to care about the greatest improvement of the soul. I tell you that virtue is not given by money, but that from virtue comes money and every other good of man, public as well as private. This is my teaching, and if this is the doctrine which corrupts the youth, I am a mischievous person. But if any one says that this is not my teaching, he is speaking an untruth. Wherefore, O men of Athens, I say to you, do as Anytus bids or not as Anytus bids, and either acquit me or not; but whichever you do, understand that I shall never alter my ways, not even if I have to die many times.

Men of Athens, do not interrupt, but hear me; there was an understanding between us that you should hear me to the end: I have something more to say, at which you may be inclined to cry out; but I believe that to hear me will be good for you, and therefore I beg that you will not cry out. I would have you know, that if you kill such an one as I am, you will injure yourselves more than you will injure me. Nothing will injure me, not Meletus nor yet Anytus—they cannot, for a bad man is not permitted to injure a better than himself. I do not deny that Anytus may, perhaps, kill him, or drive him into exile, or deprive him of civil rights; and he may imagine, and others may imagine, that he is inflicting a great injury upon him: but there I do not agree. For the evil of doing as he is doing—the evil of unjustly taking away the life of another—is greater far.

And now, Athenians, I am not going to argue for my own sake, as you may think, but for yours, that you may not sin against the God by condemning me, who am his gift to you. For if you kill me you will not easily find a successor to me, who, if I may use such a ludicrous figure of speech, am a sort of gadfly, given to the state by God; and the state is a great and noble steed who is tardy in his motions owing to his very size, and requires to be stirred into life. I am that gadfly which God has attached to the state, and all day long and in all places am always fastening upon you, arousing and persuading and reproaching you. You will not easily find another like me, and therefore I would advise you to spare me. I dare say that you may feel out of temper (like a person who is suddenly awakened from sleep), and you think that you might easily strike me dead as Anytus advises, and then you would sleep on for the remainder of your lives, unless God in his care of you sent you another gadfly. When I say that I am given to you by God, the proof of my mission is this:—if I had been like other men, I should not have neglected all my own concerns or patiently seen the neglect of them during all these years, and have been doing yours, coming to you individually like a father or elder brother, exhorting you to regard virtue; such conduct, I say, would be unlike human nature. If I had gained anything, or if my exhortations had been paid, there would have been some sense in my doing so; but now, as you will perceive, not even the impudence of my accusers dares to say that I have ever exacted or sought pay of any one; of that they have no witness. And I have a sufficient witness to the truth of what I say—my poverty.

Some one may wonder why I go about in private giving advice and busying myself with the concerns of others, but do not venture to come forward in public and advise the state. I will tell you why. You have heard me speak at sundry times and in divers places of an oracle or sign which comes to me, and is the divinity which Meletus ridicules in the indictment. This sign, which is a kind of voice, first began to come to me when I was a child; it always forbids but never commands me to do anything which I am going to do. This is what deters me from being a politician. And rightly, as I think. For I am certain, O men of Athens, that if I had engaged in politics, I should have perished long ago, and done no good either to you or to myself. And do not be offended at my telling you the truth: for the truth is, that no man who goes to war with you or any other multitude, honestly striving against the many lawless and unrighteous deeds which are done in a state, will save his life; he who will fight for the right, if he would live even for a brief space, must have a private station and not a public one.

I can give you convincing evidence of what I say, not words only, but what you value far more—actions. Let me relate to you a passage of my own life which will prove to you that I should never have yielded to injustice from any fear of death, and that 'as I should have refused to yield' I must have died at once. I will tell you a tale of the courts, not very interesting perhaps, but nevertheless true. The only office of state which I ever held, O men of Athens, was that of senator: the tribe Antiochis, which is my tribe, had the presidency at the trial of the generals who had not taken up the bodies of the slain after the battle of Arginusae; and you proposed to try them in a body, contrary to law, as you all thought afterwards; but at the time I was the only one of the

Prytanes who was opposed to the illegality, and I gave my vote against you; and when the orators threatened to impeach and arrest me, and you called and shouted, I made up my mind that I would run the risk, having law and justice with me, rather than take part in your injustice because I feared imprisonment and death. This happened in the days of the democracy. But when the oligarchy of the Thirty was in power, they sent for me and four others into the rotunda, and bade us bring Leon the Salaminian from Salamis, as they wanted to put him to death. This was a specimen of the sort of commands which they were always giving with the view of implicating as many as possible in their crimes; and then I showed, not in word only but in deed, that, if I may be allowed to use such an expression, I cared not a straw for death, and that my great and only care was lest I should do an unrighteous or unholy thing. For the strong arm of that oppressive power did not frighten me into doing wrong; and when we came out of the rotunda the other four went to Salamis and fetched Leon, but I went quietly home. For which I might have lost my life, had not the power of the Thirty shortly afterwards come to an end. And many will witness to my words.

Now do you really imagine that I could have survived all these years, if I had led a public life, supposing that like a good man I had always maintained the right and had made justice, as I ought, the first thing? No indeed, men of Athens, neither I nor any other man. But I have been always the same in all my actions, public as well as private, and never have I yielded any base compliance to those who are slanderously termed my disciples, or to any other. Not that I have any regular disciples. But if any one likes to come and hear me while I am pursuing my mission, whether he be young or old, he is not excluded. Nor do I converse only with those who pay; but any one, whether he be rich or poor, may ask and answer me and listen to my words; and whether he turns out to be a bad man or a good one, neither result can be justly imputed to me; for I never taught or professed to teach him anything. And if any one says that he has ever learned or heard anything from me in private which all the world has not heard, let me tell you that he is lying.

But I shall be asked, Why do people delight in continually conversing with you? I have told you already, Athenians, the whole truth about this matter: they like to hear the cross-examination of the pretenders to wisdom; there is amusement in it. Now this duty of cross-examining other men has been imposed upon me by God; and has been signified to me by oracles, visions, and in every way in which the will of divine power was ever intimated to any one. This is true, O Athenians, or, if not true, would be soon refuted. If I am or have been corrupting the youth, those of them who are now grown up and have become sensible that I gave them bad advice in the days of their youth should come forward as accusers, and take their revenge; or if they do not like to come themselves, some of their relatives, fathers, brothers, or other kinsmen, should say what evil their families have suffered at my hands. Now is their time. Many of them I see in the court. There is Crito, who is of the same age and of the same deme with myself, and there is Critobulus his son, whom I also see. Then again there is Lysanias of Sphettus, who is the father of Aeschines—he is present; and also there is Antiphon of Cephisus, who is the father of Epigenes; and there are the brothers of several who have associated with me. There is Nicostratus the son of Theosdotides, and the brother of Theodotus (now Theodotus himself is dead, and therefore he, at any rate, will not seek to stop him); and there is Paralus the son of Demodocus, who had a brother Theages; and Adeimantus the son of Ariston, whose brother Plato is present; and Aeantodorus, who is the brother of Apollodorus, whom I also see. I might mention a great many others, some of whom Meletus should have produced as witnesses in the course of his speech; and let him still produce them, if he has forgotten—I will make way for him. And let him say, if he has any testimony of the sort which he can produce. Nay, Athenians, the very opposite is the truth. For all these are ready to witness on behalf of the corrupter, of the injurer of their kindred, as Meletus and Anytus call me; not the corrupted youth only—there might have been a motive for that—but their uncorrupted elder relatives. Why should they too support me with their testimony? Why, indeed, except for the sake of truth and justice, and because they know that I am speaking the truth, and that Meletus is a liar.

Well, Athenians, this and the like of this is all the defence which I have to offer. Yet a word more. Perhaps there may be some one who is offended at me, when he calls to mind how he himself on a similar, or even a less serious occasion, prayed and entreated the judges with many tears, and how he produced his children in court, which was a moving spectacle, together with a host of relations and friends; whereas I, who am probably in danger of my life, will do none of these things. The contrast may occur to his mind, and he may be set against me, and vote in anger because he is displeased at me on this account. Now if there be such a person among you,—mind, I do not say that there is,— to him I may fairly reply: My friend, I am a man, and like other men, a creature of flesh and blood, and not 'of wood or stone,' as Homer says; and I have a family, yes, and sons, O Athenians, three in number, one almost a man, and two others who are still young; and yet I will not bring any of them hither in order to petition you for an acquittal. And why not? Not from any self-assertion or want of respect for you. Whether I am or am not afraid of death is another question, of which I will not now speak. But, having regard to public opinion, I feel that such conduct would be discreditable to myself, and to you, and to the whole state. One who has reached my years, and who has a name for wisdom, ought not to demean himself. Whether this opinion of me be deserved or not, at any rate the world has decided that Socrates is in some way superior to other men. And if those among you who are said to be superior in wisdom and courage, and any other virtue, demean themselves in this way, how shameful is their conduct! I have seen men of reputation, when they have been condemned, behaving in the strangest manner: they seemed to fancy that they were going to suffer something dreadful if they died, and that they could be immortal if you only allowed them to live; and I think that such are a dishonour to the state, and that any stranger coming in would have said of them that the most eminent men of Athens, to whom the Athenians themselves give honour and command, are no better than women. And I say that these things ought not to be done by those of us who have a reputation; and if they are done, you ought not to permit them; you ought rather to show that you are far more disposed to condemn the man who gets up a doleful scene and makes the city ridiculous, than him who holds his peace.

But, setting aside the question of public opinion, there seems to be something wrong in asking a favour of a judge, and thus procuring an acquittal, instead of informing and convincing him. For his duty is, not to make a present of justice, but to give judgment; and he has sworn that he will judge according to the laws, and not according to his own good pleasure; and we ought not to encourage you, nor should you allow yourselves to be encouraged, in this habit of perjury—there can be no piety in that. Do not then require me to do what I consider dishonourable and impious and wrong, especially now, when I am being tried for impiety on the indictment of Meletus. For if, O men of Athens, by force of persuasion and entreaty I could overpower your oaths, then I should be teaching you to believe that there are no gods, and in defending should simply convict myself of the charge of not believing in them. But that is not so—far otherwise. For I do believe that there are gods, and in a sense higher than that in which any of my accusers believe in them. And to you and to God I commit my cause, to be determined by you as is best for you and me.

* * * * *

There are many reasons why I am not grieved, O men of Athens, at the vote of condemnation. I expected it, and am only surprised that the votes are so nearly equal; for I had thought that the majority against me would have been far larger; but now, had thirty votes gone over to the other side, I should have been acquitted. And I may say, I think, that I have escaped Meletus. I may say more; for without the assistance of Anytus and Lycon, any one may see that he would not have had a fifth part of the votes, as the law requires, in which case he would have incurred a fine of a thousand drachmae.

And so he proposes death as the penalty. And what shall I propose on my part, O men of Athens? Clearly that which is my due. And what is my due? What return shall be made to the man who has never had the wit to be idle during his whole life; but has been careless of what the many care for—wealth, and family interests, and military offices, and speaking in the assembly, and magistracies, and plots, and parties. Reflecting that I was really too honest a man to be a politician and live, I did not go where I could do no good to you or to myself; but where I could do the greatest good privately to every one of you, thither I went, and sought to persuade every man among you that he must look to himself, and seek virtue and wisdom before he looks to his private interests, and look to the state before he looks to the interests of the state; and that this should be the order which he observes in all his actions. What shall be done to such an one? Doubtless some good thing, O men of Athens, if he has his reward; and the good should be of a kind suitable to him. What would be a reward suitable to a poor man who is your benefactor, and who desires leisure that he may instruct you? There can be no reward so fitting as maintenance in the Prytaneum, O men of Athens, a reward which he deserves far more than the citizen who has won the prize at Olympia in the horse or chariot race, whether the chariots were drawn by two horses or by many. For I am in want, and he has enough; and he only gives you the appearance of happiness, and I give you the reality. And if I am to estimate the penalty fairly, I should say that maintenance in the Prytaneum is the just return.

Perhaps you think that I am braving you in what I am saying now, as in what I said before about the tears and prayers. But this is not so. I speak rather because I am convinced that I never intentionally wronged any one, although I cannot convince you—the time has been too short; if there were a law at Athens, as there is in other cities, that a capital cause should not be decided in one day, then I believe that I should have convinced you. But I cannot in a moment refute great slanders; and, as I am convinced that I never wronged another, I will assuredly not wrong myself. I will not say of myself that I deserve any evil, or propose any penalty. Why should I? because I am afraid of the penalty of death which Meletus proposes? When I do not know whether death is a good or an evil, why should I propose a penalty which would certainly be an evil? Shall I say imprisonment? And why should I live in prison, and be the slave of the magistrates of the year—of the Eleven? Or shall the penalty be a fine, and imprisonment until the fine is paid? There is the same objection. I should have to lie in prison, for money I have none, and cannot pay. And if I say exile (and this may possibly be the penalty which you will affix), I must indeed be blinded by the love of life, if I am so irrational as to expect that when you, who are my own citizens, cannot endure my discourses and words, and have found them so grievous and odious that you will have no more of them, others are likely to endure me. No indeed, men of Athens, that is not very likely. And what a life should I lead, at my age, wandering from city to city, ever changing my place of exile, and always being driven out! For I am quite sure that wherever I go, there, as here, the young men will flock to me; and if I drive them away, their elders will drive me out at their request; and if I let them come, their fathers and friends will drive me out for their sakes.

Some one will say: Yes, Socrates, but cannot you hold your tongue, and then you may go into a foreign city, and no one will interfere with you? Now I have great difficulty in making you understand my answer to this. For if I tell you that to do as you say would be a disobedience to the God, and therefore that I cannot hold my tongue, you will not believe that I am serious; and if I say again that daily to discourse about virtue, and of those other things about which you hear me examining myself and others, is the greatest good of man, and that the unexamined life is not worth living, you are still less likely to believe me. Yet I say what is true, although a thing of which it is hard for me to persuade you. Also, I have never been accustomed to think that I deserve to suffer any harm. Had I money I might have estimated the offence at what I was able to pay, and not have been much the worse. But I have none, and therefore I must ask you to proportion the fine to my means. Well, perhaps I could afford a mina, and therefore I propose that penalty: Plato, Crito, Critobulus, and Apollodorus, my friends here, bid me say thirty minae, and they will be the sureties. Let thirty minae be the penalty; for which sum they will be ample security to you.

* * * * *

Not much time will be gained, O Athenians, in return for the evil name which you will get from the detractors of the city, who will say that you killed Socrates, a wise man; for they will call me wise, even although I am not wise, when they want to reproach you. If you had waited a little while, your desire would have been fulfilled in the course of nature. For I am far advanced in years, as you may perceive, and not far from death. I am speaking now not to all of you, but only to those who have condemned me to death. And I have another thing to say to them: you think that I was convicted because I had no words of the sort which would have procured my acquittal—I mean, if I had thought fit to leave nothing undone or unsaid. Not so; the deficiency which led to my conviction was not of words—certainly not. But I had not the boldness or impudence or inclination to address you as you would have liked me to do, weeping and wailing and lamenting, and saying and doing many things which you have been accustomed to hear from others, and which, as I maintain, are unworthy of me. I thought at the time that I ought not to do anything common or mean when in danger: nor do I now repent of the style of my defence; I would rather die having spoken after my manner, than speak in your manner and live. For neither in war nor yet at law ought I or any man to use every way of escaping death. Often in battle there can be no doubt that if a man will throw away his arms, and fall on his knees before his pursuers, he may escape death; and in other dangers there are other ways of escaping death, if a man is willing to say and do anything. The difficulty, my friends, is not to avoid death, but to avoid unrighteousness; for that runs faster than death. I am old and move slowly, and the slower runner has overtaken me, and my accusers are keen and quick, and the faster runner, who is unrighteousness, has overtaken them. And now I depart hence condemned by you to suffer the penalty of death,—they too go their ways condemned by the truth to suffer the penalty of villainy and wrong; and I must abide by my award—let them abide by theirs. I suppose that these things may be regarded as fated,—and I think that they are well.

And now, O men who have condemned me, I would fain prophesy to you; for I am about to die, and in the hour of death men are gifted with prophetic power. And I prophesy to you who are my murderers, that immediately after my departure punishment far heavier than you have inflicted on me will surely await you. Me you have killed because you wanted to escape the accuser, and not to give an account of your lives. But that will not be as you suppose: far otherwise. For I say that there will be more accusers of you than there are now; accusers whom hitherto I have restrained: and as they are younger they will be more inconsiderate with you, and you will be more offended at them. If you think that by killing men you can prevent some one from censuring your evil lives, you are mistaken; that is not a way of escape which is either possible or honourable; the easiest and the noblest way is not to be disabling others, but to be improving yourselves. This is the prophecy which I utter before my departure to the judges who have condemned me.

Friends, who would have acquitted me, I would like also to talk with you about the thing which has come to pass, while the magistrates are busy, and before I go to the place at which I must die. Stay then a little, for we may as well talk with one another while there is time. You are my friends, and I should like to show you the meaning of this event which has happened to me. O my judges—for you I may truly call judges—I should like to tell you of a wonderful circumstance. Hitherto the divine faculty of which the internal oracle is the source has constantly been in the habit of opposing me even about trifles, if I was going to make a slip or error in any matter; and now as you see there has come upon me that which may be thought, and is generally believed to be, the last and worst evil. But the oracle made no sign of opposition, either when I was leaving my house in the morning, or when I was on my way to the court, or while I was speaking, at anything which I was going to say; and yet I have often been stopped in the middle of a speech, but now in nothing I either said or did touching the matter in hand has the oracle opposed me. What do I take to be the explanation of this silence? I will tell you. It is an intimation that what has happened to me is a good, and that those of us who think that death is an evil are in error. For the customary sign would surely have opposed me had I been going to evil and not to good.

Let us reflect in another way, and we shall see that there is great reason to hope that death is a good; for one of two things—either death is a state of nothingness and utter unconsciousness, or, as men say, there is a change and migration of the soul from this world to another. Now if you suppose that there is no consciousness, but a sleep like the sleep of him who is undisturbed even by dreams, death will be an unspeakable gain. For if a person were to select the night in which his sleep was undisturbed even by dreams, and were to compare with this the other days and nights of his life, and then were to tell us how many days and nights he had passed in the course of his life better and more pleasantly than this one, I think that any man, I will not say a private man, but even the great king will not find many such days or nights, when compared with the others. Now if death be of such a nature, I say that to die is gain; for eternity is then only a single night. But if death is the journey to another place, and there, as men say, all the dead abide, what good, O my friends and judges, can be greater than this? If indeed when the pilgrim arrives in the world below, he is delivered from the professors of justice in this world, and finds the true judges who are said to give judgment there, Minos and Rhadamanthus and Aeacus and Triptolemus, and other sons of God who were righteous in their own life, that pilgrimage will be worth making. What would not a man give if he might converse with Orpheus and Musaeus and Hesiod and Homer? Nay, if this be true, let me die again and again. I myself, too, shall have a wonderful interest in there meeting and conversing with Palamedes, and Ajax the son of Telamon, and any other ancient hero who has suffered death through an unjust judgment; and there will be no small pleasure, as I think, in comparing my own sufferings with theirs. Above all, I shall then be able to continue my search into true and false knowledge; as in this world, so also in the next; and I shall find out who is wise, and who pretends to be wise, and is not. What would not a man give, O judges, to be able to examine the leader of the great Trojan expedition; or Odysseus or Sisyphus, or numberless others, men and women too! What infinite delight would there be in conversing with them and asking them questions! In another world they do not put a man to death for asking questions: assuredly not. For besides being happier than we are, they will be immortal, if what is said is true.

Wherefore, O judges, be of good cheer about death, and know of a certainty, that no evil can happen to a good man, either in life or after death. He and his are not neglected by the gods; nor has my own approaching end happened by mere chance. But I see clearly that the time had arrived when it was better for me to die and be released from trouble; wherefore the oracle gave no sign. For which reason, also, I am not angry with my condemners, or with my accusers; they have done me no harm, although they did not mean to do me any good; and for this I may gently blame them.

Still I have a favour to ask of them. When my sons are grown up, I would ask you, O my friends, to punish them; and I would have you trouble them, as I have troubled you, if they seem to care about riches, or anything, more than about virtue; or if they pretend to be something when they are really nothing,—then reprove them, as I have reproved you, for not caring about that for which they ought to care, and thinking that they are something when they are really nothing. And if you do this, both I and my sons will have received justice at your hands.

The hour of departure has arrived, and we go our ways—I to die, and you to live. Which is better God only knows.

Crito

INTRODUCTION

The Crito seems intended to exhibit the character of Socrates in one light only, not as the philosopher, fulfilling a divine mission and trusting in the will of heaven, but simply as the good citizen, who having been unjustly condemned is willing to give up his life in obedience to the laws of the state...

The days of Socrates are drawing to a close; the fatal ship has been seen off Sunium, as he is informed by his aged friend and contemporary Crito, who visits him before the dawn has broken; he himself has been warned in a dream that on the third day he must depart. Time is precious, and Crito has come early in order to gain his consent to a plan of escape. This can be easily accomplished by his friends, who will incur no danger in making the attempt to save him, but will be disgraced for ever if they allow him to perish. He should think of his duty to his children, and not play into the hands of his enemies. Money is already provided by Crito as well as by Simmias and others, and he will have no difficulty in finding friends in Thessaly and other places.

Socrates is afraid that Crito is but pressing upon him the opinions of the many: whereas, all his life long he has followed the dictates of reason only and the opinion of the one wise or skilled man. There was a time when Crito himself had allowed the propriety of this. And although some one will say 'the many can kill us,' that makes no difference; but a good life, in other words, a just and honourable life, is alone to be valued. All considerations of loss of reputation or injury to his children should be dismissed: the only question is whether he would be right in attempting to escape. Crito, who is a disinterested person not having the fear of death before his eyes, shall answer this for him. Before he was condemned they had often held discussions, in which they agreed that no man should either do evil, or return evil for evil, or betray the right. Are these principles to be altered because the circumstances of Socrates are altered? Crito admits that they remain the same. Then is his escape consistent with the maintenance of them? To this Crito is unable or unwilling to reply.

Socrates proceeds:—Suppose the Laws of Athens to come and remonstrate with him: they will ask 'Why does he seek to overturn them?' and if he replies, 'they have injured him,' will not the Laws answer, 'Yes, but was that the agreement? Has he any objection to make to them which would justify him in overturning them? Was he not brought into the world and educated by their help, and are they not his parents? He might have left Athens and gone where he pleased, but he has lived there for seventy years more constantly than any other citizen.' Thus he has clearly shown that he acknowledged the agreement, which he cannot now break without dishonour to himself and danger to his friends. Even in the course of the trial he might have proposed exile as the penalty, but then he declared that he preferred death to exile. And whither will he direct his footsteps? In any well-ordered state the Laws will consider him as an enemy. Possibly in a land of misrule like Thessaly he may be welcomed at first, and the unseemly narrative of his escape will be regarded by the inhabitants as an amusing tale. But if he offends them he will have to learn another sort of lesson. Will he continue to give lectures in virtue? That would hardly be decent. And how will his children be the gainers if he takes them into Thessaly, and deprives them of Athenian citizenship? Or if he leaves them behind, does he expect that they will be better taken care of by his friends because he is in Thessaly? Will not true friends care for them equally whether he is alive or dead?

Finally, they exhort him to think of justice first, and of life and children afterwards. He may now depart in peace and innocence, a sufferer and not a doer of evil. But if he breaks agreements, and returns evil for evil, they will be angry with him while he lives; and their brethren the Laws of the world below will receive him as an enemy. Such is the mystic voice which is always murmuring in his ears.

That Socrates was not a good citizen was a charge made against him during his lifetime, which has been often repeated in later ages. The crimes of Alcibiades, Critias, and Charmides, who had been his pupils, were still recent in the memory of the now restored democracy. The fact that he had been neutral in the death-struggle of Athens was not likely to conciliate popular good-will. Plato, writing probably in the next generation, undertakes the defence of his friend and master in this particular, not to the Athenians of his day, but to posterity and the world at large.

Whether such an incident ever really occurred as the visit of Crito and the proposal of escape is uncertain: Plato could easily have invented far more than that (Phaedr.); and in the selection of Crito, the aged friend, as the fittest person to make the proposal to Socrates, we seem to recognize the hand of the artist. Whether any one who has been subjected by the laws of his country to an unjust judgment is right in attempting to escape, is a thesis about which casuists might disagree. Shelley (Prose Works) is of opinion that Socrates 'did well to die,' but not for the 'sophistical' reasons which Plato has put into his mouth. And there would be no difficulty in arguing that Socrates should have lived and preferred to a glorious death the good which he might still be able to perform. 'A rhetorician would have had much to say upon that point.' It may be observed however that Plato never intended to answer the question of casuistry, but only to exhibit the ideal of patient virtue which refuses to do the least evil in order to avoid the greatest, and to show his master maintaining in death the opinions which he had professed in his life. Not 'the world,' but the 'one wise man,' is still the paradox of Socrates in his last hours. He must be guided by reason, although her conclusions may be fatal to him. The remarkable sentiment that the wicked can do neither good nor evil is true, if taken in the sense, which he means, of moral evil; in his own words, 'they cannot make a man wise or foolish.'

This little dialogue is a perfect piece of dialectic, in which granting the 'common principle,' there is no escaping from the conclusion. It is anticipated at the beginning by the dream of Socrates and the parody of Homer. The personification of the Laws, and of their brethren the Laws in the world below, is one of the noblest and boldest figures of speech which occur in Plato.

CRITO

PERSONS OF THE DIALOGUE: Socrates, Crito.

SCENE: The Prison of Socrates.

SOCRATES: Why have you come at this hour, Crito? it must be quite early.

CRITO: Yes, certainly.

SOCRATES: What is the exact time?

CRITO: The dawn is breaking.

SOCRATES: I wonder that the keeper of the prison would let you in.

CRITO: He knows me because I often come, Socrates; moreover. I have done him a kindness.

SOCRATES: And are you only just arrived?

CRITO: No, I came some time ago.

SOCRATES: Then why did you sit and say nothing, instead of at once awakening me?

CRITO: I should not have liked myself, Socrates, to be in such great trouble and unrest as you are—indeed I should not: I have been watching with amazement your peaceful slumbers; and for that reason I did not awake you, because I wished to minimize the pain. I have always thought you to be of a happy disposition; but never did I see anything like the easy, tranquil manner in which you bear this calamity.

SOCRATES: Why, Crito, when a man has reached my age he ought not to be repining at the approach of death.

CRITO: And yet other old men find themselves in similar misfortunes, and age does not prevent them from repining.

SOCRATES: That is true. But you have not told me why you come at this early hour.

CRITO: I come to bring you a message which is sad and painful; not, as I believe, to yourself, but to all of us who are your friends, and saddest of all to me.

SOCRATES: What? Has the ship come from Delos, on the arrival of which I am to die?

CRITO: No, the ship has not actually arrived, but she will probably be here to-day, as persons who have come from Sunium tell me that they have left her there; and therefore to-morrow, Socrates, will be the last day of your life.

SOCRATES: Very well, Crito; if such is the will of God, I am willing; but my belief is that there will be a delay of a day.

CRITO: Why do you think so?

SOCRATES: I will tell you. I am to die on the day after the arrival of the ship?

CRITO: Yes; that is what the authorities say.

SOCRATES: But I do not think that the ship will be here until to-morrow; this I infer from a vision which I had last night, or rather only just now, when you fortunately allowed me to sleep.

CRITO: And what was the nature of the vision?

SOCRATES: There appeared to me the likeness of a woman, fair and comely, clothed in bright raiment, who called to me and said: O Socrates, 'The third day hence to fertile Phthia shalt thou go.' (Homer, Il.)

CRITO: What a singular dream, Socrates!

SOCRATES: There can be no doubt about the meaning, Crito, I think.

CRITO: Yes; the meaning is only too clear. But, oh! my beloved Socrates, let me entreat you once more to take my advice and escape. For if you die I shall not only lose a friend who can never be replaced, but there is another evil: people who do not know you and me will believe that I might have saved you if I had been willing to give money, but that I did not care. Now, can there be a worse disgrace than this—that I should be thought to value money more than the life of a friend? For the many will not be persuaded that I wanted you to escape, and that you refused.

SOCRATES: But why, my dear Crito, should we care about the opinion of the many? Good men, and they are the only persons who are worth considering, will think of these things truly as they occurred.

CRITO: But you see, Socrates, that the opinion of the many must be regarded, for what is now happening shows that they can do the greatest evil to any one who has lost their good opinion.

SOCRATES: I only wish it were so, Crito; and that the many could do the greatest evil; for then they would also be able to do the greatest good—and what a fine thing this would be! But in reality they can do neither; for they cannot make a man either wise or foolish; and whatever they do is the result of chance.

CRITO: Well, I will not dispute with you; but please to tell me, Socrates, whether you are not acting out of regard to me and your other friends: are you not afraid that if you escape from prison we may get into trouble with the informers for having stolen you away, and lose either the whole or a great part of our property; or that even a worse evil may happen to us? Now, if you fear on our account, be at ease; for in order to save you, we ought surely to run this, or even a greater risk; be persuaded, then, and do as I say.

SOCRATES: Yes, Crito, that is one fear which you mention, but by no means the only one.

CRITO: Fear not—there are persons who are willing to get you out of prison at no great cost; and as for the informers they are far from being exorbitant in their demands—a little money will satisfy them. My means, which are certainly ample, are at your service, and if you have a scruple about spending all mine, here are strangers who will give you the use of theirs; and one of them, Simmias the Theban, has brought a large sum of money for this very purpose; and Cebes and many others are prepared to spend their money in helping you to escape. I say, therefore, do not hesitate on our account, and do not say, as you did in the court (compare Apol.), that you will have a difficulty in knowing what to do with yourself anywhere else. For men will love you in other places to which you may go, and not in Athens only; there are friends of mine in Thessaly, if you like to go to them, who will value and protect you, and no Thessalian will give you any trouble. Nor can I think that you are at all justified, Socrates, in betraying your own life when you might be saved; in acting thus you are playing into the hands of your enemies, who are hurrying on your destruction. And further I should say that you are deserting your own children; for you might bring them up and educate them; instead of which you go away and leave them, and they will have to take their chance; and if they do not meet with the usual fate of orphans, there will be small thanks to you. No man should bring children into the world who is unwilling to persevere to the end in their nurture and education. But you appear to be choosing the easier part, not the better and manlier, which would have been more becoming in one who professes to care for virtue in all his actions, like yourself. And indeed, I am ashamed not only of you, but of us who are your friends, when I reflect that the whole business will be attributed entirely to our want of courage. The trial need never have come on, or might have been managed differently; and this last act, or crowning folly, will seem to have occurred through our negligence and cowardice, who might have saved you, if we had been good for anything; and you might have saved yourself, for there was no difficulty at all. See now, Socrates, how sad and discreditable are the consequences, both to us and you. Make up your mind then, or rather have your mind already made up, for the time of deliberation is over, and there is only one thing to be done, which must be done this very night, and if we delay at all will be no longer practicable or possible; I beseech you therefore, Socrates, be persuaded by me, and do as I say.

SOCRATES: Dear Crito, your zeal is invaluable, if a right one; but if wrong, the greater the zeal the greater the danger; and therefore we ought to consider whether I shall or shall not do as you say. For I am and always have been one of those natures who must be guided by reason, whatever the reason may be which upon reflection appears to me to be the best; and now that this chance has befallen me, I cannot repudiate my own words: the principles which I have hitherto honoured and revered I still honour, and unless we can at once find other and better principles, I am certain not to agree with you; no, not even if the power of the multitude could inflict many more imprisonments, confiscations, deaths, frightening us like children with hobgoblin terrors (compare Apol.). What will be the fairest way of considering the question? Shall I return to your old argument about the opinions of men?—we were saying that some of them are to be regarded, and others not. Now were we right in maintaining this before I was condemned? And has the argument which was once good now proved to be talk for the sake of talking—mere childish nonsense? That is what I want to consider with your help, Crito:—whether, under my present circumstances, the argument appears to be in any way different or not; and is to be allowed by me or disallowed. That argument, which, as I believe, is maintained by many persons of authority, was to the effect, as I was saying, that the opinions of some men are to be regarded, and of other men not to be regarded. Now you, Crito, are not going to die to-morrow—at least, there is no human probability of this, and therefore you are disinterested and not liable to be deceived by the circumstances in which you are placed. Tell me then, whether I am right in saying that some opinions, and the opinions of some men only, are to be valued, and that other opinions, and the opinions of other men, are not to be valued. I ask you whether I was right in maintaining this?

CRITO: Certainly.

SOCRATES: The good are to be regarded, and not the bad?

CRITO: Yes.

SOCRATES: And the opinions of the wise are good, and the opinions of the unwise are evil?

CRITO: Certainly.

SOCRATES: And what was said about another matter? Is the pupil who devotes himself to the practice of gymnastics supposed to attend to the praise and blame and opinion of every man, or of one man only— his physician or trainer, whoever he may be?

CRITO: Of one man only.

SOCRATES: And he ought to fear the censure and welcome the praise of that one only, and not of the many?

CRITO: Clearly so.

SOCRATES: And he ought to act and train, and eat and drink in the way which seems good to his single master who has understanding, rather than according to the opinion of all other men put together?

CRITO: True.

SOCRATES: And if he disobeys and disregards the opinion and approval of the one, and regards the opinion of the many who have no understanding, will he not suffer evil?

CRITO: Certainly he will.

SOCRATES: And what will the evil be, whither tending and what affecting, in the disobedient person?

CRITO: Clearly, affecting the body; that is what is destroyed by the evil.

SOCRATES: Very good; and is not this true, Crito, of other things which we need not separately enumerate? In questions of just and unjust, fair and foul, good and evil, which are the subjects of our present consultation, ought we to follow the opinion of the many and to fear them; or the opinion of the one man who has understanding? ought we not to fear and reverence him more than all the rest of the world: and if we desert him shall we not destroy and injure that principle in us which may be assumed to be improved by justice and deteriorated by injustice;—there is such a principle?

CRITO: Certainly there is, Socrates.

SOCRATES: Take a parallel instance:—if, acting under the advice of those who have no understanding, we destroy that which is improved by health and is deteriorated by disease, would life be worth having? And that which has been destroyed is—the body?

CRITO: Yes.

SOCRATES: Could we live, having an evil and corrupted body?

CRITO: Certainly not.

SOCRATES: And will life be worth having, if that higher part of man be destroyed, which is improved by justice and depraved by injustice? Do we suppose that principle, whatever it may be in man, which has to do with justice and injustice, to be inferior to the body?

CRITO: Certainly not.

SOCRATES: More honourable than the body?

CRITO: Far more.

SOCRATES: Then, my friend, we must not regard what the many say of us: but what he, the one man who has understanding of just and unjust, will say, and what the truth will say. And therefore you begin in error when you advise that we should regard the opinion of the many about just and unjust, good and evil, honorable and dishonorable.— 'Well,' some one will say, 'but the many can kill us.'

CRITO: Yes, Socrates; that will clearly be the answer.

SOCRATES: And it is true; but still I find with surprise that the old argument is unshaken as ever. And I should like to know whether I may say the same of another proposition—that not life, but a good life, is to be chiefly valued?

CRITO: Yes, that also remains unshaken.

SOCRATES: And a good life is equivalent to a just and honorable one—that holds also?

CRITO: Yes, it does.

SOCRATES: From these premises I proceed to argue the question whether I ought or ought not to try and escape without the consent of the Athenians: and if I am clearly right in escaping, then I will make the attempt; but if not, I will abstain. The other considerations which you mention, of money and loss of character and the duty of educating one's children, are, I fear, only the doctrines of the multitude, who would be as ready to restore people to life, if they were able, as they are to put them to death—and with as little reason. But now, since the argument has thus far prevailed, the only question which remains to be considered is, whether we shall do rightly either in escaping or in suffering others to aid in our escape and paying them in money and thanks, or whether in reality we shall not do rightly; and if the latter, then death or any other calamity which may ensue on my remaining here must not be allowed to enter into the calculation.

CRITO: I think that you are right, Socrates; how then shall we proceed?

SOCRATES: Let us consider the matter together, and do you either refute me if you can, and I will be convinced; or else cease, my dear friend, from repeating to me that I ought to escape against the wishes of the Athenians: for I highly value your attempts to persuade me to do so, but I may not be persuaded against my own better judgment. And now please to consider my first position, and try how you can best answer me.

CRITO: I will.

SOCRATES: Are we to say that we are never intentionally to do wrong, or that in one way we ought and in another way we ought not to do wrong, or is doing wrong always evil and dishonorable, as I was just now saying, and as has been already acknowledged by us? Are all our former admissions which were made within a few days to be thrown away? And have we, at our age, been earnestly discoursing with one another all our life long only to discover that we are no better than children? Or, in spite of the opinion of the many, and in spite of consequences whether better or worse, shall we insist on the truth of what was then said, that injustice is always an evil and dishonour to him who acts unjustly? Shall we say so or not?

CRITO: Yes.

SOCRATES: Then we must do no wrong?

CRITO: Certainly not.

SOCRATES: Nor when injured injure in return, as the many imagine; for we must injure no one at all? (E.g. compare Rep.)

CRITO: Clearly not.

SOCRATES: Again, Crito, may we do evil?

CRITO: Surely not, Socrates.

SOCRATES: And what of doing evil in return for evil, which is the morality of the many—is that just or not?

CRITO: Not just.

SOCRATES: For doing evil to another is the same as injuring him?

CRITO: Very true.

SOCRATES: Then we ought not to retaliate or render evil for evil to any one, whatever evil we may have suffered from him. But I would have you consider, Crito, whether you really mean what you are saying. For this opinion has never been held, and never will be held, by any considerable number of persons; and those who are agreed and those who are not agreed upon this point have no common ground, and can only despise one another when they see how widely they differ. Tell me, then, whether you agree with and assent to my first principle, that neither injury nor retaliation nor warding off evil by evil is ever right. And shall that be the premise of our argument? Or do you decline and dissent from this? For so I have ever thought, and continue to think; but, if you are of another opinion, let me hear what you have to say. If, however, you remain of the same mind as formerly, I will proceed to the next step.

CRITO: You may proceed, for I have not changed my mind.

SOCRATES: Then I will go on to the next point, which may be put in the form of a question:—Ought a man to do what he admits to be right, or ought he to betray the right?

CRITO: He ought to do what he thinks right.

SOCRATES: But if this is true, what is the application? In leaving the prison against the will of the Athenians, do I wrong any? or rather do I not wrong those whom I ought least to wrong? Do I not desert the principles which were acknowledged by us to be just—what do you say?

CRITO: I cannot tell, Socrates, for I do not know.

SOCRATES: Then consider the matter in this way:—Imagine that I am about to play truant (you may call the proceeding by any name which you like), and the laws and the government come and interrogate me: 'Tell us, Socrates,' they say; 'what are you about? are you not going by an act of yours to overturn us—the laws, and the whole state, as far as in you lies? Do you imagine that a state can subsist and not be overthrown, in which the decisions of law have no power, but are set aside and trampled upon by individuals?' What will be our answer, Crito, to these and the like words? Any one, and especially a rhetorician, will have a good deal to say on behalf of the law which requires a sentence to be carried out. He will argue that this law should not be set aside; and shall we reply, 'Yes; but the state has injured us and given an unjust sentence.' Suppose I say that?

CRITO: Very good, Socrates.

SOCRATES: 'And was that our agreement with you?' the law would answer; 'or were you to abide by the sentence of the state?' And if I were to express my astonishment at their words, the law would probably add: 'Answer, Socrates, instead of opening your eyes—you are in the habit of asking and answering questions. Tell us,—What complaint have you to make against us which justifies you in attempting to destroy us and the state? In the first place did we not bring you into existence? Your father married your mother by our aid and begat you. Say whether you have any objection to urge against those of us who regulate marriage?' None, I should reply. 'Or against those of us who after birth regulate the nurture and education of children, in which you also were trained? Were not the laws, which have the charge of education, right in commanding your father to train you in music and gymnastic?' Right, I should reply. 'Well then, since you were brought into the world and nurtured and educated by us, can you deny in the first place that you are our child and slave, as your fathers were before you? And if this is true you are not on equal terms with us; nor can you think that you have a right to do to us what we are doing to you. Would you have any right to strike or revile or do any other evil to your father or your master, if you had one, because you have been struck or reviled by him, or received some other evil at his hands?—you would not say this? And because we think right to destroy you, do you think that you have any right to destroy us in return, and your country as far as in you lies? Will you, O professor of true virtue, pretend that you are justified in this? Has a philosopher like you failed to discover that our country is more to be valued and higher and holier far than mother or father or any ancestor, and more to be regarded in the eyes of the gods and of men of understanding? also to be soothed, and gently and reverently entreated when angry, even more than a father, and either to be persuaded, or if not persuaded, to be obeyed? And when we are punished by her, whether with imprisonment or stripes, the punishment is to be endured in silence; and if she lead us to wounds or death in battle, thither we follow as is right; neither may any one yield or retreat or leave his rank, but whether in battle or in a court of law, or in any other place, he must do what his city and his country order him; or he must change their view of what is just: and if he may do no violence to his father or mother, much less may he do violence to his country.' What answer shall we make to this, Crito? Do the laws speak truly, or do they not?

CRITO: I think that they do.

SOCRATES: Then the laws will say: 'Consider, Socrates, if we are speaking truly that in your present attempt you are going to do us an injury. For, having brought you into the world, and nurtured and educated you, and given you and every other citizen a share in every good which we had to give, we further proclaim to any Athenian by the liberty which we allow him, that if he does not like us when he has become of age and has seen the ways of the city, and made our acquaintance, he may go where he pleases and take his goods with him. None of us laws will forbid him or interfere with him. Any one who does not like us and the city, and who wants to emigrate to a colony or to any other city, may go where he likes, retaining his property. But he who has experience of the manner in which we order justice and administer the state, and still remains, has entered into an implied contract that he will do as we command him. And he who disobeys us is, as we maintain, thrice wrong: first, because in disobeying us he is disobeying his parents; secondly, because we are the authors of his education; thirdly, because he has made an agreement with us that he will duly obey our commands; and he neither obeys them nor convinces us that our commands are unjust; and we do not rudely impose them, but give him the alternative of obeying or convincing us;—that is what we offer, and he does neither.

'These are the sort of accusations to which, as we were saying, you, Socrates, will be exposed if you accomplish your intentions; you, above all other Athenians.' Suppose now I ask, why I rather than anybody else? they will justly retort upon me that I above all other men have acknowledged the agreement. 'There is clear proof,' they will say, 'Socrates, that we and the city were not displeasing to you. Of all Athenians you have been the most constant resident in the city, which, as you never leave, you may be supposed to love (compare Phaedr.). For you never went out of the city either to see the games, except once when you went to the Isthmus, or to any other place unless when you were on military service; nor did you travel as other men do. Nor had you any curiosity to know other states or their laws: your affections did not go beyond us and our state; we were your especial favourites, and you acquiesced in our government of you; and here in this city you begat your children, which is a proof of your satisfaction. Moreover, you might in the course of the trial, if you had liked, have fixed the penalty at banishment; the state which refuses to let you go now would have let you go then. But you pretended that you preferred death to exile (compare Apol.), and that you were not unwilling to die. And now you have forgotten these fine sentiments, and pay no respect to us the laws, of whom you are the destroyer; and are doing what only a miserable slave would do, running away and turning your back upon the compacts and agreements which you made as a citizen. And first of all answer this very question: Are we right in saying that you agreed to be governed according to us in deed, and not in word only? Is that true or not?' How shall we answer, Crito? Must we not assent?

CRITO: We cannot help it, Socrates.

SOCRATES: Then will they not say: 'You, Socrates, are breaking the covenants and agreements which you made with us at your leisure, not in any haste or under any compulsion or deception, but after you have had seventy years to think of them, during which time you were at liberty to leave the city, if we were not to your mind, or if our covenants appeared to you to be unfair. You had your choice, and might have gone either to Lacedaemon or Crete, both which states are often praised by you for their good government, or to some other Hellenic or foreign state. Whereas you, above all other Athenians, seemed to be so fond of the state, or, in other words, of us her laws (and who would care about a state which has no laws?), that you never stirred out of her; the halt, the blind, the maimed, were not more stationary in her than you were. And now you run away and forsake your agreements. Not so, Socrates, if you will take our advice; do not make yourself ridiculous by escaping out of the city.

'For just consider, if you transgress and err in this sort of way, what good will you do either to yourself or to your friends? That your friends will be driven into exile and deprived of citizenship, or will lose their property, is tolerably certain; and you yourself, if you fly to one of the neighbouring cities, as, for example, Thebes or Megara, both of which are well governed, will come to them as an enemy, Socrates, and their government will be against you, and all patriotic citizens will cast an evil eye upon you as a subverter of the laws, and you will confirm in the minds of the judges the justice of their own condemnation of you. For he who is a corrupter of the laws is more than likely to be a corrupter of the young and foolish portion of mankind. Will you then flee from well-ordered cities and virtuous men? and is existence worth having on these terms? Or will you go to them without shame, and talk to them, Socrates? And what will you say to them? What you say here about virtue and justice and institutions and laws being the best things among men? Would that be decent of you? Surely not. But if you go away from well-governed states to Crito's friends in Thessaly, where there is great disorder and licence, they will be charmed to hear the tale of your escape from prison, set off with ludicrous particulars of the manner in which you were wrapped in a goatskin or some other disguise, and metamorphosed as the manner is of runaways; but will there be no one to remind you that in your old age you were not ashamed to violate the most sacred laws from a miserable desire of a little more life? Perhaps not, if you keep them in a good temper; but if they are out of temper you will hear many degrading things; you will live, but how?—as the flatterer of all men, and the servant of all men; and doing what?—eating and drinking in Thessaly, having gone abroad in order that you may get a dinner. And where will be your fine sentiments about justice and virtue? Say that you wish to live for the sake of your children—you want to bring them up and educate them— will you take them into Thessaly and deprive them of Athenian citizenship? Is this the benefit which you will confer upon them? Or are you under the impression that they will be better cared for and educated here if you are still alive, although absent from them; for your friends will take care of them? Do you fancy that if you are an inhabitant of Thessaly they will take care of them, and if you are an inhabitant of the other world that they will not take care of them? Nay; but if they who call themselves friends are good for anything, they will—to be sure they will.

'Listen, then, Socrates, to us who have brought you up. Think not of life and children first, and of justice afterwards, but of justice first, that you may be justified before the princes of the world below. For neither will you nor any that belong to you be happier or holier or juster in this life, or happier in another, if you do as Crito bids. Now you depart in innocence, a sufferer and not a doer of evil; a victim, not of the laws, but of men. But if you go forth, returning evil for evil, and injury for injury, breaking the covenants and agreements which you have made with us, and wronging those whom you ought least of all to wrong, that is to say, yourself, your friends, your country, and us, we shall be angry with you while you live, and our brethren, the laws in the world below, will receive you as an enemy; for they will know that you have done your best to destroy us. Listen, then, to us and not to Crito.'

This, dear Crito, is the voice which I seem to hear murmuring in my ears, like the sound of the flute in the ears of the mystic; that voice, I say, is humming in my ears, and prevents me from hearing any other. And I know that anything more which you may say will be vain. Yet speak, if you have anything to say.

CRITO: I have nothing to say, Socrates.

SOCRATES: Leave me then, Crito, to fulfil the will of God, and to follow whither he leads.

Meno

INTRODUCTION

This Dialogue begins abruptly with a question of Meno, who asks, 'whether virtue can be taught.' Socrates replies that he does not as yet know what virtue is, and has never known anyone who did. 'Then he cannot have met Gorgias when he was at Athens.' Yes, Socrates had met him, but he has a bad memory, and has forgotten what Gorgias said. Will Meno tell him his own notion, which is probably not very different from that of Gorgias? 'O yes—nothing easier: there is the virtue of a man, of a woman, of an old man, and of a child; there is a virtue of every age and state of life, all of which may be easily described.'

Socrates reminds Meno that this is only an enumeration of the virtues and not a definition of the notion which is common to them all. In a second attempt Meno defines virtue to be 'the power of command.' But to this, again, exceptions are taken. For there must be a virtue of those who obey, as well as of those who command; and the power of command must be justly or not unjustly exercised. Meno is very ready to admit that justice is virtue: 'Would you say virtue or a virtue, for there are other virtues, such as courage, temperance, and the like; just as round is a figure, and black and white are colours, and yet there are other figures and other colours. Let Meno take the examples of figure and colour, and try to define them.' Meno confesses his inability, and after a process of interrogation, in which Socrates explains to him the nature of a 'simile in multis,' Socrates himself defines figure as 'the accompaniment of colour.' But some one may object that he does not know the meaning of the word 'colour;' and if he is a candid friend, and not a mere disputant, Socrates is willing to furnish him with a simpler and more philosophical definition, into which no disputed word is allowed to intrude: 'Figure is the limit of form.' Meno imperiously insists that he must still have a definition of colour. Some raillery follows; and at length Socrates is induced to reply, 'that colour is the effluence of form, sensible, and in due proportion to the sight.' This definition is exactly suited to the taste of Meno, who welcomes the familiar language of Gorgias and Empedocles. Socrates is of opinion that the more abstract or dialectical definition of figure is far better.

Now that Meno has been made to understand the nature of a general definition, he answers in the spirit of a Greek gentleman, and in the words of a poet, 'that virtue is to delight in things honourable, and to have the power of getting them.' This is a nearer approximation than he has yet made to a complete definition, and, regarded as a piece of proverbial or popular morality, is not far from the truth. But the objection is urged, 'that the honourable is the good,' and as every one equally desires the good, the point of the definition is contained in the words, 'the power of getting them.' 'And they must be got justly or with justice.' The definition will then stand thus: 'Virtue is the power of getting good with justice.' But justice is a part of virtue, and therefore virtue is the getting of good with a part of virtue. The definition repeats the word defined.

Meno complains that the conversation of Socrates has the effect of a torpedo's shock upon him. When he talks with other persons he has plenty to say about virtue; in the presence of Socrates, his thoughts desert him. Socrates replies that he is only the cause of perplexity in others, because he is himself perplexed. He proposes to continue the enquiry. But how, asks Meno, can he enquire either into what he knows or into what he does not know? This is a sophistical puzzle, which, as Socrates remarks, saves a great deal of trouble to him who accepts it. But the puzzle has a real difficulty latent under it, to which Socrates will endeavour to find a reply. The difficulty is the origin of knowledge:—

He has heard from priests and priestesses, and from the poet Pindar, of an immortal soul which is born again and again in successive periods of existence, returning into this world when she has paid the penalty of ancient crime, and, having wandered over all places of the upper and under world, and seen and known all things at one time or other, is by association out of one thing capable of recovering all. For nature is of one kindred; and every soul has a seed or germ which may be developed into all knowledge. The existence of this latent knowledge is further proved by the interrogation of one of Meno's slaves, who, in the skilful hands of Socrates, is made to acknowledge some elementary relations of geometrical figures. The theorem that the square of the diagonal is double the square of the side—that famous discovery of primitive mathematics, in honour of which the legendary Pythagoras is said to have sacrificed a hecatomb—is elicited from him. The first step in the process of teaching has made him conscious of his own ignorance. He has had the 'torpedo's shock' given him, and is the better for the operation. But whence had the uneducated man this knowledge? He had never learnt geometry in this world; nor was it born with him; he must therefore have had it when he was not a man. And as he always either was or was not a man, he must have always had it. (Compare Phaedo.)

After Socrates has given this specimen of the true nature of teaching, the original question of the teachableness of virtue is renewed. Again he professes a desire to know 'what virtue is' first. But he is willing to argue the question, as mathematicians say, under an hypothesis. He will assume that if virtue is knowledge, then virtue can be taught. (This was the stage of the argument at which the Protagoras concluded.)

Socrates has no difficulty in showing that virtue is a good, and that goods, whether of body or mind, must be under the direction of knowledge. Upon the assumption just made, then, virtue is teachable. But where are the teachers? There are none to be found. This is extremely discouraging. Virtue is no sooner discovered to be teachable, than the discovery follows that it is not taught. Virtue, therefore, is and is not teachable.

In this dilemma an appeal is made to Anytus, a respectable and well-to-do citizen of the old school, and a family friend of Meno, who happens to be present. He is asked 'whether Meno shall go to the Sophists and be taught.' The suggestion throws him into a rage. 'To whom, then, shall Meno go?' asks Socrates. To any Athenian gentleman—to the great Athenian statesmen of past times. Socrates replies here, as elsewhere (Laches, Prot.), that Themistocles, Pericles, and other great men, had sons to whom they would surely, if they could have done so, have imparted their own political wisdom; but no one ever heard that these sons of theirs were remarkable for anything except riding and wrestling and similar accomplishments. Anytus is angry at the imputation which is cast on his favourite statesmen, and on a class to which he supposes himself to belong; he breaks off with a significant hint. The mention of another opportunity of talking with him, and the suggestion that Meno may do the Athenian people a service by pacifying him, are evident allusions to the trial of Socrates.

Socrates returns to the consideration of the question 'whether virtue is teachable,' which was denied on the ground that there are no teachers of it: (for the Sophists are bad teachers, and the rest of the world do not profess to teach). But there is another point which we failed to observe, and in which Gorgias has never instructed Meno, nor Prodicus Socrates. This is the nature of right opinion. For virtue may be under the guidance of right opinion as well as of knowledge; and right opinion is for practical purposes as good as knowledge, but is incapable of being taught, and is also liable, like the images of Daedalus, to 'walk off,' because not bound by the tie of the cause. This is the sort of instinct which is possessed by statesmen, who are not wise or knowing persons, but only inspired or divine. The higher virtue, which is identical with knowledge, is an ideal only. If the statesman had this knowledge, and could teach what he knew, he would be like Tiresias in the world below,—'he alone has wisdom, but the rest flit like shadows.'

This Dialogue is an attempt to answer the question, Can virtue be taught? No one would either ask or answer such a question in modern times. But in the age of Socrates it was only by an effort that the mind could rise to a general notion of virtue as distinct from the particular virtues of courage, liberality, and the like. And when a hazy conception of this ideal was attained, it was only by a further effort that the question of the teachableness of virtue could be resolved.

The answer which is given by Plato is paradoxical enough, and seems rather intended to stimulate than to satisfy enquiry. Virtue is knowledge, and therefore virtue can be taught. But virtue is not taught, and therefore in this higher and ideal sense there is no virtue and no knowledge. The teaching of the Sophists is confessedly inadequate, and Meno, who is their pupil, is ignorant of the very nature of general terms. He can only produce out of their armoury the sophism, 'that you can neither enquire into what you know nor into what you do not know;' to which Socrates replies by his theory of reminiscence.

To the doctrine that virtue is knowledge, Plato has been constantly tending in the previous Dialogues. But the new truth is no sooner found than it vanishes away. 'If there is knowledge, there must be teachers; and where are the teachers?' There is no knowledge in the higher sense of systematic, connected, reasoned knowledge, such as may one day be attained, and such as Plato himself seems to see in some far off vision of a single science. And there are no teachers in the higher sense of the word; that is to say, no real teachers who will arouse the spirit of enquiry in their pupils, and not merely instruct them in rhetoric or impart to them ready- made information for a fee of 'one' or of 'fifty drachms.' Plato is desirous of deepening the notion of education, and therefore he asserts the paradox that there are no educators. This paradox, though different in form, is not really different from the remark which is often made in modern times by those who would depreciate either the methods of education commonly employed, or the standard attained—that 'there is no true education among us.'

There remains still a possibility which must not be overlooked. Even if there be no true knowledge, as is proved by 'the wretched state of education,' there may be right opinion, which is a sort of guessing or divination resting on no knowledge of causes, and incommunicable to others. This is the gift which our statesmen have, as is proved by the circumstance that they are unable to impart their knowledge to their sons. Those who are possessed of it cannot be said to be men of science or philosophers, but they are inspired and divine.

There may be some trace of irony in this curious passage, which forms the concluding portion of the Dialogue. But Plato certainly does not mean to intimate that the supernatural or divine is the true basis of human life. To him knowledge, if only attainable in this world, is of all things the most divine. Yet, like other philosophers, he is willing to admit that 'probability is the guide of life (Butler's Analogy.);' and he is at the same time desirous of contrasting the wisdom which governs the world with a higher wisdom. There are many instincts, judgments, and anticipations of the human mind which cannot be reduced to rule, and of which the grounds cannot always be given in words. A person may have some skill or latent experience which he is able to use himself and is yet unable to teach others, because he has no principles, and is incapable of collecting or arranging his ideas. He has practice, but not theory; art, but not science. This is a true fact of psychology, which is recognized by Plato in this passage. But he is far from saying, as some have imagined, that inspiration or divine grace is to be regarded as higher than knowledge. He would not have preferred the poet or man of action to the philosopher, or the virtue of custom to the virtue based upon ideas.

Also here, as in the Ion and Phaedrus, Plato appears to acknowledge an unreasoning element in the higher nature of man. The philosopher only has knowledge, and yet the statesman and the poet are inspired. There may be a sort of irony in regarding in this way the gifts of genius. But there is no reason to suppose that he is deriding them, any more than he is deriding the phenomena of love or of enthusiasm in the Symposium, or of oracles in the Apology, or of divine intimations when he is speaking of the daemonium of Socrates. He recognizes the lower form of right opinion, as well as the higher one of science, in the spirit of one who desires to include in his philosophy every aspect of human life; just as he recognizes the existence of popular opinion as a fact, and the Sophists as the expression of it.

This Dialogue contains the first intimation of the doctrine of reminiscence and of the immortality of the soul. The proof is very slight, even slighter than in the Phaedo and Republic. Because men had abstract ideas in a previous state, they must have always had them, and their souls therefore must have always existed. For they must always have been either men or not men. The fallacy of the latter words is transparent. And Socrates himself appears to be conscious of their weakness; for he adds immediately afterwards, 'I have said some things of which I am not altogether confident.' (Compare Phaedo.) It may be observed, however, that the fanciful notion of pre-existence is combined with a true but partial view of the origin and unity of knowledge, and of the association of ideas. Knowledge is prior to any particular knowledge, and exists not in the previous state of the individual, but of the race. It is potential, not actual, and can only be appropriated by strenuous exertion.

The idealism of Plato is here presented in a less developed form than in the Phaedo and Phaedrus. Nothing is said of the pre-existence of ideas of justice, temperance, and the like. Nor is Socrates positive of anything but the duty of enquiry. The doctrine of reminiscence too is explained more in accordance with fact and experience as arising out of the affinities of nature (ate tes thuseos oles suggenous ouses). Modern philosophy says that all things in nature are dependent on one another; the ancient philosopher had the same truth latent in his mind when he affirmed that out of one thing all the rest may be recovered. The subjective was converted by him into an objective; the mental phenomenon of the association of ideas (compare Phaedo) became a real chain of existences. The germs of two valuable principles of education may also be gathered from the 'words of priests and priestesses:' (1) that true knowledge is a knowledge of causes (compare Aristotle's theory of episteme); and (2) that the process of learning consists not in what is brought to the learner, but in what is drawn out of him.

Some lesser points of the dialogue may be noted, such as (1) the acute observation that Meno prefers the familiar definition, which is embellished with poetical language, to the better and truer one; or (2) the shrewd reflection, which may admit of an application to modern as well as to ancient teachers, that the Sophists having made large fortunes; this must surely be a criterion of their powers of teaching, for that no man could get a living by shoemaking who was not a good shoemaker; or (3) the remark conveyed, almost in a word, that the verbal sceptic is saved the labour of thought and enquiry (ouden dei to toiouto zeteseos). Characteristic also of the temper of the Socratic enquiry is, (4) the proposal to discuss the teachableness of virtue under an hypothesis, after the manner of the mathematicians; and (5) the repetition of the favourite doctrine which occurs so frequently in the earlier and more Socratic Dialogues, and gives a colour to all of them—that mankind only desire evil through ignorance; (6) the experiment of eliciting from the slave-boy the mathematical truth which is latent in him, and (7) the remark that he is all the better for knowing his ignorance.

The character of Meno, like that of Critias, has no relation to the actual circumstances of his life. Plato is silent about his treachery to the ten thousand Greeks, which Xenophon has recorded, as he is also silent about the crimes of Critias. He is a Thessalian Alcibiades, rich and luxurious—a spoilt child of fortune, and is described as the hereditary friend of the great king. Like Alcibiades he is inspired with an ardent desire of knowledge, and is equally willing to learn of Socrates and of the Sophists. He may be regarded as standing in the same relation to Gorgias as Hippocrates in the Protagoras to the other great Sophist. He is the sophisticated youth on whom Socrates tries his cross-examining powers, just as in the Charmides, the Lysis, and the Euthydemus, ingenuous boyhood is made the subject of a similar experiment. He is treated by Socrates in a half-playful manner suited to his character; at the same time he appears not quite to understand the process to which he is being subjected. For he is exhibited as ignorant of the very elements of dialectics, in which the Sophists have failed to instruct their disciple. His definition of virtue as 'the power and desire of attaining things honourable,' like the first definition of justice in the Republic, is taken from a poet. His answers have a sophistical ring, and at the same time show the sophistical incapacity to grasp a general notion.

Anytus is the type of the narrow-minded man of the world, who is indignant at innovation, and equally detests the popular teacher and the true philosopher. He seems, like Aristophanes, to regard the new opinions, whether of Socrates or the Sophists, as fatal to Athenian greatness. He is of the same class as Callicles in the Gorgias, but of a different variety; the immoral and sophistical doctrines of Callicles are not attributed to him. The moderation with which he is described is remarkable, if he be the accuser of Socrates, as is apparently indicated by his parting words. Perhaps Plato may have been desirous of showing that the accusation of Socrates was not to be attributed to badness or malevolence, but rather to a tendency in men's minds. Or he may have been regardless of the historical truth of the characters of his dialogue, as in the case of Meno and Critias. Like Chaerephon (Apol.) the real Anytus was a democrat, and had joined Thrasybulus in the conflict with the thirty.

The Protagoras arrived at a sort of hypothetical conclusion, that if 'virtue is knowledge, it can be taught.' In the Euthydemus, Socrates himself offered an example of the manner in which the true teacher may draw out the mind of youth; this was in contrast to the quibbling follies of the Sophists. In the Meno the subject is more developed; the foundations of the enquiry are laid deeper, and the nature of knowledge is more distinctly explained. There is a progression by antagonism of two opposite aspects of philosophy. But at the moment when we approach nearest, the truth doubles upon us and passes out of our reach. We seem to find that the ideal of knowledge is irreconcilable with experience. In human life there is indeed the profession of knowledge, but right opinion is our actual guide. There is another sort of progress from the general notions of Socrates, who asked simply, 'what is friendship?' 'what is temperance?' 'what is courage?' as in the Lysis, Charmides, Laches, to the transcendentalism of Plato, who, in the second stage of his philosophy, sought to find the nature of knowledge in a prior and future state of existence.

The difficulty in framing general notions which has appeared in this and in all the previous Dialogues recurs in the Gorgias and Theaetetus as well as in the Republic. In the Gorgias too the statesmen reappear, but in stronger opposition to the philosopher. They are no longer allowed to have a divine insight, but, though acknowledged to have been clever men and good speakers, are denounced as 'blind leaders of the blind.' The doctrine of the immortality of the soul is also carried further, being made the foundation not only of a theory of knowledge, but of a doctrine of rewards and punishments. In the Republic the relation of knowledge to virtue is described in a manner more consistent with modern distinctions. The existence of the virtues without the possession of knowledge in the higher or philosophical sense is admitted to be possible. Right opinion is again introduced in the Theaetetus as an account of knowledge, but is rejected on the ground that it is irrational (as here, because it is not bound by the tie of the cause), and also because the conception of false opinion is given up as hopeless. The doctrines of Plato are necessarily different at different times of his life, as new distinctions are realized, or new stages of thought attained by him. We are not therefore justified, in order to take away the appearance of inconsistency, in attributing to him hidden meanings or remote allusions.

There are no external criteria by which we can determine the date of the Meno. There is no reason to suppose that any of the Dialogues of Plato were written before the death of Socrates; the Meno, which appears to be one of the earliest of them, is proved to have been of a later date by the allusion of Anytus.

We cannot argue that Plato was more likely to have written, as he has done, of Meno before than after his miserable death; for we have already seen, in the examples of Charmides and Critias, that the characters in Plato are very far from resembling the same characters in history. The repulsive picture which is given of him in the Anabasis of Xenophon, where he also appears as the friend of Aristippus 'and a fair youth having lovers,' has no other trait of likeness to the Meno of Plato.

The place of the Meno in the series is doubtfully indicated by internal evidence. The main character of the Dialogue is Socrates; but to the 'general definitions' of Socrates is added the Platonic doctrine of reminiscence. The problems of virtue and knowledge have been discussed in the Lysis, Laches, Charmides, and Protagoras; the puzzle about knowing and learning has already appeared in the Euthydemus. The doctrines of immortality and pre-existence are carried further in the Phaedrus and Phaedo; the distinction between opinion and knowledge is more fully developed in the Theaetetus. The lessons of Prodicus, whom he facetiously calls his master, are still running in the mind of Socrates. Unlike the later Platonic Dialogues, the Meno arrives at no conclusion. Hence we are led to place the Dialogue at some point of time later than the Protagoras, and earlier than the Phaedrus and Gorgias. The place which is assigned to it in this work is due mainly to the desire to bring together in a single volume all the Dialogues which contain allusions to the trial and death of Socrates.

ON THE IDEAS OF PLATO

Plato's doctrine of ideas has attained an imaginary clearness and definiteness which is not to be found in his own writings. The popular account of them is partly derived from one or two passages in his Dialogues interpreted without regard to their poetical environment. It is due also to the misunderstanding of him by the Aristotelian school; and the erroneous notion has been further narrowed and has become fixed by the realism of the schoolmen. This popular view of the Platonic ideas may be summed up in some such formula as the following: 'Truth consists not in particulars, but in universals, which have a place in the mind of God, or in some far-off heaven. These were revealed to men in a former state of existence, and are recovered by reminiscence (anamnesis) or association from sensible things. The sensible things are not realities, but shadows only, in relation to the truth.' These unmeaning propositions are hardly suspected to be a caricature of a great theory of knowledge, which Plato in various ways and under many figures of speech is seeking to unfold. Poetry has been converted into dogma; and it is not remarked that the Platonic ideas are to be found only in about a third of Plato's writings and are not confined to him. The forms which they assume are numerous, and if taken literally, inconsistent with one another. At one time we are in the clouds of mythology, at another among the abstractions of mathematics or metaphysics; we pass imperceptibly from one to the other. Reason and fancy are mingled in the same passage. The ideas are sometimes described as many, coextensive with the universals of sense and also with the first principles of ethics; or again they are absorbed into the single idea of good, and subordinated to it. They are not more certain than facts, but they are equally certain (Phaedo). They are both personal and impersonal. They are abstract terms: they are also the causes of things; and they are even transformed into the demons or spirits by whose help God made the world. And the idea of good (Republic) may without violence be converted into the Supreme Being, who 'because He was good' created all things (Tim.).

It would be a mistake to try and reconcile these differing modes of thought. They are not to be regarded seriously as having a distinct meaning. They are parables, prophecies, myths, symbols, revelations, aspirations after an unknown world. They derive their origin from a deep religious and contemplative feeling, and also from an observation of curious mental phenomena. They gather up the elements of the previous philosophies, which they put together in a new form. Their great diversity shows the tentative character of early endeavours to think. They have not yet settled down into a single system. Plato uses them, though he also criticises them; he acknowledges that both he and others are always talking about them, especially about the Idea of Good; and that they are not peculiar to himself (Phaedo; Republic; Soph.). But in his later writings he seems to have laid aside the old forms of them. As he proceeds he makes for himself new modes of expression more akin to the Aristotelian logic.

Yet amid all these varieties and incongruities, there is a common meaning or spirit which pervades his writings, both those in which he treats of the ideas and those in which he is silent about them. This is the spirit of idealism, which in the history of philosophy has had many names and taken many forms, and has in a measure influenced those who seemed to be most averse to it. It has often been charged with inconsistency and fancifulness, and yet has had an elevating effect on human nature, and has exercised a wonderful charm and interest over a few spirits who have been lost in the thought of it. It has been banished again and again, but has always returned. It has attempted to leave the earth and soar heavenwards, but soon has found that only in experience could any solid foundation of knowledge be laid. It has degenerated into pantheism, but has again emerged. No other knowledge has given an equal stimulus to the mind. It is the science of sciences, which are also ideas, and under either aspect require to be defined. They can only be thought of in due proportion when conceived in relation to one another. They are the glasses through which the kingdoms of science are seen, but at a distance. All the greatest minds, except when living in an age of reaction against them, have unconsciously fallen under their power.

The account of the Platonic ideas in the Meno is the simplest and clearest, and we shall best illustrate their nature by giving this first and then comparing the manner in which they are described elsewhere, e.g. in the Phaedrus, Phaedo, Republic; to which may be added the criticism of them in the Parmenides, the personal form which is attributed to them in the Timaeus, the logical character which they assume in the

Sophist and Philebus, and the allusion to them in the Laws. In the Cratylus they dawn upon him with the freshness of a newly-discovered thought.

The Meno goes back to a former state of existence, in which men did and suffered good and evil, and received the reward or punishment of them until their sin was purged away and they were allowed to return to earth. This is a tradition of the olden time, to which priests and poets bear witness. The souls of men returning to earth bring back a latent memory of ideas, which were known to them in a former state. The recollection is awakened into life and consciousness by the sight of the things which resemble them on earth. The soul evidently possesses such innate ideas before she has had time to acquire them. This is proved by an experiment tried on one of Meno's slaves, from whom Socrates elicits truths of arithmetic and geometry, which he had never learned in this world. He must therefore have brought them with him from another.

The notion of a previous state of existence is found in the verses of Empedocles and in the fragments of Heracleitus. It was the natural answer to two questions, 'Whence came the soul? What is the origin of evil?' and prevailed far and wide in the east. It found its way into Hellas probably through the medium of Orphic and Pythagorean rites and mysteries. It was easier to think of a former than of a future life, because such a life has really existed for the race though not for the individual, and all men come into the world, if not 'trailing clouds of glory,' at any rate able to enter into the inheritance of the past. In the Phaedrus, as well as in the Meno, it is this former rather than a future life on which Plato is disposed to dwell. There the Gods, and men following in their train, go forth to contemplate the heavens, and are borne round in the revolutions of them. There they see the divine forms of justice, temperance, and the like, in their unchangeable beauty, but not without an effort more than human. The soul of man is likened to a charioteer and two steeds, one mortal, the other immortal. The charioteer and the mortal steed are in fierce conflict; at length the animal principle is finally overpowered, though not extinguished, by the combined energies of the passionate and rational elements. This is one of those passages in Plato which, partaking both of a philosophical and poetical character, is necessarily indistinct and inconsistent. The magnificent figure under which the nature of the soul is described has not much to do with the popular doctrine of the ideas. Yet there is one little trait in the description which shows that they are present to Plato's mind, namely, the remark that the soul, which had seen truths in the form of the universal, cannot again return to the nature of an animal.

In the Phaedo, as in the Meno, the origin of ideas is sought for in a previous state of existence. There was no time when they could have been acquired in this life, and therefore they must have been recovered from another. The process of recovery is no other than the ordinary law of association, by which in daily life the sight of one thing or person recalls another to our minds, and by which in scientific enquiry from any part of knowledge we may be led on to infer the whole. It is also argued that ideas, or rather ideals, must be derived from a previous state of existence because they are more perfect than the sensible forms of them which are given by experience. But in the Phaedo the doctrine of ideas is subordinate to the proof of the immortality of the soul. 'If the soul existed in a previous state, then it will exist in a future state, for a law of alternation pervades all things.' And, 'If the ideas exist, then the soul exists; if not, not.' It is to be observed, both in the Meno and the Phaedo, that Socrates expresses himself with diffidence. He speaks in the Phaedo of the words with which he has comforted himself and his friends, and will not be too confident that the description which he has given of the soul and her mansions is exactly true, but he 'ventures to think that something of the kind is true.' And in the Meno, after dwelling upon the immortality of the soul, he adds, 'Of some things which I have said I am not altogether confident' (compare Apology; Gorgias). From this class of uncertainties he exempts the difference between truth and appearance, of which he is absolutely convinced.

In the Republic the ideas are spoken of in two ways, which though not contradictory are different. In the tenth book they are represented as the genera or general ideas under which individuals having a common name are contained. For example, there is the bed which the carpenter makes, the picture of the bed which is drawn by the painter, the bed existing in nature of which God is the author. Of the latter all visible beds are only the shadows or reflections. This and similar illustrations or explanations are put forth, not for their own sake, or as an exposition of Plato's theory of ideas, but with a view of showing that poetry and the mimetic arts are concerned with an inferior part of the soul and a lower kind of knowledge. On the other hand, in the 6th and 7th books of the Republic we reach the highest and most perfect conception, which Plato is able to attain, of the nature of knowledge. The ideas are now finally seen to be one as well as many, causes as well as ideas, and to have a unity which is the idea of good and the cause of all the rest. They seem, however, to have lost their first aspect of universals under which individuals are contained, and to have been converted into forms of another kind, which are inconsistently regarded from the one side as images or ideals of justice, temperance, holiness and the like; from the other as hypotheses, or mathematical truths or principles.

In the Timaeus, which in the series of Plato's works immediately follows the Republic, though probably written some time afterwards, no mention occurs of the doctrine of ideas. Geometrical forms and arithmetical ratios furnish the laws according to which the world is created. But though the conception of the ideas as genera or species is forgotten or laid aside, the distinction of the visible and intellectual is as firmly maintained as ever. The *idea* of good likewise disappears and is superseded by the conception of a personal God, who works according to a final cause or principle of goodness which he himself is. No doubt is expressed by Plato, either in the Timaeus or in any other dialogue, of the truths which he conceives to be the first and highest. It is not the existence of God or the idea of good which he approaches in a tentative or hesitating manner, but the investigations of physiology. These he regards, not seriously, as a part of philosophy, but as an innocent recreation (Tim.).

Passing on to the Parmenides, we find in that dialogue not an exposition or defence of the doctrine of ideas, but an assault upon them, which is put into the mouth of the veteran Parmenides, and might be ascribed to Aristotle himself, or to one of his disciples. The doctrine which is assailed takes two or three forms, but fails in any of them to escape the dialectical difficulties which are urged against it. It is admitted that there are ideas of all things, but the manner in which individuals partake of them, whether of the whole or of the part, and in which they become like them, or how ideas can be either within or without the sphere of human knowledge, or how the human and divine can have any relation to each other, is held to be incapable of explanation. And yet, if there are no universal ideas, what becomes of philosophy? (Parmenides.) In the Sophist the theory of ideas is spoken of as a doctrine held not by Plato, but by another sect of philosophers, called 'the Friends of Ideas,' probably the Megarians, who were very distinct from him, if not opposed to him (Sophist). Nor in what may be termed Plato's abridgement of the history of philosophy (Soph.), is any mention made such as we find in the first book of Aristotle's Metaphysics, of the derivation of such a theory or of any part of it from the Pythagoreans, the Eleatics, the Heracleiteans, or even from Socrates. In the Philebus, probably one of the latest of the Platonic Dialogues, the conception of a personal or semi-personal deity expressed under the figure of mind, the king of all, who is also the cause, is retained. The one and many of the Phaedrus and Theaetetus is still working in the mind of Plato, and the correlation of ideas, not of 'all with all,' but of 'some with some,' is asserted and explained. But they are spoken of in a different manner, and are not supposed to be recovered from a former state of existence. The metaphysical conception of truth passes into a psychological one, which is continued in the Laws, and is the final form of the Platonic philosophy, so far as can be gathered from his own writings (see especially Laws). In the Laws he harps once more on the old string, and returns to general notions:—these he acknowledges to be many, and yet he insists that they are also one. The guardian must be made to recognize the truth, for which he has contended long ago in the Protagoras, that the virtues are four, but they are also in some sense one (Laws; compare Protagoras).

So various, and if regarded on the surface only, inconsistent, are the statements of Plato respecting the doctrine of ideas. If we attempted to harmonize or to combine them, we should make out of them, not a system, but the caricature of a system. They are the ever-varying expression of Plato's Idealism. The terms used in them are in their substance and general meaning the same, although they seem to be different. They pass from the subject to the object, from earth (diesseits) to heaven (jenseits) without regard to the gulf which later theology and philosophy have made between them. They are also intended to supplement or explain each other. They relate to a subject of which Plato himself would have said that 'he was not confident of the precise form of his own statements, but was strong in the belief that something of the kind was true.' It is the spirit, not the letter, in which they agree—the spirit which places the divine above the human, the spiritual above the material, the one above the many, the mind before the body.

The stream of ancient philosophy in the Alexandrian and Roman times widens into a lake or sea, and then disappears underground to reappear after many ages in a distant land. It begins to flow again under new conditions, at first confined between high and narrow banks, but finally spreading over the continent of Europe. It is and is not the same with ancient philosophy. There is a great deal in modern philosophy which is inspired by ancient. There is much in ancient philosophy which was 'born out of due time; and before men were capable of understanding it. To the fathers of modern philosophy, their own thoughts appeared to be new and original, but they carried with them an echo or shadow of the past, coming back by recollection from an elder world. Of this the enquirers of the seventeenth century, who to themselves appeared to be working out independently the enquiry into all truth, were unconscious. They stood in a new relation to theology and natural philosophy, and for a time maintained towards both an attitude of reserve and separation. Yet the similarities between modern and ancient thought are greater far than the differences. All philosophy, even that part of it which is said to be based upon experience, is really ideal; and ideas are not only derived from facts, but they are also prior to them and extend far beyond them, just as the mind is prior to the senses.

Early Greek speculation culminates in the ideas of Plato, or rather in the single idea of good. His followers, and perhaps he himself, having arrived at this elevation, instead of going forwards went backwards from philosophy to psychology, from ideas to numbers. But what we perceive to be the real meaning of them, an explanation of the nature and origin of knowledge, will always continue to be one of the first problems of philosophy.

Plato also left behind him a most potent instrument, the forms of logic—arms ready for use, but not yet taken out of their armoury. They were the late birth of the early Greek philosophy, and were the only part of it which has had an uninterrupted hold on the mind of Europe. Philosophies come and go; but the detection of fallacies, the framing of definitions, the invention of methods still continue to be the main elements of the reasoning process.

Modern philosophy, like ancient, begins with very simple conceptions. It is almost wholly a reflection on self. It might be described as a quickening into life of old words and notions latent in the semi-barbarous Latin, and putting a new meaning into them. Unlike ancient philosophy, it has been unaffected by impressions derived from outward nature: it arose within the limits of the mind itself. From the time of Descartes to Hume and Kant it has had little or nothing to do with facts of science. On the other hand, the ancient and mediaeval logic retained a continuous influence over it, and a form like that of mathematics was easily impressed upon it; the principle of ancient philosophy which is most apparent in it is scepticism; we must doubt nearly every traditional or received notion, that we may hold fast one or two. The being of God in a personal or impersonal form was a mental necessity to the first thinkers of modern times: from this alone all other ideas could be deduced. There had been an obscure presentiment of 'cognito, ergo sum' more than 2000 years previously. The Eleatic notion that being and thought were the same was revived in a new form by Descartes. But now it gave birth to consciousness and self-reflection: it awakened the 'ego' in human nature. The mind naked and abstract has no other certainty but the conviction of its own existence. 'I think, therefore I am;' and this thought is God thinking in me, who has also communicated to the reason of man his own attributes of thought and extension—these are truly imparted to him because God is true (compare Republic). It has been often remarked that Descartes, having begun by dismissing all presuppositions, introduces several: he passes almost at once from scepticism to dogmatism. It is more important for the illustration of Plato to observe that he, like Plato, insists that God is true and incapable of deception (Republic)—that he proceeds from general ideas, that many elements of mathematics may be found in him. A certain influence of mathematics both on the form and substance of their philosophy is discernible in both of them. After making the greatest opposition between thought and extension, Descartes, like Plato, supposes them to be reunited for a time, not in their own nature but by a special divine act (compare Phaedrus), and he also supposes all the parts of the human body to meet in the pineal gland, that alone affording a principle of unity in the material frame of man. It is characteristic of the first period of modern philosophy, that having begun (like the Presocratics) with a few general notions,

Descartes first falls absolutely under their influence, and then quickly discards them. At the same time he is less able to observe facts, because they are too much magnified by the glasses through which they are seen. The common logic says 'the greater the extension, the less the comprehension,' and we may put the same thought in another way and say of abstract or general ideas, that the greater the abstraction of them, the less are they capable of being applied to particular and concrete natures.

Not very different from Descartes in his relation to ancient philosophy is his successor Spinoza, who lived in the following generation. The system of Spinoza is less personal and also less dualistic than that of Descartes. In this respect the difference between them is like that between Xenophanes and Parmenides. The teaching of Spinoza might be described generally as the Jewish religion reduced to an abstraction and taking the form of the Eleatic philosophy. Like Parmenides, he is overpowered and intoxicated with the idea of Being or God. The greatness of both philosophies consists in the immensity of a thought which excludes all other thoughts; their weakness is the necessary separation of this thought from actual existence and from practical life. In neither of them is there any clear opposition between the inward and outward world. The substance of Spinoza has two attributes, which alone are cognizable by man, thought and extension; these are in extreme opposition to one another, and also in inseparable identity. They may be regarded as the two aspects or expressions under which God or substance is unfolded to man. Here a step is made beyond the limits of the Eleatic philosophy. The famous theorem of Spinoza, 'Omnis determinatio est negatio,' is already contained in the 'negation is relation' of Plato's Sophist. The grand description of the philosopher in Republic VI, as the spectator of all time and all existence, may be paralleled with another famous expression of Spinoza, 'Contemplatio rerum sub specie eternitatis.' According to Spinoza finite objects are unreal, for they are conditioned by what is alien to them, and by one another. Human beings are included in the number of them. Hence there is no reality in human action and no place for right and wrong. Individuality is accident. The boasted freedom of the will is only a consciousness of necessity. Truth, he says, is the direction of the reason towards the infinite, in which all things repose; and herein lies the secret of man's well-being. In the exaltation of the reason or intellect, in the denial of the voluntariness of evil (Timaeus; Laws) Spinoza approaches nearer to Plato than in his conception of an infinite substance. As Socrates said that virtue is knowledge, so Spinoza would have maintained that knowledge alone is good, and what contributes to knowledge useful. Both are equally far from any real experience or observation of nature. And the same difficulty is found in both when we seek to apply their ideas to life and practice.

There is a gulf fixed between the infinite substance and finite objects or individuals of Spinoza, just as there is between the ideas of Plato and the world of sense.

Removed from Spinoza by less than a generation is the philosopher Leibnitz, who after deepening and intensifying the opposition between mind and matter, reunites them by his preconcerted harmony (compare again Phaedrus). To him all the particles of matter are living beings which reflect on one another, and in the least of them the whole is contained. Here we catch a reminiscence both of the omoiomere, or similar particles of Anaxagoras, and of the world-animal of the Timaeus.

In Bacon and Locke we have another development in which the mind of man is supposed to receive knowledge by a new method and to work by observation and experience. But we may remark that it is the idea of experience, rather than experience itself, with which the mind is filled. It is a symbol of knowledge rather than the reality which is vouchsafed to us. The Organon of Bacon is not much nearer to actual facts than the Organon of Aristotle or the Platonic idea of good. Many of the old rags and ribbons which defaced the garment of philosophy have been stripped off, but some of them still adhere. A crude conception of the ideas of Plato survives in the 'forms' of Bacon. And on the other hand, there are many passages of Plato in which the importance of the investigation of facts is as much insisted upon as by Bacon. Both are almost equally superior to the illusions of language, and are constantly crying out against them, as against other idols.

Locke cannot be truly regarded as the author of sensationalism any more than of idealism. His system is based upon experience, but with him experience includes reflection as well as sense. His analysis and construction of ideas has no foundation in fact; it is only the dialectic of the mind 'talking to herself.' The philosophy of Berkeley is but the transposition of two words. For objects of sense he would substitute sensations. He imagines himself to have changed the relation of the human mind towards God and nature; they remain the same as before, though he has drawn the imaginary line by which they are divided at a different point. He has annihilated the outward world, but it instantly reappears governed by the same laws and described under the same names.

A like remark applies to David Hume, of whose philosophy the central principle is the denial of the relation of cause and effect. He would deprive men of a familiar term which they can ill afford to lose; but he seems not to have observed that this alteration is merely verbal and does not in any degree affect the nature of things. Still less did he remark that he was arguing from the necessary imperfection of language against the most certain facts. And here, again, we may find a parallel with the ancients. He goes beyond facts in his scepticism, as they did in their idealism. Like the ancient Sophists, he relegates the more important principles of ethics to custom and probability. But crude and unmeaning as this philosophy is, it exercised a great influence on his successors, not unlike that which Locke exercised upon Berkeley and Berkeley upon Hume himself. All three were both sceptical and ideal in almost equal degrees. Neither they nor their predecessors had any true conception of language or of the history of philosophy. Hume's paradox has been forgotten by the world, and did not any more than the scepticism of the ancients require to be seriously refuted. Like some other philosophical paradoxes, it would have been better left to die out. It certainly could not be refuted by a philosophy such as Kant's, in which, no less than in the previously mentioned systems, the history of the human mind and the nature of language are almost wholly ignored, and the certainty of objective knowledge is transferred to the subject; while absolute truth is reduced to a figment, more abstract and narrow than Plato's ideas, of 'thing in itself,' to which, if we reason strictly, no predicate can be applied.

The question which Plato has raised respecting the origin and nature of ideas belongs to the infancy of philosophy; in modern times it would no longer be asked. Their origin is only their history, so far as we know it; there can be no other. We may trace them in language, in philosophy, in mythology, in poetry, but we cannot argue a priori about them. We may attempt to shake them off, but they are always returning, and in every sphere of science and human action are tending to go beyond facts. They are thought to be innate, because they have been familiar to us all our lives, and we can no longer dismiss them from our mind. Many of them express relations of terms to which nothing exactly or nothing at all in rerum natura corresponds. We are not such free agents in the use of them as we sometimes imagine. Fixed ideas have taken the most complete possession of some thinkers who have been most determined to renounce them, and have been vehemently affirmed when they could be least explained and were incapable of proof. The world has often been led away by a word to which no distinct meaning could be attached. Abstractions such as 'authority,' 'equality,' 'utility,' 'liberty,' 'pleasure,' 'experience,' 'consciousness,' 'chance,' 'substance,' 'matter,' 'atom,' and a heap of other metaphysical and theological terms, are the source of quite as much error and illusion and have as little relation to actual facts as the ideas of Plato. Few students of theology or philosophy have sufficiently reflected how quickly the bloom of a philosophy passes away; or how hard it is for one age to understand the writings of another; or how nice a judgment is required of those who are seeking to express the philosophy of one age in the terms of another. The 'eternal truths' of which metaphysicians speak have hardly ever lasted more than a generation. In our own day schools or systems of philosophy which have once been famous have died before the founders of them. We are still, as in Plato's age, groping about for a new method more comprehensive than any of those which now prevail; and also more permanent. And we seem to see at a distance the promise of such a method, which can hardly be any other than the method of idealized experience, having roots which strike far down into the history of philosophy. It is a method which does not divorce the present from the past, or the part from the whole, or the abstract from the concrete, or theory from fact, or the divine from the human, or one science from another, but labours to connect them. Along such a road we have proceeded a few steps, sufficient, perhaps, to make us reflect on the want of method which prevails in our own day. In another age, all the branches of knowledge, whether relating to God or man or nature, will become the knowledge of 'the revelation of a single science' (Symp.), and all things, like the stars in heaven, will shed their light upon one another.

MENO

PERSONS OF THE DIALOGUE: Meno, Socrates, A
Slave of Meno (Boy), Anytus.

MENO: Can you tell me, Socrates, whether virtue is acquired by teaching or by practice; or if neither by teaching nor by practice, then whether it comes to man by nature, or in what other way?

SOCRATES: O Meno, there was a time when the Thessalians were famous among the other Hellenes only for their riches and their riding; but now, if I am not mistaken, they are equally famous for their wisdom, especially at Larissa, which is the native city of your friend Aristippus. And this is Gorgias' doing; for when he came there, the flower of the Aleuadae, among them your admirer Aristippus, and the other chiefs of the Thessalians, fell in love with his wisdom. And he has taught you the habit of answering questions in a grand and bold style, which becomes those who know, and is the style in which he himself answers all comers; and any Hellene who likes may ask him anything. How different is our lot! my dear Meno. Here at Athens there is a dearth of the commodity, and all wisdom seems to have emigrated from us to you. I am certain that if you were to ask any Athenian whether virtue was natural or acquired, he would laugh in your face, and say: 'Stranger, you have far too good an opinion of me, if you think that I can answer your question. For I literally do not know what virtue is, and much less whether it is acquired by teaching or not.' And I myself, Meno, living as I do in this region of poverty, am as poor as the rest of the world; and I confess with shame that I know literally nothing about virtue; and when I do not know the 'quid' of anything how can I know the 'quale'? How, if I knew nothing at all of Meno, could I tell if he was fair, or the opposite of fair; rich and noble, or the reverse of rich and noble? Do you think that I could?

MENO: No, indeed. But are you in earnest, Socrates, in saying that you do not know what virtue is? And am I to carry back this report of you to Thessaly?

SOCRATES: Not only that, my dear boy, but you may say further that I have never known of any one else who did, in my judgment.

MENO: Then you have never met Gorgias when he was at Athens?

SOCRATES: Yes, I have.

MENO: And did you not think that he knew?

SOCRATES: I have not a good memory, Meno, and therefore I cannot now tell what I thought of him at the time. And I dare say that he did know, and that you know what he said: please, therefore, to remind me of what he said; or, if you would rather, tell me your own view; for I suspect that you and he think much alike.

MENO: Very true.

SOCRATES: Then as he is not here, never mind him, and do you tell me: By the gods, Meno, be generous, and tell me what you say that virtue is; for I shall be truly delighted to find that I have been mistaken, and that you and Gorgias do really have this knowledge; although I have been just saying that I have never found anybody who had.

MENO: There will be no difficulty, Socrates, in answering your question. Let us take first the virtue of a man—he should know how to administer the state, and in the administration of it to benefit his friends and harm his enemies; and he must also be careful not to suffer harm himself. A woman's virtue, if you wish to know about that, may also be easily described: her duty is to order her house, and keep what is indoors, and obey her husband. Every age, every condition of life, young or old, male or female, bond or free, has a different virtue: there are virtues numberless, and no lack of definitions of them; for virtue is relative to the actions and ages of each of us in all that we do. And the same may be said of vice, Socrates. (Compare Arist. Pol.)

SOCRATES: How fortunate I am, Meno! When I ask you for one virtue, you present me with a swarm of them (Compare Theaet.), which are in your keeping. Suppose that I carry on the figure of the swarm, and ask of you, What is the nature of the bee? and you answer that there are many kinds of bees, and I reply: But do bees differ as bees, because there are many and different kinds of them; or are they not rather to be distinguished by some other quality, as for example beauty, size, or shape? How would you answer me?

MENO: I should answer that bees do not differ from one another, as bees.

SOCRATES: And if I went on to say: That is what I desire to know, Meno; tell me what is the quality in which they do not differ, but are all alike;—would you be able to answer?

MENO: I should.

SOCRATES: And so of the virtues, however many and different they may be, they have all a common nature which makes them virtues; and on this he who would answer the question, 'What is virtue?' would do well to have his eye fixed: Do you understand?

MENO: I am beginning to understand; but I do not as yet take hold of the question as I could wish.

SOCRATES: When you say, Meno, that there is one virtue of a man, another of a woman, another of a child, and so on, does this apply only to virtue, or would you say the same of health, and size, and strength? Or is the nature of health always the same, whether in man or woman?

MENO: I should say that health is the same, both in man and woman.

SOCRATES: And is not this true of size and strength? If a woman is strong, she will be strong by reason of the same form and of the same strength subsisting in her which there is in the man. I mean to say that strength, as strength, whether of man or woman, is the same. Is there any difference?

MENO: I think not.

SOCRATES: And will not virtue, as virtue, be the same, whether in a child or in a grown-up person, in a woman or in a man?

MENO: I cannot help feeling, Socrates, that this case is different from the others.

SOCRATES: But why? Were you not saying that the virtue of a man was to order a state, and the virtue of a woman was to order a house?

MENO: I did say so.

SOCRATES: And can either house or state or anything be well ordered without temperance and without justice?

MENO: Certainly not.

SOCRATES: Then they who order a state or a house temperately or justly order them with temperance and justice?

MENO: Certainly.

SOCRATES: Then both men and women, if they are to be good men and women, must have the same virtues of temperance and justice?

MENO: True.

SOCRATES: And can either a young man or an elder one be good, if they are intemperate and unjust?

MENO: They cannot.

SOCRATES: They must be temperate and just?

MENO: Yes.

SOCRATES: Then all men are good in the same way, and by

participation in the same virtues?

MENO: Such is the inference.

SOCRATES: And they surely would not have been good in the same way, unless their virtue had been the same?

MENO: They would not.

SOCRATES: Then now that the sameness of all virtue has been proven, try and remember what you and Gorgias say that virtue is.

MENO: Will you have one definition of them all?

SOCRATES: That is what I am seeking.

MENO: If you want to have one definition of them all, I know not what to say, but that virtue is the power of governing mankind.

SOCRATES: And does this definition of virtue include all virtue? Is virtue the same in a child and in a slave, Meno? Can the child govern his father, or the slave his master; and would he who governed be any longer a slave?

MENO: I think not, Socrates.

SOCRATES: No, indeed; there would be small reason in that. Yet once more, fair friend; according to you, virtue is 'the power of governing;' but do you not add 'justly and not unjustly'?

MENO: Yes, Socrates; I agree there; for justice is virtue.

SOCRATES: Would you say 'virtue,' Meno, or 'a virtue'?

MENO: What do you mean?

SOCRATES: I mean as I might say about anything; that a round, for example, is 'a figure' and not simply 'figure,' and I should adopt this mode of speaking, because there are other figures.

MENO: Quite right; and that is just what I am saying about virtue—that there are other virtues as well as justice.

SOCRATES: What are they? tell me the names of them, as I would tell you the names of the other figures if you asked me.

MENO: Courage and temperance and wisdom and magnanimity are virtues; and there are many others.

SOCRATES: Yes, Meno; and again we are in the same case: in searching after one virtue we have found many, though not in the same way as before; but we have been unable to find the common virtue which runs through them all.

MENO: Why, Socrates, even now I am not able to follow you in the attempt to get at one common notion of virtue as of other things.

SOCRATES: No wonder; but I will try to get nearer if I can, for you know that all things have a common notion. Suppose now that some one asked you the question which I asked before: Meno, he would say, what is figure? And if you answered 'roundness,' he would reply to you, in my way of speaking, by asking whether you would say that roundness is 'figure' or 'a figure;' and you would answer 'a figure.'

MENO: Certainly.

SOCRATES: And for this reason—that there are other figures?

MENO: Yes.

SOCRATES: And if he proceeded to ask, What other figures are there? you would have told him.

MENO: I should.

SOCRATES: And if he similarly asked what colour is, and you answered whiteness, and the questioner rejoined, Would you say that whiteness is colour or a colour? you would reply, A colour, because there are other colours as well.

MENO: I should.

SOCRATES: And if he had said, Tell me what they are?—you would have told him of other colours which are colours just as much as whiteness.

MENO: Yes.

SOCRATES: And suppose that he were to pursue the matter in my way, he would say: Ever and anon we are landed in particulars, but this is not what I want; tell me then, since you call them by a common name, and say that they are all figures, even when opposed to one another, what is that common nature which you designate as figure—which contains straight as well as round, and is no more one than the other—that would be your mode of speaking?

MENO: Yes.

SOCRATES: And in speaking thus, you do not mean to say that the round is round any more than straight, or the straight any more straight than round?

MENO: Certainly not.

SOCRATES: You only assert that the round figure is not more a figure than the straight, or the straight than the round?

MENO: Very true.

SOCRATES: To what then do we give the name of figure? Try and answer. Suppose that when a person asked you this question either about figure or colour, you were to reply, Man, I do not understand what you want, or know what you are saying; he would look rather astonished and say: Do you not understand that I am looking for the 'simile in multis'? And then he might put the question in another form: Meno, he might say, what is that 'simile in multis' which you call figure, and which includes not only round and straight figures, but all? Could you not answer that question, Meno? I wish that you would try; the attempt will be good practice with a view to the answer about virtue.

MENO: I would rather that you should answer, Socrates.

SOCRATES: Shall I indulge you?

MENO: By all means.

SOCRATES: And then you will tell me about virtue?

MENO: I will.

SOCRATES: Then I must do my best, for there is a prize to be won.

MENO: Certainly.

SOCRATES: Well, I will try and explain to you what figure is. What do you say to this answer?—Figure is the only thing which always follows colour. Will you be satisfied with it, as I am sure that I should be, if you would let me have a similar definition of virtue?

MENO: But, Socrates, it is such a simple answer.

SOCRATES: Why simple?

MENO: Because, according to you, figure is that which always follows colour.

(SOCRATES: Granted.)

MENO: But if a person were to say that he does not know what colour is, any more than what figure is—what sort of answer would you have given him?

SOCRATES: I should have told him the truth. And if he were a philosopher of the eristic and antagonistic sort, I should say to him: You have my answer, and if I am wrong, your business is to take up the argument and refute me. But if we were friends, and were talking as you and I are now, I should reply in a milder strain and more in the dialectician's vein; that is to say, I should not only speak the truth, but I should make use of premises which the person interrogated would be willing to admit. And this is the way in which I shall endeavour to approach you. You will acknowledge, will you not, that there is such a thing as an end, or termination, or extremity?—all which words I use in the same sense, although I am aware that Prodicus might draw distinctions about them: but still you, I am sure, would speak of a thing as ended or terminated—that is all which I am saying—not anything very difficult.

MENO: Yes, I should; and I believe that I understand your meaning.

SOCRATES: And you would speak of a surface and also of a solid, as for example in geometry.

MENO: Yes.

SOCRATES: Well then, you are now in a condition to understand my definition of figure. I define figure to be that in which the solid ends; or, more concisely, the limit of solid.

MENO: And now, Socrates, what is colour?

SOCRATES: You are outrageous, Meno, in thus plaguing a poor old man to give you an answer, when you will not take the trouble of remembering what is Gorgias' definition of virtue.

MENO: When you have told me what I ask, I will tell you, Socrates.

SOCRATES: A man who was blindfolded has only to hear you talking, and he would know that you are a fair creature and have still many lovers.

MENO: Why do you think so?

SOCRATES: Why, because you always speak in imperatives: like all beauties when they are in their prime, you are tyrannical; and also, as I suspect, you have found out that I have weakness for the fair, and therefore to humour you I must answer.

MENO: Please do.

SOCRATES: Would you like me to answer you after the manner of Gorgias, which is familiar to you?

MENO: I should like nothing better.

SOCRATES: Do not he and you and Empedocles say that there are certain effluences of existence?

MENO: Certainly.

SOCRATES: And passages into which and through which the effluences pass?

MENO: Exactly.

SOCRATES: And some of the effluences fit into the passages, and some of them are too small or too large?

MENO: True.

SOCRATES: And there is such a thing as sight?

MENO: Yes.

SOCRATES: And now, as Pindar says, 'read my meaning:'— colour is an effluence of form, commensurate with sight, and palpable to sense.

MENO: That, Socrates, appears to me to be an admirable answer.

SOCRATES: Why, yes, because it happens to be one which you have been in the habit of hearing: and your wit will have discovered, I suspect, that you may explain in the same way the nature of sound and smell, and of many other similar phenomena.

MENO: Quite true.

SOCRATES: The answer, Meno, was in the orthodox solemn vein, and therefore was more acceptable to you than the other answer about figure.

MENO: Yes.

SOCRATES: And yet, O son of Alexidemus, I cannot help thinking that the other was the better; and I am sure that you would be of the same opinion, if you would only stay and be initiated, and were not compelled, as you said yesterday, to go away before the mysteries.

MENO: But I will stay, Socrates, if you will give me many such answers.

SOCRATES: Well then, for my own sake as well as for yours, I will do my very best; but I am afraid that I shall not be able to give you very many as good: and now, in your turn, you are to fulfil your promise, and tell me what virtue is in the universal; and do not make a singular into a plural, as the facetious say of those who break a thing, but deliver virtue to me whole and sound, and not broken into a number of pieces: I have given you the pattern.

MENO: Well then, Socrates, virtue, as I take it, is when he, who desires the honourable, is able to provide it for himself; so the poet says, and I say too—'Virtue is the desire of things honourable and the power of attaining them.'

SOCRATES: And does he who desires the honourable also desire the good?

MENO: Certainly.

SOCRATES: Then are there some who desire the evil and others who desire the good? Do not all men, my dear sir, desire good?

MENO: I think not.

SOCRATES: There are some who desire evil?

MENO: Yes.

SOCRATES: Do you mean that they think the evils which they desire, to be good; or do they know that they are evil and yet desire them?

MENO: Both, I think.

SOCRATES: And do you really imagine, Meno, that a man knows evils to be evils and desires them notwithstanding?

MENO: Certainly I do.

SOCRATES: And desire is of possession?

MENO: Yes, of possession.

SOCRATES: And does he think that the evils will do good to him who possesses them, or does he know that they will do him harm?

MENO: There are some who think that the evils will do them good, and others who know that they will do them harm.

SOCRATES: And, in your opinion, do those who think that they will do them good know that they are evils?

MENO: Certainly not.

SOCRATES: Is it not obvious that those who are ignorant of their nature do not desire them; but they desire what they suppose to be goods although they are really evils; and if they are mistaken and suppose the evils to be goods they really desire goods?

MENO: Yes, in that case.

SOCRATES: Well, and do those who, as you say, desire evils, and think that evils are hurtful to the possessor of them, know that they will be hurt by them?

MENO: They must know it.

SOCRATES: And must they not suppose that those who are hurt are miserable in proportion to the hurt which is inflicted upon them?

MENO: How can it be otherwise?

SOCRATES: But are not the miserable ill-fated?

MENO: Yes, indeed.

SOCRATES: And does any one desire to be miserable and ill-fated?

MENO: I should say not, Socrates.

SOCRATES: But if there is no one who desires to be miserable, there is no one, Meno, who desires evil; for what is misery but the desire and possession of evil?

MENO: That appears to be the truth, Socrates, and I admit that nobody desires evil.

SOCRATES: And yet, were you not saying just now that virtue is the desire and power of attaining good?

MENO: Yes, I did say so.

SOCRATES: But if this be affirmed, then the desire of good is common to all, and one man is no better than another in that respect?

MENO: True.

SOCRATES: And if one man is not better than another in desiring good, he must be better in the power of attaining it?

MENO: Exactly.

SOCRATES: Then, according to your definition, virtue would appear to be the power of attaining good?

MENO: I entirely approve, Socrates, of the manner in which you now view this matter.

SOCRATES: Then let us see whether what you say is true from another point of view; for very likely you may be right:—You affirm virtue to be the power of attaining goods?

MENO: Yes.

SOCRATES: And the goods which you mean are such as health and wealth and the possession of gold and silver, and having office and honour in the state—those are what you would call goods?

MENO: Yes, I should include all those.

SOCRATES: Then, according to Meno, who is the hereditary friend of the great king, virtue is the power of getting silver and gold; and would you add that they must be gained piously, justly, or do you deem this to be of no consequence? And is any mode of acquisition, even if unjust and dishonest, equally to be deemed virtue?

MENO: Not virtue, Socrates, but vice.

SOCRATES: Then justice or temperance or holiness, or some other part of virtue, as would appear, must accompany the acquisition, and without them the mere acquisition of good will not be virtue.

MENO: Why, how can there be virtue without these?

SOCRATES: And the non-acquisition of gold and silver in a dishonest manner for oneself or another, or in other words the want of them, may be equally virtue?

MENO: True.

SOCRATES: Then the acquisition of such goods is no more virtue than the non-acquisition and want of them, but whatever is accompanied by justice or honesty is virtue, and whatever is devoid of justice is vice.

MENO: It cannot be otherwise, in my judgment.

SOCRATES: And were we not saying just now that justice, temperance, and the like, were each of them a part of virtue?

MENO: Yes.

SOCRATES: And so, Meno, this is the way in which you mock me.

MENO: Why do you say that, Socrates?

SOCRATES: Why, because I asked you to deliver virtue into my hands whole and unbroken, and I gave you a pattern according to which you were to frame your answer; and you have forgotten already, and tell me that virtue is the power of attaining good justly, or with justice; and justice you acknowledge to be a part of virtue.

MENO: Yes.

SOCRATES: Then it follows from your own admissions, that virtue is doing what you do with a part of virtue; for justice and the like are said by you to be parts of virtue.

MENO: What of that?

SOCRATES: What of that! Why, did not I ask you to tell me the nature of virtue as a whole? And you are very far from telling me this; but declare every action to be virtue which is done with a part of virtue; as though you had told me and I must already know the whole of virtue, and this too when frittered away into little pieces. And, therefore, my dear Meno, I fear that I must begin again and repeat the same question: What is virtue? for otherwise, I can only say, that every action done with a part of virtue is virtue; what else is the meaning of saying that every action done with justice is virtue? Ought I not to ask the question over again; for can any one who does not know virtue know a part of virtue?

MENO: No; I do not say that he can.

SOCRATES: Do you remember how, in the example of figure, we rejected any answer given in terms which were as yet unexplained or unadmitted?

MENO: Yes, Socrates; and we were quite right in doing so.

SOCRATES: But then, my friend, do not suppose that we can explain to any one the nature of virtue as a whole through some unexplained portion of virtue, or anything at all in that fashion; we should only have to ask over again the old question, What is virtue? Am I not right?

MENO: I believe that you are.

SOCRATES: Then begin again, and answer me, What, according to you and your friend Gorgias, is the definition of virtue?

MENO: O Socrates, I used to be told, before I knew you, that you were always doubting yourself and making others doubt; and now you are casting your spells over me, and I am simply getting bewitched and enchanted, and am at my wits' end. And if I may venture to make a jest upon you, you seem to me both in your appearance and in your power over others to be very like the flat torpedo fish, who torpifies those who come near him and touch him, as you have now torpified me, I think. For my soul and my tongue are really torpid, and I do not know how to answer you; and though I have been delivered of an infinite variety of speeches about virtue before now, and to many persons—and very good ones they were, as I thought—at this moment I cannot even say what virtue is. And I think that you are very wise in not voyaging and going away from home, for if you did in other places as you do in Athens, you would be cast into prison as a magician.

SOCRATES: You are a rogue, Meno, and had all but caught me.

MENO: What do you mean, Socrates?

SOCRATES: I can tell why you made a simile about me.

MENO: Why?

SOCRATES: In order that I might make another simile about you. For I know that all pretty young gentlemen like to have pretty similes made about them—as well they may—but I shall not return the compliment. As to my being a torpedo, if the torpedo is torpid as well as the cause of torpidity in others, then indeed I am a torpedo, but not otherwise; for I perplex others, not because I am clear, but because I am utterly perplexed myself. And now I know not what virtue is, and you seem to be in the same case, although you did once perhaps know before you touched me. However, I have no objection to join with you in the enquiry.

MENO: And how will you enquire, Socrates, into that which you do not know? What will you put forth as the subject of enquiry? And if you find what you want, how will you ever know that this is the thing which you did not know?

SOCRATES: I know, Meno, what you mean; but just see what a tiresome dispute you are introducing. You argue that a man cannot enquire either about that which he knows, or about that which he does not know; for if he knows, he has no need to enquire; and if not, he cannot; for he does not know the very subject about which he is to enquire (Compare Aristot. Post. Anal.).

MENO: Well, Socrates, and is not the argument sound?

SOCRATES: I think not.

MENO: Why not?

SOCRATES: I will tell you why: I have heard from certain wise men and women who spoke of things divine that—

MENO: What did they say?

SOCRATES: They spoke of a glorious truth, as I conceive.

MENO: What was it? and who were they?

SOCRATES: Some of them were priests and priestesses, who had studied how they might be able to give a reason of their profession:

there have been poets also, who spoke of these things by inspiration, like Pindar, and many others who were inspired. And they say—mark, now, and see whether their words are true—they say that the soul of man is immortal, and at one time has an end, which is termed dying, and at another time is born again, but is never destroyed. And the moral is, that a man ought to live always in perfect holiness.

'For in the ninth year Persephone sends the souls of those from whom she has received the penalty of ancient crime back again from beneath into the light of the sun above, and these are they who become noble kings and mighty men and great in wisdom and are called saintly heroes in after ages.'

The soul, then, as being immortal, and having been born again many times, and having seen all things that exist, whether in this world or in the world below, has knowledge of them all; and it is no wonder that she should be able to call to remembrance all that she ever knew about virtue, and about everything; for as all nature is akin, and the soul has learned all things; there is no difficulty in her eliciting or as men say learning, out of a single recollection all the rest, if a man is strenuous and does not faint; for all enquiry and all learning is but recollection. And therefore we ought not to listen to this sophistical argument about the impossibility of enquiry: for it will make us idle; and is sweet only to the sluggard; but the other saying will make us active and inquisitive. In that confiding, I will gladly enquire with you into the nature of virtue.

MENO: Yes, Socrates; but what do you mean by saying that we do not learn, and that what we call learning is only a process of recollection? Can you teach me how this is?

SOCRATES: I told you, Meno, just now that you were a rogue, and now you ask whether I can teach you, when I am saying that there is no teaching, but only recollection; and thus you imagine that you will involve me in a contradiction.

MENO: Indeed, Socrates, I protest that I had no such intention. I only asked the question from habit; but if you can prove to me that what you say is true, I wish that you would.

SOCRATES: It will be no easy matter, but I will try to please you to the utmost of my power. Suppose that you call one of your numerous attendants, that I may demonstrate on him.

MENO: Certainly. Come hither, boy.

SOCRATES: He is Greek, and speaks Greek, does he not?

MENO: Yes, indeed; he was born in the house.

SOCRATES: Attend now to the questions which I ask him, and observe whether he learns of me or only remembers.

MENO: I will.

SOCRATES: Tell me, boy, do you know that a figure like this is a square?

BOY: I do.

SOCRATES: And you know that a square figure has these four lines equal?

BOY: Certainly.

SOCRATES: And these lines which I have drawn through the middle of the square are also equal?

BOY: Yes.

SOCRATES: A square may be of any size?

BOY: Certainly.

SOCRATES: And if one side of the figure be of two feet, and the other side be of two feet, how much will the whole be? Let me explain: if in one direction the space was of two feet, and in the other direction of one foot, the whole would be of two feet taken once?

BOY: Yes.

SOCRATES: But since this side is also of two feet, there are twice two feet?

BOY: There are.

SOCRATES: Then the square is of twice two feet?

BOY: Yes.

SOCRATES: And how many are twice two feet? count and tell me.

BOY: Four, Socrates.

SOCRATES: And might there not be another square twice as large as this, and having like this the lines equal?

BOY: Yes.

SOCRATES: And of how many feet will that be?

BOY: Of eight feet.

SOCRATES: And now try and tell me the length of the line which forms the side of that double square: this is two feet—what will that be?

BOY: Clearly, Socrates, it will be double.

SOCRATES: Do you observe, Meno, that I am not teaching the boy anything, but only asking him questions; and now he fancies that he knows how long a line is necessary in order to produce a figure of eight square feet; does he not?

MENO: Yes.

SOCRATES: And does he really know?

MENO: Certainly not.

SOCRATES: He only guesses that because the square is double, the line is double.

MENO: True.

SOCRATES: Observe him while he recalls the steps in regular order. (To the Boy:) Tell me, boy, do you assert that a double space comes from a double line? Remember that I am not speaking of an oblong, but of a figure equal every way, and twice the size of this—that is to say of eight feet; and I want to know whether you still say that a double square comes from double line?

BOY: Yes.

SOCRATES: But does not this line become doubled if we add another such line here?

BOY: Certainly.

SOCRATES: And four such lines will make a space containing eight feet?

BOY: Yes.

SOCRATES: Let us describe such a figure: Would you not say that this is the figure of eight feet?

BOY: Yes.

SOCRATES: And are there not these four divisions in the figure, each of which is equal to the figure of four feet?

BOY: True.

SOCRATES: And is not that four times four?

BOY: Certainly.

SOCRATES: And four times is not double?

BOY: No, indeed.

SOCRATES: But how much?

BOY: Four times as much.

SOCRATES: Therefore the double line, boy, has given a space, not twice, but four times as much.

BOY: True.

SOCRATES: Four times four are sixteen—are they not?

BOY: Yes.

SOCRATES: What line would give you a space of eight feet, as this gives one of sixteen feet;—do you see?

BOY: Yes.

SOCRATES: And the space of four feet is made from this half line?

BOY: Yes.

SOCRATES: Good; and is not a space of eight feet twice the size of this, and half the size of the other?

BOY: Certainly.

SOCRATES: Such a space, then, will be made out of a line greater than this one, and less than that one?

BOY: Yes; I think so.

SOCRATES: Very good; I like to hear you say what you think. And now tell me, is not this a line of two feet and that of four?

BOY: Yes.

SOCRATES: Then the line which forms the side of eight feet ought to be more than this line of two feet, and less than the other of four feet?

BOY: It ought.

SOCRATES: Try and see if you can tell me how much it will be.

BOY: Three feet.

SOCRATES: Then if we add a half to this line of two, that will be the line of three. Here are two and there is one; and on the other side, here are two also and there is one: and that makes the figure of which you speak?

BOY: Yes.

SOCRATES: But if there are three feet this way and three feet that way, the whole space will be three times three feet?

BOY: That is evident.

SOCRATES: And how much are three times three feet?

BOY: Nine.

SOCRATES: And how much is the double of four?

BOY: Eight.

SOCRATES: Then the figure of eight is not made out of a line of three?

BOY: No.

SOCRATES: But from what line?—tell me exactly; and if you would rather not reckon, try and show me the line.

BOY: Indeed, Socrates, I do not know.

SOCRATES: Do you see, Meno, what advances he has made in his power of recollection? He did not know at first, and he does not know now, what is the side of a figure of eight feet: but then he thought that he knew, and answered confidently as if he knew, and had no difficulty; now he has a difficulty, and neither knows nor fancies that he knows.

MENO: True.

SOCRATES: Is he not better off in knowing his ignorance?

MENO: I think that he is.

SOCRATES: If we have made him doubt, and given him the 'torpedo's shock,' have we done him any harm?

MENO: I think not.

SOCRATES: We have certainly, as would seem, assisted him in some degree to the discovery of the truth; and now he will wish to remedy his ignorance, but then he would have been ready to tell all the world again and again that the double space should have a double side.

MENO: True.

SOCRATES: But do you suppose that he would ever have enquired into or learned what he fancied that he knew, though he was really ignorant of it, until he had fallen into perplexity under the idea that he did not know, and had desired to know?

MENO: I think not, Socrates.

SOCRATES: Then he was the better for the torpedo's touch?

MENO: I think so.

SOCRATES: Mark now the farther development. I shall only ask him, and not teach him, and he shall share the enquiry with me: and do you watch and see if you find me telling or explaining anything to him, instead of eliciting his opinion. Tell me, boy, is not this a square of four feet which I have drawn?

BOY: Yes.

SOCRATES: And now I add another square equal to the former one?

BOY: Yes.

SOCRATES: And a third, which is equal to either of them?

BOY: Yes.

SOCRATES: Suppose that we fill up the vacant corner?

BOY: Very good.

SOCRATES: Here, then, there are four equal spaces?

BOY: Yes.

SOCRATES: And how many times larger is this space than this other?

BOY: Four times.

SOCRATES: But it ought to have been twice only, as you will remember.

BOY: True.

SOCRATES: And does not this line, reaching from corner to corner, bisect each of these spaces?

BOY: Yes.

SOCRATES: And are there not here four equal lines which contain this space?

BOY: There are.

SOCRATES: Look and see how much this space is.

BOY: I do not understand.

SOCRATES: Has not each interior line cut off half of the four spaces?

BOY: Yes.

SOCRATES: And how many spaces are there in this section?

BOY: Four.

SOCRATES: And how many in this?

BOY: Two.

SOCRATES: And four is how many times two?

BOY: Twice.

SOCRATES: And this space is of how many feet?

BOY: Of eight feet.

SOCRATES: And from what line do you get this figure?

BOY: From this.

SOCRATES: That is, from the line which extends from corner to corner of the figure of four feet?

BOY: Yes.

SOCRATES: And that is the line which the learned call the diagonal. And if this is the proper name, then you, Meno's slave, are prepared to affirm that the double space is the square of the diagonal?

BOY: Certainly, Socrates.

SOCRATES: What do you say of him, Meno? Were not all these answers given out of his own head?

MENO: Yes, they were all his own.

SOCRATES: And yet, as we were just now saying, he did not know?

MENO: True.

SOCRATES: But still he had in him those notions of his—had he not?

MENO: Yes.

SOCRATES: Then he who does not know may still have true notions of that which he does not know?

MENO: He has.

SOCRATES: And at present these notions have just been stirred up in him, as in a dream; but if he were frequently asked the same questions, in different forms, he would know as well as any one at last?

MENO: I dare say.

SOCRATES: Without any one teaching him he will recover his knowledge for himself, if he is only asked questions?

MENO: Yes.

SOCRATES: And this spontaneous recovery of knowledge in him is recollection?

MENO: True.

SOCRATES: And this knowledge which he now has must he not either have acquired or always possessed?

MENO: Yes.

SOCRATES: But if he always possessed this knowledge he would always have known; or if he has acquired the knowledge he could not have acquired it in this life, unless he has been taught geometry; for he may be made to do the same with all geometry and every other branch of knowledge. Now, has any one ever taught him all this? You must know about him, if, as you say, he was born and bred in your house.

MENO: And I am certain that no one ever did teach him.

SOCRATES: And yet he has the knowledge?

MENO: The fact, Socrates, is undeniable.

SOCRATES: But if he did not acquire the knowledge in this life, then he must have had and learned it at some other time?

MENO: Clearly he must.

SOCRATES: Which must have been the time when he was not a man?

MENO: Yes.

SOCRATES: And if there have been always true thoughts in him, both at the time when he was and was not a man, which only need to be awakened into knowledge by putting questions to him, his soul must have always possessed this knowledge, for he always either was or was not a man?

MENO: Obviously.

SOCRATES: And if the truth of all things always existed in the soul, then the soul is immortal. Wherefore be of good cheer, and try to recollect what you do not know, or rather what you do not remember.

MENO: I feel, somehow, that I like what you are saying.

SOCRATES: And I, Meno, like what I am saying. Some things I have said of which I am not altogether confident. But that we shall be better and braver and less helpless if we think that we ought to enquire, than we should have been if we indulged in the idle fancy that there was no knowing and no use in seeking to know what we do not know;—that is a theme upon which I am ready to fight, in word and deed, to the utmost of my power.

MENO: There again, Socrates, your words seem to me excellent.

SOCRATES: Then, as we are agreed that a man should enquire about that which he does not know, shall you and I make an effort to enquire together into the nature of virtue?

MENO: By all means, Socrates. And yet I would much rather return to my original question, Whether in seeking to acquire virtue we should regard it as a thing to be taught, or as a gift of nature, or as coming to men in some other way?

SOCRATES: Had I the command of you as well as of myself, Meno, I would not have enquired whether virtue is given by instruction or not, until we had first ascertained 'what it is.' But as you think only of controlling me who am your slave, and never of controlling yourself,—such being your notion of freedom, I must yield to you, for you are irresistible. And therefore I have now to enquire into the qualities of a thing of which I do not as yet know the nature. At any rate, will you condescend a little, and allow the question 'Whether virtue is given by instruction, or in any other way,' to be argued upon hypothesis? As the geometrician, when he is asked whether a certain triangle is capable being inscribed in a certain circle (Or, whether a certain area is capable of being inscribed as a triangle in a certain circle.), will reply: 'I cannot tell you as yet; but I will offer a hypothesis which may assist us in forming a conclusion: If the figure be such that when you have produced a given side of it (Or, when you apply it to the given line, i.e. the diameter of the circle (autou).), the given area of the triangle falls short by an area corresponding to the part produced (Or, similar to the area so applied.), then one consequence follows, and if this is impossible then some other; and therefore I wish to assume a hypothesis before I tell you whether this triangle is capable of being inscribed in the circle':—that is a geometrical hypothesis. And we too, as we know not the nature and qualities of virtue, must ask, whether virtue is or is not taught, under a hypothesis: as thus, if virtue is of such a class of mental goods, will it be taught or not? Let the first hypothesis be that virtue is or is not knowledge,—in that case will it be taught or not? or, as we were just now saying, 'remembered'? For there is no use in disputing about the name. But is virtue taught or not? or rather, does not every one see that knowledge alone is taught?

MENO: I agree.

SOCRATES: Then if virtue is knowledge, virtue will be taught?

MENO: Certainly.

SOCRATES: Then now we have made a quick end of this question: if virtue is of such a nature, it will be taught; and if not, not?

MENO: Certainly.

SOCRATES: The next question is, whether virtue is knowledge or of another species?

MENO: Yes, that appears to be the question which comes next in order.

SOCRATES: Do we not say that virtue is a good?—This is a hypothesis which is not set aside.

MENO: Certainly.

SOCRATES: Now, if there be any sort of good which is distinct from knowledge, virtue may be that good; but if knowledge embraces all good, then we shall be right in thinking that virtue is knowledge?

MENO: True.

SOCRATES: And virtue makes us good?

MENO: Yes.

SOCRATES: And if we are good, then we are profitable; for all good things are profitable?

MENO: Yes.

SOCRATES: Then virtue is profitable?

MENO: That is the only inference.

SOCRATES: Then now let us see what are the things which severally profit us. Health and strength, and beauty and wealth—these, and the like of these, we call profitable?

MENO: True.

SOCRATES: And yet these things may also sometimes do us harm: would you not think so?

MENO: Yes.

SOCRATES: And what is the guiding principle which makes them profitable or the reverse? Are they not profitable when they are rightly used, and hurtful when they are not rightly used?

MENO: Certainly.

SOCRATES: Next, let us consider the goods of the soul: they are temperance, justice, courage, quickness of apprehension, memory, magnanimity, and the like?

MENO: Surely.

SOCRATES: And such of these as are not knowledge, but of another sort, are sometimes profitable and sometimes hurtful; as, for example, courage wanting prudence, which is only a sort of confidence? When a man has no sense he is harmed by courage, but when he has sense he is profited?

MENO: True.

SOCRATES: And the same may be said of temperance and quickness of apprehension; whatever things are learned or done with sense are profitable, but when done without sense they are hurtful?

MENO: Very true.

SOCRATES: And in general, all that the soul attempts or endures, when under the guidance of wisdom, ends in happiness; but when she is under the guidance of folly, in the opposite?

MENO: That appears to be true.

SOCRATES: If then virtue is a quality of the soul, and is admitted to be profitable, it must be wisdom or prudence, since none of the things of the soul are either profitable or hurtful in themselves, but they are all made profitable or hurtful by the addition of wisdom or of folly; and therefore if virtue is profitable, virtue must be a sort of wisdom or prudence?

MENO: I quite agree.

SOCRATES: And the other goods, such as wealth and the like, of which we were just now saying that they are sometimes good and sometimes evil, do not they also become profitable or hurtful, accordingly as the soul guides and uses them rightly or wrongly; just as the things of the soul herself are benefited when under the guidance of wisdom and harmed by folly?

MENO: True.

SOCRATES: And the wise soul guides them rightly, and the foolish soul wrongly.

MENO: Yes.

SOCRATES: And is not this universally true of human nature? All other things hang upon the soul, and the things of the soul herself hang upon wisdom, if they are to be good; and so wisdom is inferred to be that which profits—and virtue, as we say, is profitable?

MENO: Certainly.

SOCRATES: And thus we arrive at the conclusion that virtue is either wholly or partly wisdom?

MENO: I think that what you are saying, Socrates, is very true.

SOCRATES: But if this is true, then the good are not by nature good?

MENO: I think not.

SOCRATES: If they had been, there would assuredly have been

discerners of characters among us who would have known our future great men; and on their showing we should have adopted them, and when we had got them, we should have kept them in the citadel out of the way of harm, and set a stamp upon them far rather than upon a piece of gold, in order that no one might tamper with them; and when they grew up they would have been useful to the state?

MENO: Yes, Socrates, that would have been the right way.

SOCRATES: But if the good are not by nature good, are they made good by instruction?

MENO: There appears to be no other alternative, Socrates. On the supposition that virtue is knowledge, there can be no doubt that virtue is taught.

SOCRATES: Yes, indeed; but what if the supposition is erroneous?

MENO: I certainly thought just now that we were right.

SOCRATES: Yes, Meno; but a principle which has any soundness should stand firm not only just now, but always.

MENO: Well; and why are you so slow of heart to believe that knowledge is virtue?

SOCRATES: I will try and tell you why, Meno. I do not retract the assertion that if virtue is knowledge it may be taught; but I fear that I have some reason in doubting whether virtue is knowledge: for consider now and say whether virtue, and not only virtue but anything that is taught, must not have teachers and disciples?

MENO: Surely.

SOCRATES: And conversely, may not the art of which neither teachers nor disciples exist be assumed to be incapable of being taught?

MENO: True; but do you think that there are no teachers of virtue?

SOCRATES: I have certainly often enquired whether there were any, and taken great pains to find them, and have never succeeded; and many have assisted me in the search, and they were the persons whom I thought the most likely to know. Here at the moment when he is wanted we fortunately have sitting by us Anytus, the very person of whom we should make enquiry; to him then let us repair. In the first place, he is the son of a wealthy and wise father, Anthemion, who acquired his wealth, not by accident or gift, like Ismenias the Theban (who has recently made himself as rich as Polycrates), but by his own skill and industry, and who is a well- conditioned, modest man, not insolent, or overbearing, or annoying; moreover, this son of his has received a good education, as the Athenian people certainly appear to think, for they choose him to fill the highest offices. And these are the sort of men from whom you are likely to learn whether there are any teachers of virtue, and who they are. Please, Anytus, to help me and your friend Meno in answering our question, Who are the teachers? Consider the matter thus: If we wanted Meno to be a good physician, to whom should we send him? Should we not send him to the physicians?

ANYTUS: Certainly.

SOCRATES: Or if we wanted him to be a good cobbler, should we not send him to the cobblers?

ANYTUS: Yes.

SOCRATES: And so forth?

ANYTUS: Yes.

SOCRATES: Let me trouble you with one more question. When we say that we should be right in sending him to the physicians if we wanted him to be a physician, do we mean that we should be right in sending him to those who profess the art, rather than to those who do not, and to those who demand payment for teaching the art, and profess to teach it to any one who will come and learn? And if these were our reasons, should we not be right in sending him?

ANYTUS: Yes.

SOCRATES: And might not the same be said of flute-playing, and of the other arts? Would a man who wanted to make another a flute-player refuse to send him to those who profess to teach the art for money, and be plaguing other persons to give him instruction, who are not professed teachers and who never had a single disciple in that branch of knowledge which he wishes him to acquire—would not such conduct be the height of folly?

ANYTUS: Yes, by Zeus, and of ignorance too.

SOCRATES: Very good. And now you are in a position to advise with me about my friend Meno. He has been telling me, Anytus, that he desires to attain that kind of wisdom and virtue by which men order the state or the house, and honour their parents, and know when to receive and when to send away citizens and strangers, as a good man should. Now, to whom should he go in order that he may learn this virtue? Does not the previous argument imply clearly that we should send him to those who profess and avouch that they are the common teachers of all Hellas, and are ready to impart instruction to any one who likes, at a fixed price?

ANYTUS: Whom do you mean, Socrates?

SOCRATES: You surely know, do you not, Anytus, that these are the people whom mankind call Sophists?

ANYTUS: By Heracles, Socrates, forbear! I only hope that no friend or kinsman or acquaintance of mine, whether citizen or stranger, will ever be so mad as to allow himself to be corrupted by them; for they are a manifest pest and corrupting influence to those who have to do with them.

SOCRATES: What, Anytus? Of all the people who profess that they know how to do men good, do you mean to say that these are the only ones who not only do them no good, but positively corrupt those who are entrusted to them, and in return for this disservice have the face to demand money? Indeed, I cannot believe you; for I know of a single man, Protagoras, who made more out of his craft than the illustrious Pheidias, who created such noble works, or any ten other statuaries. How could that be? A mender of old shoes, or patcher up of clothes, who made the shoes or clothes worse than he received them, could not have remained thirty days undetected, and would very soon have starved; whereas during more than forty years, Protagoras was corrupting all Hellas, and sending his disciples from him worse than he received them, and he was never found out. For, if I am not mistaken, he was about seventy years old at his death, forty of which were spent in the practice of his profession; and during all that time he had a good reputation, which to this day he retains: and not only Protagoras, but many others are well spoken of; some who lived before him, and others who are still living. Now, when you say that they deceived and corrupted the youth, are they to be supposed to have corrupted them consciously or unconsciously? Can those who were deemed by many to be the wisest men of Hellas have been out of their minds?

ANYTUS: Out of their minds! No, Socrates; the young men who gave their money to them were out of their minds, and their relations and guardians who entrusted their youth to the care of these men were still more out of their minds, and most of all, the cities who allowed them to come in, and did not drive them out, citizen and stranger alike.

SOCRATES: Has any of the Sophists wronged you, Anytus? What makes you so angry with them?

ANYTUS: No, indeed, neither I nor any of my belongings has ever had, nor would I suffer them to have, anything to do with them.

SOCRATES: Then you are entirely unacquainted with them?

ANYTUS: And I have no wish to be acquainted.

SOCRATES: Then, my dear friend, how can you know whether a thing is good or bad of which you are wholly ignorant?

ANYTUS: Quite well; I am sure that I know what manner of men these are, whether I am acquainted with them or not.

SOCRATES: You must be a diviner, Anytus, for I really cannot make out, judging from your own words, how, if you are not acquainted with them, you know about them. But I am not enquiring of you who are the teachers who will corrupt Meno (let them be, if you please, the Sophists); I only ask you to tell him who there is in this great city who will teach him how to become eminent in the virtues which I was just now describing. He is the friend of your family, and you will oblige him.

ANYTUS: Why do you not tell him yourself?

SOCRATES: I have told him whom I supposed to be the teachers of these things; but I learn from you that I am utterly at fault, and I dare say that you are right. And now I wish that you, on your part, would tell me to whom among the Athenians he should go. Whom would you name?

ANYTUS: Why single out individuals? Any Athenian gentleman, taken at random, if he will mind him, will do far more good to him than the Sophists.

SOCRATES: And did those gentlemen grow of themselves; and without having been taught by any one, were they nevertheless able to teach others that which they had never learned themselves?

ANYTUS: I imagine that they learned of the previous generation of gentlemen. Have there not been many good men in this city?

SOCRATES: Yes, certainly, Anytus; and many good statesmen also there always have been and there are still, in the city of Athens. But the question is whether they were also good teachers of their own virtue;—not whether there are, or have been, good men in this part of the world, but whether virtue can be taught, is the question which we have been discussing. Now, do we mean to say that the good men of our own and of other times knew how to impart to others that virtue which they had themselves; or is virtue a thing incapable of being communicated or imparted by one man to another? That is the question which I and Meno have been arguing. Look at the matter in your own way: Would you not admit that Themistocles was a good man?

ANYTUS: Certainly; no man better.

SOCRATES: And must not he then have been a good teacher, if any man ever was a good teacher, of his own virtue?

ANYTUS: Yes certainly,—if he wanted to be so.

SOCRATES: But would he not have wanted? He would, at any rate, have desired to make his own son a good man and a gentleman; he could not have been jealous of him, or have intentionally abstained from imparting to him his own virtue. Did you never hear that he made his son Cleophantus a famous horseman; and had him taught to stand upright on horseback and hurl a javelin, and to do many other marvellous things; and in anything which could be learned from a master he was well trained? Have you not heard from our elders of him?

ANYTUS: I have.

SOCRATES: Then no one could say that his son showed any want of capacity?

ANYTUS: Very likely not.

SOCRATES: But did any one, old or young, ever say in your hearing that Cleophantus, son of Themistocles, was a wise or good man, as his father was?

ANYTUS: I have certainly never heard any one say so.

SOCRATES: And if virtue could have been taught, would his father Themistocles have sought to train him in these minor accomplishments, and allowed him who, as you must remember, was his own son, to be no better than his neighbours in those qualities in which he himself excelled?

ANYTUS: Indeed, indeed, I think not.

SOCRATES: Here was a teacher of virtue whom you admit to be among the best men of the past. Let us take another,—Aristides, the son of Lysimachus: would you not acknowledge that he was a good man?

ANYTUS: To be sure I should.

SOCRATES: And did not he train his son Lysimachus better than any other Athenian in all that could be done for him by the help of masters? But what has been the result? Is he a bit better than any other mortal? He is an acquaintance of yours, and you see what he is like. There is Pericles, again, magnificent in his wisdom; and he, as you are aware, had two sons, Paralus and Xanthippus.

ANYTUS: I know.

SOCRATES: And you know, also, that he taught them to be unrivalled horsemen, and had them trained in music and gymnastics and all sorts of arts—in these respects they were on a level with the best—and had he no wish to make good men of them? Nay, he must have wished it. But virtue, as I suspect, could not be taught. And that you may not suppose the incompetent teachers to be only the meaner sort of Athenians and few in number, remember again that Thucydides had two sons, Melesias and Stephanus, whom, besides giving them a good education in other things, he trained in wrestling, and they were the best wrestlers in Athens: one of them he committed to the care of Xanthias, and the other of Eudorus, who had the reputation of being the most celebrated wrestlers of that day. Do you remember them?

ANYTUS: I have heard of them.

SOCRATES: Now, can there be a doubt that Thucydides, whose children were taught things for which he had to spend money, would have taught them to be good men, which would have cost him nothing, if virtue could have been taught? Will you reply that he was a mean man, and had not many friends among the Athenians and allies? Nay, but he was of a great family, and a man of influence at Athens and in all Hellas, and, if virtue could have been taught, he would have found out some Athenian or foreigner who would have made good men of his sons, if he could not himself spare the time from cares of state. Once more, I suspect, friend Anytus, that virtue is not a thing which can be taught?

ANYTUS: Socrates, I think that you are too ready to speak evil of men: and, if you will take my advice, I would recommend you to be careful. Perhaps there is no city in which it is not easier to do men harm than to do them good, and this is certainly the case at Athens, as I believe that you know.

SOCRATES: O Meno, think that Anytus is in a rage. And he may well be in a rage, for he thinks, in the first place, that I am defaming these gentlemen; and in the second place, he is of opinion that he is one of them himself. But some day he will know what is the meaning of defamation, and if he ever does, he will forgive me. Meanwhile I will return to you, Meno; for I suppose that there are gentlemen in your region too?

MENO: Certainly there are.

SOCRATES: And are they willing to teach the young? and do they profess to be teachers? and do they agree that virtue is taught?

MENO: No indeed, Socrates, they are anything but agreed; you may hear them saying at one time that virtue can be taught, and then again the reverse.

SOCRATES: Can we call those teachers who do not acknowledge the possibility of their own vocation?

MENO: I think not, Socrates.

SOCRATES: And what do you think of these Sophists, who are the only professors? Do they seem to you to be teachers of virtue?

MENO: I often wonder, Socrates, that Gorgias is never heard promising to teach virtue: and when he hears others promising he only laughs at them; but he thinks that men should be taught to speak.

SOCRATES: Then do you not think that the Sophists are teachers?

MENO: I cannot tell you, Socrates; like the rest of the world, I am in doubt, and sometimes I think that they are teachers and sometimes not.

SOCRATES: And are you aware that not you only and other politicians have doubts whether virtue can be taught or not, but that Theognis the poet says the very same thing?

MENO: Where does he say so?

SOCRATES: In these elegiac verses (Theog.):

'Eat and drink and sit with the mighty, and make yourself agreeable to them; for from the good you will learn what is good, but if you mix with the bad you will lose the intelligence which you already have.'

Do you observe that here he seems to imply that virtue can be taught?

MENO: Clearly.

SOCRATES: But in some other verses he shifts about and says (Theog.):

'If understanding could be created and put into a man, then they' (who were able to perform this feat) 'would have obtained great rewards.'

And again:—

'Never would a bad son have sprung from a good sire, for he

would have heard the voice of instruction; but not by teaching will you ever make a bad man into a good one.'

And this, as you may remark, is a contradiction of the other.

MENO: Clearly.

SOCRATES: And is there anything else of which the professors are affirmed not only not to be teachers of others, but to be ignorant themselves, and bad at the knowledge of that which they are professing to teach? or is there anything about which even the acknowledged 'gentlemen' are sometimes saying that 'this thing can be taught,' and sometimes the opposite? Can you say that they are teachers in any true sense whose ideas are in such confusion?

MENO: I should say, certainly not.

SOCRATES: But if neither the Sophists nor the gentlemen are teachers, clearly there can be no other teachers?

MENO: No.

SOCRATES: And if there are no teachers, neither are there disciples?

MENO: Agreed.

SOCRATES: And we have admitted that a thing cannot be taught of which there are neither teachers nor disciples?

MENO: We have.

SOCRATES: And there are no teachers of virtue to be found anywhere?

MENO: There are not.

SOCRATES: And if there are no teachers, neither are there scholars?

MENO: That, I think, is true.

SOCRATES: Then virtue cannot be taught?

MENO: Not if we are right in our view. But I cannot believe, Socrates, that there are no good men: And if there are, how did they come into existence?

SOCRATES: I am afraid, Meno, that you and I are not good for much, and that Gorgias has been as poor an educator of you as Prodicus has been of me. Certainly we shall have to look to ourselves, and try to find some one who will help in some way or other to improve us. This I say, because I observe that in the previous discussion none of us remarked that right and good action is possible to man under other guidance than that of knowledge (*episteme*);—and indeed if this be denied, there is no seeing how there can be any good men at all.

MENO: How do you mean, Socrates?

SOCRATES: I mean that good men are necessarily useful or profitable. Were we not right in admitting this? It must be so.

MENO: Yes.

SOCRATES: And in supposing that they will be useful only if they are true guides to us of action—there we were also right?

MENO: Yes.

SOCRATES: But when we said that a man cannot be a good guide unless he have knowledge (*phrhonesis*), this we were wrong.

MENO: What do you mean by the word 'right'?

SOCRATES: I will explain. If a man knew the way to Larissa, or anywhere else, and went to the place and led others thither, would he not be a right and good guide?

MENO: Certainly.

SOCRATES: And a person who had a right opinion about the way, but had never been and did not know, might be a good guide also, might he not?

MENO: Certainly.

SOCRATES: And while he has true opinion about that which the other knows, he will be just as good a guide if he thinks the truth, as he who knows the truth?

MENO: Exactly.

SOCRATES: Then true opinion is as good a guide to correct action as knowledge; and that was the point which we omitted in our speculation about the nature of virtue, when we said that knowledge only is the guide of right action; whereas there is also right opinion.

MENO: True.

SOCRATES: Then right opinion is not less useful than knowledge?

MENO: The difference, Socrates, is only that he who has knowledge will always be right; but he who has right opinion will sometimes be right, and sometimes not.

SOCRATES: What do you mean? Can he be wrong who has right opinion, so long as he has right opinion?

MENO: I admit the cogency of your argument, and therefore, Socrates, I wonder that knowledge should be preferred to right opinion—or why they should ever differ.

SOCRATES: And shall I explain this wonder to you?

MENO: Do tell me.

SOCRATES: You would not wonder if you had ever observed the images of Daedalus (Compare Euthyphro); but perhaps you have not got them in your country?

MENO: What have they to do with the question?

SOCRATES: Because they require to be fastened in order to keep them, and if they are not fastened they will play truant and run away.

MENO: Well, what of that?

SOCRATES: I mean to say that they are not very valuable possessions if they are at liberty, for they will walk off like runaway slaves; but when fastened, they are of great value, for they are really beautiful works of art. Now this is an illustration of the nature of true opinions: while they abide with us they are beautiful and fruitful, but they run away out of the human soul, and do not remain long, and therefore they are not of much value until they are fastened by the tie of the cause; and this fastening of them, friend Meno, is recollection, as you and I have agreed to call it. But when they are bound, in the first place, they have the nature of knowledge; and, in the second place, they are abiding. And this is why knowledge is more honourable and excellent than true opinion, because fastened by a chain.

MENO: What you are saying, Socrates, seems to be very like the truth.

SOCRATES: I too speak rather in ignorance; I only conjecture. And yet that knowledge differs from true opinion is no matter of conjecture with me. There are not many things which I profess to know, but this is most certainly one of them.

MENO: Yes, Socrates; and you are quite right in saying so.

SOCRATES: And am I not also right in saying that true opinion leading the way perfects action quite as well as knowledge?

MENO: There again, Socrates, I think you are right.

SOCRATES: Then right opinion is not a whit inferior to knowledge, or less useful in action; nor is the man who has right opinion inferior to him who has knowledge?

MENO: True.

SOCRATES: And surely the good man has been acknowledged by us to be useful?

MENO: Yes.

SOCRATES: Seeing then that men become good and useful to states, not only because they have knowledge, but because they have right opinion, and that neither knowledge nor right opinion is given to man by nature or acquired by him—do you imagine either of them to be given by nature?

MENO: Not I.

SOCRATES: Then if they are not given by nature, neither are the good by nature good?

MENO: Certainly not.

SOCRATES: And nature being excluded, then came the question whether virtue is acquired by teaching?

MENO: Yes.

SOCRATES: If virtue was wisdom (or knowledge), then, as we thought, it was taught?

MENO: Yes.

SOCRATES: And if it was taught it was wisdom?

MENO: Certainly.

SOCRATES: And if there were teachers, it might be taught; and if there were no teachers, not?

MENO: True.

SOCRATES: But surely we acknowledged that there were no teachers of virtue?

MENO: Yes.

SOCRATES: Then we acknowledged that it was not taught, and was not wisdom?

MENO: Certainly.

SOCRATES: And yet we admitted that it was a good?

MENO: Yes.

SOCRATES: And the right guide is useful and good?

MENO: Certainly.

SOCRATES: And the only right guides are knowledge and true opinion—these are the guides of man; for things which happen by chance are not under the guidance of man: but the guides of man are true opinion and knowledge.

MENO: I think so too.

SOCRATES: But if virtue is not taught, neither is virtue knowledge.

MENO: Clearly not.

SOCRATES: Then of two good and useful things, one, which is knowledge, has been set aside, and cannot be supposed to be our guide in political life.

MENO: I think not.

SOCRATES: And therefore not by any wisdom, and not because they were wise, did Themistocles and those others of whom Anytus spoke govern states. This was the reason why they were unable to make others like themselves—because their virtue was not grounded on knowledge.

MENO: That is probably true, Socrates.

SOCRATES: But if not by knowledge, the only alternative which remains is that statesmen must have guided states by right opinion, which is in politics what divination is in religion; for diviners and also prophets say many things truly, but they know not what they say.

MENO: So I believe.

SOCRATES: And may we not, Meno, truly call those men 'divine' who, having no understanding, yet succeed in many a grand deed and word?

MENO: Certainly.

SOCRATES: Then we shall also be right in calling divine those whom we were just now speaking of as diviners and prophets, including the whole tribe of poets. Yes, and statesmen above all may be said to be divine and illumined, being inspired and possessed of God, in which condition they say many grand things, not knowing what they say.

MENO: Yes.

SOCRATES: And the women too, Meno, call good men divine—

do they not? and the Spartans, when they praise a good man, say 'that he is a divine man.'

MENO: And I think, Socrates, that they are right; although very likely our friend Anytus may take offence at the word.

SOCRATES: I do not care; as for Anytus, there will be another opportunity of talking with him. To sum up our enquiry—the result seems to be, if we are at all right in our view, that virtue is neither natural nor acquired, but an instinct given by God to the virtuous. Nor is the instinct accompanied by reason, unless there may be supposed to be among statesmen some one who is capable of educating statesmen. And if there be such an one, he may be said to be among the living what Homer says that Tiresias was among the dead, 'he alone has understanding; but the rest are flitting shades'; and he and his virtue in like manner will be a reality among shadows.

MENO: That is excellent, Socrates.

SOCRATES: Then, Meno, the conclusion is that virtue comes to the virtuous by the gift of God. But we shall never know the certain truth until, before asking how virtue is given, we enquire into the actual nature of virtue. I fear that I must go away, but do you, now that you are persuaded yourself, persuade our friend Anytus. And do not let him be so exasperated; if you can conciliate him, you will have done good service to the Athenian people.

Phaedo

INTRODUCTION

After an interval of some months or years, and at Phlius, a town of Peloponnesus, the tale of the last hours of Socrates is narrated to Echecrates and other Phliasians by Phaedo the 'beloved disciple.' The Dialogue necessarily takes the form of a narrative, because Socrates has to be described acting as well as speaking. The minutest particulars of the event are interesting to distant friends, and the narrator has an equal interest in them.

During the voyage of the sacred ship to and from Delos, which has occupied thirty days, the execution of Socrates has been deferred. (Compare Xen. Mem.) The time has been passed by him in conversation with a select company of disciples. But now the holy season is over, and the disciples meet earlier than usual in order that they may converse with Socrates for the last time. Those who were present, and those who might have been expected to be present, are mentioned by name. There are Simmias and Cebes (Crito), two disciples of Philolaus whom Socrates 'by his enchantments has attracted from Thebes' (Mem.), Crito the aged friend, the attendant of the prison, who is as good as a friend—these take part in the conversation. There are present also, Hermogenes, from whom Xenophon derived his information about the trial of Socrates (Mem.), the 'madman' Apollodorus (Symp.), Euclid and Terpsion from Megara (compare Theaet.), Ctesippus, Antisthenes, Menexenus, and some other less-known members of the Socratic circle, all of whom are silent auditors. Aristippus, Cleombrotus, and Plato are noted as absent. Almost as soon as the friends of Socrates enter the prison Xanthippe and her children are sent home in the care of one of Crito's servants. Socrates himself has just been released from chains, and is led by this circumstance to make the natural remark that 'pleasure follows pain.' (Observe that Plato is preparing the way for his doctrine of the alternation of opposites.) 'Aesop would have represented them in a fable as a two-headed creature of the gods.' The mention of Aesop reminds Cebes of a question which had been asked by Evenus the poet (compare Apol.): 'Why Socrates, who was not a poet, while in prison had been putting Aesop into verse?'—'Because several times in his life he had been warned in dreams that he should practise music; and as he was about to die and was not certain of what was meant, he wished to fulfil the admonition in the letter as well as in the spirit, by writing verses as well as by cultivating philosophy. Tell this to Evenus; and say that I would have him follow me in death.' 'He is not at all the sort of man to comply with your request, Socrates.' 'Why, is he not a philosopher?' 'Yes.' 'Then he will be willing to die, although he will not take his own life, for that is held to be unlawful.'

Cebes asks why suicide is thought not to be right, if death is to be accounted a good? Well, (1) according to one explanation, because man is a prisoner, who must not open the door of his prison and run away— this is the truth in a 'mystery.' Or (2) rather, because he is not his own property, but a possession of the gods, and has no right to make away with that which does not belong to him. But why, asks Cebes, if he is a possession of the gods, should he wish to die and leave them? For he is under their protection; and surely he cannot take better care of himself than they take of him. Simmias explains that Cebes is really referring to Socrates, whom they think too unmoved at the prospect of leaving the gods and his friends. Socrates answers that he is going to other gods who are wise and good, and perhaps to better friends; and he professes that he is ready to defend himself against the charge of Cebes. The company shall be his judges, and he hopes that he will be more successful in convincing them than he had been in convincing the court.

The philosopher desires death—which the wicked world will insinuate that he also deserves: and perhaps he does, but not in any sense which they are capable of understanding. Enough of them: the real question is, What is the nature of that death which he desires? Death is the separation of soul and body—and the philosopher desires such a separation. He would like to be freed from the dominion of bodily pleasures and of the senses, which are always perturbing his mental vision. He wants to get rid of eyes and ears, and with the light of the mind only to behold the light of truth. All the evils and impurities and necessities of men come from the body. And death separates him from these corruptions, which in life he cannot wholly lay aside. Why then should he repine when the hour of separation arrives? Why, if he is dead while he lives, should he fear that other death, through which alone he can behold wisdom in her purity?

Besides, the philosopher has notions of good and evil unlike those of other men. For they are courageous because they are afraid of greater dangers, and temperate because they desire greater pleasures. But he disdains this balancing of pleasures and pains, which is the exchange of commerce and not of virtue. All the virtues, including wisdom, are regarded by him only as purifications of the soul. And this was the meaning of the founders of the mysteries when they said, 'Many are the wand-bearers but few are the mystics.' (Compare Matt. xxii.: 'Many are called but few are chosen.') And in the hope that he is one of these mystics, Socrates is now departing. This is his answer to any one who charges him with indifference at the prospect of leaving the gods and his friends.

Still, a fear is expressed that the soul upon leaving the body may vanish away like smoke or air. Socrates in answer appeals first of all to the old Orphic tradition that the souls of the dead are in the world below, and that the living come from them. This he attempts to found on a philosophical assumption that all opposites—e.g. less, greater; weaker, stronger; sleeping, waking; life, death—are generated out of each other. Nor can the process of generation be only a passage from living to dying, for then all would end in death. The perpetual sleeper (Endymion) would be no longer distinguished from the rest of mankind. The circle of nature is not complete unless the living come from the dead as well as pass to them.

The Platonic doctrine of reminiscence is then adduced as a confirmation of the pre-existence of the soul. Some proofs of this doctrine are demanded. One proof given is the same as that of the Meno, and is derived from the latent knowledge of mathematics, which may be elicited from an unlearned person when a diagram is presented to him. Again, there is a power of association, which from seeing Simmias may remember Cebes, or from seeing a picture of Simmias may remember Simmias. The lyre may recall the player of the lyre, and equal pieces of wood or stone may be associated with the higher notion of absolute equality. But here observe that material equalities fall short of the conception of absolute equality with which they are compared, and which is the measure of them. And the measure or standard must be prior to that which is measured, the idea of equality prior to the visible equals. And if prior to them, then prior also to the perceptions of the senses which recall them, and therefore either given before birth or at birth. But all men have not this knowledge, nor have any without a process of reminiscence; which is a proof that it is not innate or given at birth, unless indeed it was given and taken away at the same instant. But if not given to men in birth, it must have been given before birth—this is the only alternative which remains. And if we had ideas in a former state, then our souls must have existed and must have had intelligence in a former state. The pre-existence of the soul stands or falls with the doctrine of ideas.

It is objected by Simmias and Cebes that these arguments only prove a former and not a future existence. Socrates answers this objection by recalling the previous argument, in which he had shown that the living come from the dead. But the fear that the soul at departing may vanish into air (especially if there is a wind blowing at the time) has not yet been charmed away. He proceeds: When we fear that the soul will vanish away, let us ask ourselves what is that which we suppose to be liable to dissolution? Is it the simple or the compound, the unchanging or the changing, the invisible idea or the visible object of sense? Clearly the latter and not the former; and therefore not the soul, which in her own pure thought is unchangeable, and only when using the senses descends into the region of change. Again, the soul commands, the body serves: in this respect too the soul is akin to the divine, and the body to the mortal. And in every point of view the soul is the image of divinity and immortality, and the body of the human and mortal. And whereas the body is liable to speedy dissolution, the soul is almost if not quite indissoluble. (Compare Tim.) Yet even the body may be preserved for ages by the embalmer's art: how unlikely, then, that the soul will perish and be dissipated into air while on her way to the good and wise God! She has been gathered into herself, holding aloof from the body, and practising death all her life long, and she is now finally released from the errors and follies and passions of men, and for ever dwells in the company of the gods.

But the soul which is polluted and engrossed by the corporeal, and has no eye except that of the senses, and is weighed down by the bodily appetites, cannot attain to this abstraction. In her fear of the world below she lingers about the sepulchre, loath to leave the body which she loved, a ghostly apparition, saturated with sense, and therefore visible. At length entering into some animal of a nature congenial to her former life of sensuality or violence, she takes the form of an ass, a wolf or a kite. And of these earthly souls the happiest are those who have practised virtue without philosophy; they are allowed to pass into gentle and social natures, such as bees and ants. (Compare Republic, Meno.) But only the philosopher who departs pure is permitted to enter the company of the gods. (Compare Phaedrus.) This is the reason why he abstains from fleshly lusts, and not because he fears loss or disgrace, which is the motive of other men. He too has been a captive, and the willing agent of his own captivity. But philosophy has spoken to him, and he has heard her voice; she has gently entreated him, and brought him out of the 'miry clay,' and purged away the mists of passion and the illusions of sense which envelope him; his soul has escaped from the influence of pleasures and pains, which are like nails fastening her to the body. To that prison-house she will not return; and therefore she abstains from bodily pleasures—not from a desire of having more or greater ones, but because she knows that only when calm and free from the dominion of the body can she behold the light of truth.

Simmias and Cebes remain in doubt; but they are unwilling to raise objections at such a time. Socrates wonders at their reluctance. Let them regard him rather as the swan, who, having sung the praises of Apollo all his life long, sings at his death more lustily than ever. Simmias acknowledges that there is cowardice in not probing truth to the bottom. 'And if truth divine and inspired is not to be had, then let a man take the best of human notions, and upon this frail bark let him sail through life.' He proceeds to state his difficulty: It has been argued that the soul is invisible and incorporeal, and therefore immortal, and prior to the body. But is not the soul acknowledged to be a harmony, and has she not the same relation to the body, as the harmony—which like her is invisible—has to the lyre? And yet the harmony does not survive the lyre. Cebes has also an objection, which like Simmias he expresses in a figure. He is willing to admit that the soul is more lasting than the body. But the more lasting nature of the soul does not prove her immortality; for after having worn out many bodies in a single life, and many more in successive births and deaths, she may at last perish, or, as Socrates afterwards restates the objection, the very act of birth may be the beginning of her death, and her last body may survive her, just as the coat of an old weaver is left behind him after he is dead, although a man is more lasting than his coat. And he who would prove the immortality of the soul, must prove not only that the soul outlives one or many bodies, but that she outlives them all.

The audience, like the chorus in a play, for a moment interpret the feelings of the actors; there is a temporary depression, and then the enquiry is resumed. It is a melancholy reflection that arguments, like men, are apt to be deceivers; and those who have been often deceived become distrustful both of arguments and of friends. But this unfortunate experience should not make us either haters of men or haters of arguments. The want of health and truth is not in the argument, but in ourselves. Socrates, who is about to die, is sensible of his own weakness; he desires to be impartial, but he cannot help feeling that he has too great an interest in the truth of the argument. And therefore he would have his friends examine and refute him, if they think that he is in error.

At his request Simmias and Cebes repeat their objections. They do not go to the length of denying the pre-existence of ideas. Simmias is of opinion that the soul is a harmony of the body. But the admission of the pre- existence of ideas, and therefore of the soul, is at variance with this. (Compare a parallel difficulty in Theaet.) For a harmony is an effect, whereas the soul is not an effect, but a cause; a harmony follows, but the soul leads; a harmony admits of degrees, and the soul has no degrees. Again, upon the supposition that the soul is a harmony, why is one soul better than another? Are they more or less harmonized, or is there one harmony within another? But the soul does not admit of degrees, and cannot therefore be more or less harmonized. Further, the soul is often engaged in resisting the affections of the body, as Homer describes Odysseus 'rebuking his heart.' Could he have written this under the idea that the soul is a harmony of the body? Nay rather, are we not contradicting Homer and ourselves in affirming anything of the sort?

The goddess Harmonia, as Socrates playfully terms the argument of Simmias, has been happily disposed of; and now an answer has to be given to the Theban Cadmus. Socrates recapitulates the argument of Cebes, which, as he remarks, involves the whole question of natural growth or causation; about this he proposes to narrate his own mental experience. When he was young he had puzzled himself with physics: he had enquired into the growth and decay of animals, and the origin of thought, until at last he began to doubt the self-evident fact that growth is the result of eating and drinking; and so he arrived at the conclusion that he was not meant for such enquiries. Nor was he less perplexed with notions of comparison and number. At first he had imagined himself to understand differences of greater and less, and to know that ten is two more than eight, and the like. But now those very notions appeared to him to contain a contradiction. For how can one be divided into two? Or two be compounded into one? These are difficulties which Socrates cannot answer. Of generation and destruction he knows nothing. But he has a confused notion of another method in which matters of this sort are to be investigated. (Compare Republic; Charm.)

Then he heard some one reading out of a book of Anaxagoras, that mind is the cause of all things. And he said to himself: If mind is the cause of all things, surely mind must dispose them all for the best. The new teacher will show me this 'order of the best' in man and nature. How great had been his hopes and how great his disappointment! For he found that his new friend was anything but consistent in his use of mind as a cause, and that he soon introduced winds, waters, and other eccentric notions. (Compare Arist. Metaph.) It was as if a person had said that Socrates is sitting here because he is made up of bones and muscles, instead of telling the true reason—that he is here because the

Athenians have thought good to sentence him to death, and he has thought good to await his sentence. Had his bones and muscles been left by him to their own ideas of right, they would long ago have taken themselves off. But surely there is a great confusion of the cause and condition in all this. And this confusion also leads people into all sorts of erroneous theories about the position and motions of the earth. None of them know how much stronger than any Atlas is the power of the best. But this 'best' is still undiscovered; and in enquiring after the cause, we can only hope to attain the second best.

Now there is a danger in the contemplation of the nature of things, as there is a danger in looking at the sun during an eclipse, unless the precaution is taken of looking only at the image reflected in the water, or in a glass. (Compare Laws; Republic.) 'I was afraid,' says Socrates, 'that I might injure the eye of the soul. I thought that I had better return to the old and safe method of ideas. Though I do not mean to say that he who contemplates existence through the medium of ideas sees only through a glass darkly, any more than he who contemplates actual effects.'

If the existence of ideas is granted to him, Socrates is of opinion that he will then have no difficulty in proving the immortality of the soul. He will only ask for a further admission:—that beauty is the cause of the beautiful, greatness the cause of the great, smallness of the small, and so on of other things. This is a safe and simple answer, which escapes the contradictions of greater and less (greater by reason of that which is smaller!), of addition and subtraction, and the other difficulties of relation. These subtleties he is for leaving to wiser heads than his own; he prefers to test ideas by the consistency of their consequences, and, if asked to give an account of them, goes back to some higher idea or hypothesis which appears to him to be the best, until at last he arrives at a resting-place. (Republic; Phil.)

The doctrine of ideas, which has long ago received the assent of the Socratic circle, is now affirmed by the Phliasian auditor to command the assent of any man of sense. The narrative is continued; Socrates is desirous of explaining how opposite ideas may appear to co-exist but do not really co-exist in the same thing or person. For example, Simmias may be said to have greatness and also smallness, because he is greater than Socrates and less than Phaedo. And yet Simmias is not really great and also small, but only when compared to Phaedo and Socrates. I use the illustration, says Socrates, because I want to show you not only that ideal opposites exclude one another, but also the opposites in us. I, for example, having the attribute of smallness remain small, and cannot become great: the smallness which is in me drives out greatness.

One of the company here remarked that this was inconsistent with the old assertion that opposites generated opposites. But that, replies

Socrates, was affirmed, not of opposite ideas either in us or in nature, but of opposition in the concrete—not of life and death, but of individuals living and dying. When this objection has been removed, Socrates proceeds: This doctrine of the mutual exclusion of opposites is not only true of the opposites themselves, but of things which are inseparable from them. For example, cold and heat are opposed; and fire, which is inseparable from heat, cannot co-exist with cold, or snow, which is inseparable from cold, with heat. Again, the number three excludes the number four, because three is an odd number and four is an even number, and the odd is opposed to the even. Thus we are able to proceed a step beyond 'the safe and simple answer.' We may say, not only that the odd excludes the even, but that the number three, which participates in oddness, excludes the even. And in like manner, not only does life exclude death, but the soul, of which life is the inseparable attribute, also excludes death. And that of which life is the inseparable attribute is by the force of the terms imperishable. If the odd principle were imperishable, then the number three would not perish but remove, on the approach of the even principle. But the immortal is imperishable; and therefore the soul on the approach of death does not perish but removes.

Thus all objections appear to be finally silenced. And now the application has to be made: If the soul is immortal, 'what manner of persons ought we to be?' having regard not only to time but to eternity. For death is not the end of all, and the wicked is not released from his evil by death; but every one carries with him into the world below that which he is or has become, and that only.

For after death the soul is carried away to judgment, and when she has received her punishment returns to earth in the course of ages. The wise soul is conscious of her situation, and follows the attendant angel who guides her through the windings of the world below; but the impure soul wanders hither and thither without companion or guide, and is carried at last to her own place, as the pure soul is also carried away to hers. 'In order that you may understand this, I must first describe to you the nature and conformation of the earth.'

Now the whole earth is a globe placed in the centre of the heavens, and is maintained there by the perfection of balance. That which we call the earth is only one of many small hollows, wherein collect the mists and waters and the thick lower air; but the true earth is above, and is in a finer and subtler element. And if, like birds, we could fly to the surface of the air, in the same manner that fishes come to the top of the sea, then we should behold the true earth and the true heaven and the true stars. Our earth is everywhere corrupted and corroded; and even the land which is fairer than the sea, for that is a mere chaos or waste of water and mud and sand, has nothing to show in comparison of the other world. But the heavenly earth is of divers colours, sparkling with jewels brighter than gold and whiter than any snow, having flowers and fruits innumerable. And the inhabitants dwell some on the shore of the sea of air, others in 'islets of the blest,' and they hold converse with the gods, and behold the sun, moon and stars as they truly are, and their other blessedness is of a piece with this.

The hollows on the surface of the globe vary in size and shape from that which we inhabit: but all are connected by passages and perforations in the interior of the earth. And there is one huge chasm or opening called Tartarus, into which streams of fire and water and liquid mud are ever flowing; of these small portions find their way to the surface and form seas and rivers and volcanoes. There is a perpetual inhalation and exhalation of the air rising and falling as the waters pass into the depths of the earth and return again, in their course forming lakes and rivers, but never descending below the centre of the earth; for on either side the rivers flowing either way are stopped by a precipice. These rivers are many and mighty, and there are four principal ones, Oceanus, Acheron, Pyriphlegethon, and Cocytus. Oceanus is the river which encircles the earth; Acheron takes an opposite direction, and after flowing under the earth through desert places, at last reaches the Acherusian lake,—this is the river at which the souls of the dead await their return to earth. Pyriphlegethon is a stream of fire, which coils round the earth and flows into the depths of Tartarus. The fourth river, Cocytus, is that which is called by the poets the Stygian river, and passes into and forms the lake Styx, from the waters of which it gains new and strange powers. This river, too, falls into Tartarus.

The dead are first of all judged according to their deeds, and those who are incurable are thrust into Tartarus, from which they never come out. Those who have only committed venial sins are first purified of them, and then rewarded for the good which they have done. Those who have committed crimes, great indeed, but not unpardonable, are thrust into Tartarus, but are cast forth at the end of a year by way of Pyriphlegethon or Cocytus, and these carry them as far as the Acherusian lake, where they call upon their victims to let them come out of the rivers into the lake. And if they prevail, then they are let out and their sufferings cease: if not, they are borne unceasingly into Tartarus and back again, until they at last obtain mercy. The pure souls also receive their reward, and have their abode in the upper earth, and a select few in still fairer 'mansions.'

Socrates is not prepared to insist on the literal accuracy of this description, but he is confident that something of the kind is true. He who has sought after the pleasures of knowledge and rejected the pleasures of the body, has reason to be of good hope at the approach of death; whose voice is already speaking to him, and who will one day be heard calling all men.

The hour has come at which he must drink the poison, and not much remains to be done. How shall they bury him? That is a question which he refuses to entertain, for they are burying, not him, but his dead body. His friends had once been sureties that he would remain, and they shall now be sureties that he has run away. Yet he would not die without the customary ceremonies of washing and burial. Shall he make a libation of the poison? In the spirit he will, but not in the letter. One request he utters in the very act of death, which has been a puzzle to after ages. With a sort of irony he remembers that a trifling religious duty is still unfulfilled, just as above he desires before he departs to compose a few verses in order to satisfy a scruple about a dream—unless, indeed, we suppose him to mean, that he was now restored to health, and made the customary offering to Asclepius in token of his recovery.

...

1. The doctrine of the immortality of the soul has sunk deep into the heart of the human race; and men are apt to rebel against any examination of the nature or grounds of their belief. They do not like to acknowledge that this, as well as the other 'eternal ideas; of man, has a history in time, which may be traced in Greek poetry or philosophy, and also in the Hebrew Scriptures. They convert feeling into reasoning, and throw a network of dialectics over that which is really a deeply-rooted instinct. In the same temper which Socrates reproves in himself they are disposed to think that even fallacies will do no harm, for they will die with them, and while they live they will gain by the delusion. And when they consider the numberless bad arguments which have been pressed into the service of theology, they say, like the companions of Socrates, 'What argument can we ever trust again?' But there is a better and higher spirit to be gathered from the Phaedo, as well as from the other writings of Plato, which says that first principles should be most constantly reviewed (Phaedo and Crat.), and that the highest subjects demand of us the greatest accuracy (Republic); also that we must not become misologists because arguments are apt to be deceivers.

2. In former ages there was a customary rather than a reasoned belief in the immortality of the soul. It was based on the authority of the Church, on the necessity of such a belief to morality and the order of society, on the evidence of an historical fact, and also on analogies and figures of speech which filled up the void or gave an expression in words to a cherished instinct. The mass of mankind went on their way busy with the affairs of this life, hardly stopping to think about another. But in our own day the question has been reopened, and it is doubtful whether the belief which in the first ages of Christianity was the strongest motive of action can survive the conflict with a scientific age in which the rules of evidence are stricter and the mind has become more sensitive to criticism. It has faded into the distance by a natural

process as it was removed further and further from the historical fact on which it has been supposed to rest. Arguments derived from material things such as the seed and the ear of corn or transitions in the life of animals from one state of being to another (the chrysalis and the butterfly) are not 'in pari materia' with arguments from the visible to the invisible, and are therefore felt to be no longer applicable. The evidence to the historical fact seems to be weaker than was once supposed: it is not consistent with itself, and is based upon documents which are of unknown origin. The immortality of man must be proved by other arguments than these if it is again to become a living belief. We must ask ourselves afresh why we still maintain it, and seek to discover a foundation for it in the nature of God and in the first principles of morality.

3. At the outset of the discussion we may clear away a confusion. We certainly do not mean by the immortality of the soul the immortality of fame, which whether worth having or not can only be ascribed to a very select class of the whole race of mankind, and even the interest in these few is comparatively short-lived. To have been a benefactor to the world, whether in a higher or a lower sphere of life and thought, is a great thing: to have the reputation of being one, when men have passed out of the sphere of earthly praise or blame, is hardly worthy of consideration. The memory of a great man, so far from being immortal, is really limited to his own generation:—so long as his friends or his disciples are alive, so long as his books continue to be read, so long as his political or military successes fill a page in the history of his country. The praises which are bestowed upon him at his death hardly last longer than the flowers which are strewed upon his coffin or the 'immortelles' which are laid upon his tomb. Literature makes the most of its heroes, but the true man is well aware that far from enjoying an immortality of fame, in a generation or two, or even in a much shorter time, he will be forgotten and the world will get on without him.

4. Modern philosophy is perplexed at this whole question, which is sometimes fairly given up and handed over to the realm of faith. The perplexity should not be forgotten by us when we attempt to submit the Phaedo of Plato to the requirements of logic. For what idea can we form of the soul when separated from the body? Or how can the soul be united with the body and still be independent? Is the soul related to the body as the ideal to the real, or as the whole to the parts, or as the subject to the object, or as the cause to the effect, or as the end to the means? Shall we say with Aristotle, that the soul is the entelechy or form of an organized living body? or with Plato, that she has a life of her own? Is the Pythagorean image of the harmony, or that of the monad, the truer expression? Is the soul related to the body as sight to the eye, or as the boatman to his boat? (Arist. de Anim.) And in another

state of being is the soul to be conceived of as vanishing into infinity, hardly possessing an existence which she can call her own, as in the pantheistic system of Spinoza: or as an individual informing another body and entering into new relations, but retaining her own character? (Compare Gorgias.) Or is the opposition of soul and body a mere illusion, and the true self neither soul nor body, but the union of the two in the 'I' which is above them? And is death the assertion of this individuality in the higher nature, and the falling away into nothingness of the lower? Or are we vainly attempting to pass the boundaries of human thought? The body and the soul seem to be inseparable, not only in fact, but in our conceptions of them; and any philosophy which too closely unites them, or too widely separates them, either in this life or in another, disturbs the balance of human nature. No thinker has perfectly adjusted them, or been entirely consistent with himself in describing their relation to one another. Nor can we wonder that Plato in the infancy of human thought should have confused mythology and philosophy, or have mistaken verbal arguments for real ones.

5. Again, believing in the immortality of the soul, we must still ask the question of Socrates, 'What is that which we suppose to be immortal?' Is it the personal and individual element in us, or the spiritual and universal? Is it the principle of knowledge or of goodness, or the union of the two? Is it the mere force of life which is determined to be, or the consciousness of self which cannot be got rid of, or the fire of genius which refuses to be extinguished? Or is there a hidden being which is allied to the Author of all existence, who is because he is perfect, and to whom our ideas of perfection give us a title to belong? Whatever answer is given by us to these questions, there still remains the necessity of allowing the permanence of evil, if not for ever, at any rate for a time, in order that the wicked 'may not have too good a bargain.' For the annihilation of evil at death, or the eternal duration of it, seem to involve equal difficulties in the moral government of the universe. Sometimes we are led by our feelings, rather than by our reason, to think of the good and wise only as existing in another life. Why should the mean, the weak, the idiot, the infant, the herd of men who have never in any proper sense the use of reason, reappear with blinking eyes in the light of another world? But our second thought is that the hope of humanity is a common one, and that all or none will be partakers of immortality. Reason does not allow us to suppose that we have any greater claims than others, and experience may often reveal to us unexpected flashes of the higher nature in those whom we had despised. Why should the wicked suffer any more than ourselves? had we been placed in their circumstances should we have been any better than they? The worst of men are objects of pity rather than of anger to the philanthropist; must they not be equally such to divine benevolence? Even more than the good they have need of another life;

not that they may be punished, but that they may be educated. These are a few of the reflections which arise in our minds when we attempt to assign any form to our conceptions of a future state.

There are some other questions which are disturbing to us because we have no answer to them. What is to become of the animals in a future state? Have we not seen dogs more faithful and intelligent than men, and men who are more stupid and brutal than any animals? Does their life cease at death, or is there some 'better thing reserved' also for them? They may be said to have a shadow or imitation of morality, and imperfect moral claims upon the benevolence of man and upon the justice of God. We cannot think of the least or lowest of them, the insect, the bird, the inhabitants of the sea or the desert, as having any place in a future world, and if not all, why should those who are specially attached to man be deemed worthy of any exceptional privilege? When we reason about such a subject, almost at once we degenerate into nonsense. It is a passing thought which has no real hold on the mind. We may argue for the existence of animals in a future state from the attributes of God, or from texts of Scripture ('Are not two sparrows sold for one farthing?' etc.), but the truth is that we are only filling up the void of another world with our own fancies. Again, we often talk about the origin of evil, that great bugbear of theologians, by which they frighten us into believing any superstition. What answer can be made to the old commonplace, 'Is not God the author of evil, if he knowingly permitted, but could have prevented it?' Even if we assume that the inequalities of this life are rectified by some transposition of human beings in another, still the existence of the very least evil if it could have been avoided, seems to be at variance with the love and justice of God. And so we arrive at the conclusion that we are carrying logic too far, and that the attempt to frame the world according to a rule of divine perfection is opposed to experience and had better be given up. The case of the animals is our own. We must admit that the Divine Being, although perfect himself, has placed us in a state of life in which we may work together with him for good, but we are very far from having attained to it.

6. Again, ideas must be given through something; and we are always prone to argue about the soul from analogies of outward things which may serve to embody our thoughts, but are also partly delusive. For we cannot reason from the natural to the spiritual, or from the outward to the inward. The progress of physiological science, without bringing us nearer to the great secret, has tended to remove some erroneous notions respecting the relations of body and mind, and in this we have the advantage of the ancients. But no one imagines that any seed of immortality is to be discerned in our mortal frames. Most people have been content to rest their belief in another life on the agreement of the more enlightened part of mankind, and on the

inseparable connection of such a doctrine with the existence of a God—also in a less degree on the impossibility of doubting about the continued existence of those whom we love and reverence in this world. And after all has been said, the figure, the analogy, the argument, are felt to be only approximations in different forms to an expression of the common sentiment of the human heart. That we shall live again is far more certain than that we shall take any particular form of life.

7. When we speak of the immortality of the soul, we must ask further what we mean by the word immortality. For of the duration of a living being in countless ages we can form no conception; far less than a three years' old child of the whole of life. The naked eye might as well try to see the furthest star in the infinity of heaven. Whether time and space really exist when we take away the limits of them may be doubted; at any rate the thought of them when unlimited us so overwhelming to us as to lose all distinctness. Philosophers have spoken of them as forms of the human mind, but what is the mind without them? As then infinite time, or an existence out of time, which are the only possible explanations of eternal duration, are equally inconceivable to us, let us substitute for them a hundred or a thousand years after death, and ask not what will be our employment in eternity, but what will happen to us in that definite portion of time; or what is now happening to those who passed out of life a hundred or a thousand years ago. Do we imagine that the wicked are suffering torments, or that the good are singing the praises of God, during a period longer than that of a whole life, or of ten lives of men? Is the suffering physical or mental? And does the worship of God consist only of praise, or of many forms of service? Who are the wicked, and who are the good, whom we venture to divide by a hard and fast line; and in which of the two classes should we place ourselves and our friends? May we not suspect that we are making differences of kind, because we are unable to imagine differences of degree?—putting the whole human race into heaven or hell for the greater convenience of logical division? Are we not at the same time describing them both in superlatives, only that we may satisfy the demands of rhetoric? What is that pain which does not become deadened after a thousand years? or what is the nature of that pleasure or happiness which never wearies by monotony? Earthly pleasures and pains are short in proportion as they are keen; of any others which are both intense and lasting we have no experience, and can form no idea. The words or figures of speech which we use are not consistent with themselves. For are we not imagining Heaven under the similitude of a church, and Hell as a prison, or perhaps a madhouse or chamber of horrors? And yet to beings constituted as we are, the monotony of singing psalms would be as great an infliction as the pains of hell, and might be even pleasantly interrupted by them. Where are

the actions worthy of rewards greater than those which are conferred on the greatest benefactors of mankind? And where are the crimes which according to Plato's merciful reckoning,—more merciful, at any rate, than the eternal damnation of so-called Christian teachers,—for every ten years in this life deserve a hundred of punishment in the life to come? We should be ready to die of pity if we could see the least of the sufferings which the writers of Infernos and Purgatorios have attributed to the damned. Yet these joys and terrors seem hardly to exercise an appreciable influence over the lives of men. The wicked man when old, is not, as Plato supposes (Republic), more agitated by the terrors of another world when he is nearer to them, nor the good in an ecstasy at the joys of which he is soon to be the partaker. Age numbs the sense of both worlds; and the habit of life is strongest in death. Even the dying mother is dreaming of her lost children as they were forty or fifty years before, 'pattering over the boards,' not of reunion with them in another state of being. Most persons when the last hour comes are resigned to the order of nature and the will of God. They are not thinking of Dante's Inferno or Paradiso, or of the Pilgrim's Progress. Heaven and hell are not realities to them, but words or ideas; the outward symbols of some great mystery, they hardly know what. Many noble poems and pictures have been suggested by the traditional representations of them, which have been fixed in forms of art and can no longer be altered. Many sermons have been filled with descriptions of celestial or infernal mansions. But hardly even in childhood did the thought of heaven and hell supply the motives of our actions, or at any time seriously affect the substance of our belief.

8. Another life must be described, if at all, in forms of thought and not of sense. To draw pictures of heaven and hell, whether in the language of Scripture or any other, adds nothing to our real knowledge, but may perhaps disguise our ignorance. The truest conception which we can form of a future life is a state of progress or education—a progress from evil to good, from ignorance to knowledge. To this we are led by the analogy of the present life, in which we see different races and nations of men, and different men and women of the same nation, in various states or stages of cultivation; some more and some less developed, and all of them capable of improvement under favourable circumstances. There are punishments too of children when they are growing up inflicted by their parents, of elder offenders which are imposed by the law of the land, of all men at all times of life, which are attached by the laws of nature to the performance of certain actions. All these punishments are really educational; that is to say, they are not intended to retaliate on the offender, but to teach him a lesson. Also there is an element of chance in them, which is another name for our ignorance of the laws of nature. There is evil too inseparable from good (compare Lysis); not always punished here, as good is not always

rewarded. It is capable of being indefinitely diminished; and as knowledge increases, the element of chance may more and more disappear.

For we do not argue merely from the analogy of the present state of this world to another, but from the analogy of a probable future to which we are tending. The greatest changes of which we have had experience as yet are due to our increasing knowledge of history and of nature. They have been produced by a few minds appearing in three or four favoured nations, in a comparatively short period of time. May we be allowed to imagine the minds of men everywhere working together during many ages for the completion of our knowledge? May not the science of physiology transform the world? Again, the majority of mankind have really experienced some moral improvement; almost every one feels that he has tendencies to good, and is capable of becoming better. And these germs of good are often found to be developed by new circumstances, like stunted trees when transplanted to a better soil. The differences between the savage and the civilized man, or between the civilized man in old and new countries, may be indefinitely increased. The first difference is the effect of a few thousand, the second of a few hundred years. We congratulate ourselves that slavery has become industry; that law and constitutional government have superseded despotism and violence; that an ethical religion has taken the place of Fetichism. There may yet come a time when the many may be as well off as the few; when no one will be weighed down by excessive toil; when the necessity of providing for the body will not interfere with mental improvement; when the physical frame may be strengthened and developed; and the religion of all men may become a reasonable service.

Nothing therefore, either in the present state of man or in the tendencies of the future, as far as we can entertain conjecture of them, would lead us to suppose that God governs us vindictively in this world, and therefore we have no reason to infer that he will govern us vindictively in another. The true argument from analogy is not, 'This life is a mixed state of justice and injustice, of great waste, of sudden casualties, of disproportionate punishments, and therefore the like inconsistencies, irregularities, injustices are to be expected in another;' but 'This life is subject to law, and is in a state of progress, and therefore law and progress may be believed to be the governing principles of another.' All the analogies of this world would be against unmeaning punishments inflicted a hundred or a thousand years after an offence had been committed. Suffering there might be as a part of education, but not hopeless or protracted; as there might be a retrogression of individuals or of bodies of men, yet not such as to interfere with a plan for the improvement of the whole (compare Laws.)

9. But some one will say: That we cannot reason from the seen to the unseen, and that we are creating another world after the image of this, just as men in former ages have created gods in their own likeness. And we, like the companions of Socrates, may feel discouraged at hearing our favourite 'argument from analogy' thus summarily disposed of. Like himself, too, we may adduce other arguments in which he seems to have anticipated us, though he expresses them in different language. For we feel that the soul partakes of the ideal and invisible; and can never fall into the error of confusing the external circumstances of man with his higher self; or his origin with his nature. It is as repugnant to us as it was to him to imagine that our moral ideas are to be attributed only to cerebral forces. The value of a human soul, like the value of a man's life to himself, is inestimable, and cannot be reckoned in earthly or material things. The human being alone has the consciousness of truth and justice and love, which is the consciousness of God. And the soul becoming more conscious of these, becomes more conscious of her own immortality.

10. The last ground of our belief in immortality, and the strongest, is the perfection of the divine nature. The mere fact of the existence of God does not tend to show the continued existence of man. An evil God or an indifferent God might have had the power, but not the will, to preserve us. He might have regarded us as fitted to minister to his service by a succession of existences,—like the animals, without attributing to each soul an incomparable value. But if he is perfect, he must will that all rational beings should partake of that perfection which he himself is. In the words of the Timaeus, he is good, and therefore he desires that all other things should be as like himself as possible. And the manner in which he accomplishes this is by permitting evil, or rather degrees of good, which are otherwise called evil. For all progress is good relatively to the past, and yet may be comparatively evil when regarded in the light of the future. Good and evil are relative terms, and degrees of evil are merely the negative aspect of degrees of good. Of the absolute goodness of any finite nature we can form no conception; we are all of us in process of transition from one degree of good or evil to another. The difficulties which are urged about the origin or existence of evil are mere dialectical puzzles, standing in the same relation to Christian philosophy as the puzzles of the Cynics and Megarians to the philosophy of Plato. They arise out of the tendency of the human mind to regard good and evil both as relative and absolute; just as the riddles about motion are to be explained by the double conception of space or matter, which the human mind has the power of regarding either as continuous or discrete.

In speaking of divine perfection, we mean to say that God is just and true and loving, the author of order and not of disorder, of good and not of evil. Or rather, that he is justice, that he is truth, that he is love, that he is order, that he is the very progress of which we were speaking; and that wherever these qualities are present, whether in the human soul or in the order of nature, there is God. We might still see him everywhere, if we had not been mistakenly seeking for him apart from us, instead of in us; away from the laws of nature, instead of in them. And we become united to him not by mystical absorption, but by partaking, whether consciously or unconsciously, of that truth and justice and love which he himself is.

Thus the belief in the immortality of the soul rests at last on the belief in God. If there is a good and wise God, then there is a progress of mankind towards perfection; and if there is no progress of men towards perfection, then there is no good and wise God. We cannot suppose that the moral government of God of which we see the beginnings in the world and in ourselves will cease when we pass out of life.

11. Considering the 'feebleness of the human faculties and the uncertainty of the subject,' we are inclined to believe that the fewer our words the better. At the approach of death there is not much said; good men are too honest to go out of the world professing more than they know. There is perhaps no important subject about which, at any time, even religious people speak so little to one another. In the fulness of life the thought of death is mostly awakened by the sight or recollection of the death of others rather than by the prospect of our own. We must also acknowledge that there are degrees of the belief in immortality, and many forms in which it presents itself to the mind. Some persons will say no more than that they trust in God, and that they leave all to Him. It is a great part of true religion not to pretend to know more than we do. Others when they quit this world are comforted with the hope 'That they will see and know their friends in heaven.' But it is better to leave them in the hands of God and to be assured that 'no evil shall touch them.' There are others again to whom the belief in a divine personality has ceased to have any longer a meaning; yet they are satisfied that the end of all is not here, but that something still remains to us, 'and some better thing for the good than for the evil.' They are persuaded, in spite of their theological nihilism, that the ideas of justice and truth and holiness and love are realities. They cherish an enthusiastic devotion to the first principles of morality. Through these they see, or seem to see, darkly, and in a figure, that the soul is immortal.

But besides differences of theological opinion which must ever prevail about things unseen, the hope of immortality is weaker or stronger in men at one time of life than at another; it even varies from day to day. It comes and goes; the mind, like the sky, is apt to be overclouded. Other generations of men may have sometimes lived under an 'eclipse of faith,' to us the total disappearance of it might be compared to the 'sun falling from heaven.' And we may sometimes have to begin again and acquire the belief for ourselves; or to win it back again when it is lost. It is really weakest in the hour of death. For Nature, like a kind mother or nurse, lays us to sleep without frightening us; physicians, who are the witnesses of such scenes, say that under ordinary circumstances there is no fear of the future. Often, as Plato tells us, death is accompanied 'with pleasure.' (Tim.) When the end is still uncertain, the cry of many a one has been, 'Pray, that I may be taken.' The last thoughts even of the best men depend chiefly on the accidents of their bodily state. Pain soon overpowers the desire of life; old age, like the child, is laid to sleep almost in a moment. The long experience of life will often destroy the interest which mankind have in it. So various are the feelings with which different persons draw near to death; and still more various the forms in which imagination clothes it. For this alternation of feeling compare the Old Testament,—Psalm vi.; Isaiah; Eccles.

12. When we think of God and of man in his relation to God; of the imperfection of our present state and yet of the progress which is observable in the history of the world and of the human mind; of the depth and power of our moral ideas which seem to partake of the very nature of God Himself; when we consider the contrast between the physical laws to which we are subject and the higher law which raises us above them and is yet a part of them; when we reflect on our capacity of becoming the 'spectators of all time and all existence,' and of framing in our own minds the ideal of a perfect Being; when we see how the human mind in all the higher religions of the world, including Buddhism, notwithstanding some aberrations, has tended towards such a belief—we have reason to think that our destiny is different from that of animals; and though we cannot altogether shut out the childish fear that the soul upon leaving the body may 'vanish into thin air,' we have still, so far as the nature of the subject admits, a hope of immortality with which we comfort ourselves on sufficient grounds. The denial of the belief takes the heart out of human life; it lowers men to the level of the material. As Goethe also says, 'He is dead even in this world who has no belief in another.'

13. It is well also that we should sometimes think of the forms of thought under which the idea of immortality is most naturally presented to us. It is clear that to our minds the risen soul can no longer be described, as in a picture, by the symbol of a creature half-bird, half-human, nor in any other form of sense. The multitude of angels, as in Milton, singing the Almighty 's praises, are a noble image, and may furnish a theme for the poet or the painter, but they are no longer an adequate expression of the kingdom of God which is within us. Neither is there any mansion, in this world or another, in which the departed can be imagined to dwell and carry on their occupations. When this

earthly tabernacle is dissolved, no other habitation or building can take them in: it is in the language of ideas only that we speak of them.

First of all there is the thought of rest and freedom from pain; they have gone home, as the common saying is, and the cares of this world touch them no more. Secondly, we may imagine them as they were at their best and brightest, humbly fulfilling their daily round of duties— selfless, childlike, unaffected by the world; when the eye was single and the whole body seemed to be full of light; when the mind was clear and saw into the purposes of God. Thirdly, we may think of them as possessed by a great love of God and man, working out His will at a further stage in the heavenly pilgrimage. And yet we acknowledge that these are the things which eye hath not seen nor ear heard and therefore it hath not entered into the heart of man in any sensible manner to conceive them. Fourthly, there may have been some moments in our own lives when we have risen above ourselves, or been conscious of our truer selves, in which the will of God has superseded our wills, and we have entered into communion with Him, and been partakers for a brief season of the Divine truth and love, in which like Christ we have been inspired to utter the prayer, 'I in them, and thou in me, that we may be all made perfect in one.' These precious moments, if we have ever known them, are the nearest approach which we can make to the idea of immortality.

14. Returning now to the earlier stage of human thought which is represented by the writings of Plato, we find that many of the same questions have already arisen: there is the same tendency to materialism; the same inconsistency in the application of the idea of mind; the same doubt whether the soul is to be regarded as a cause or as an effect; the same falling back on moral convictions. In the Phaedo the soul is conscious of her divine nature, and the separation from the body which has been commenced in this life is perfected in another. Beginning in mystery, Socrates, in the intermediate part of the Dialogue, attempts to bring the doctrine of a future life into connection with his theory of knowledge. In proportion as he succeeds in this, the individual seems to disappear in a more general notion of the soul; the contemplation of ideas 'under the form of eternity' takes the place of past and future states of existence. His language may be compared to that of some modern philosophers, who speak of eternity, not in the sense of perpetual duration of time, but as an ever- present quality of the soul. Yet at the conclusion of the Dialogue, having 'arrived at the end of the intellectual world' (Republic), he replaces the veil of mythology, and describes the soul and her attendant genius in the language of the mysteries or of a disciple of Zoroaster. Nor can we fairly demand of Plato a consistency which is wanting among ourselves, who acknowledge that another world is beyond the range of human thought, and yet are always seeking to represent the mansions of

heaven or hell in the colours of the painter, or in the descriptions of the poet or rhetorician.

15. The doctrine of the immortality of the soul was not new to the Greeks in the age of Socrates, but, like the unity of God, had a foundation in the popular belief. The old Homeric notion of a gibbering ghost flitting away to Hades; or of a few illustrious heroes enjoying the isles of the blest; or of an existence divided between the two; or the Hesiodic, of righteous spirits, who become guardian angels,—had given place in the mysteries and the Orphic poets to representations, partly fanciful, of a future state of rewards and punishments. (Laws.) The reticence of the Greeks on public occasions and in some part of their literature respecting this 'underground' religion, is not to be taken as a measure of the diffusion of such beliefs. If Pericles in the funeral oration is silent on the consolations of immortality, the poet Pindar and the tragedians on the other hand constantly assume the continued existence of the dead in an upper or under world. Darius and Laius are still alive; Antigone will be dear to her brethren after death; the way to the palace of Cronos is found by those who 'have thrice departed from evil.' The tragedy of the Greeks is not 'rounded' by this life, but is deeply set in decrees of fate and mysterious workings of powers beneath the earth. In the caricature of Aristophanes there is also a witness to the common sentiment. The Ionian and Pythagorean philosophies arose, and some new elements were added to the popular belief. The individual must find an expression as well as the world. Either the soul was supposed to exist in the form of a magnet, or of a particle of fire, or of light, or air, or water; or of a number or of a harmony of number; or to be or have, like the stars, a principle of motion (Arist. de Anim.). At length Anaxagoras, hardly distinguishing between life and mind, or between mind human and divine, attained the pure abstraction; and this, like the other abstractions of Greek philosophy, sank deep into the human intelligence. The opposition of the intelligible and the sensible, and of God to the world, supplied an analogy which assisted in the separation of soul and body. If ideas were separable from phenomena, mind was also separable from matter; if the ideas were eternal, the mind that conceived them was eternal too. As the unity of God was more distinctly acknowledged, the conception of the human soul became more developed. The succession, or alternation of life and death, had occurred to Heracleitus. The Eleatic Parmenides had stumbled upon the modern thesis, that 'thought and being are the same.' The Eastern belief in transmigration defined the sense of individuality; and some, like Empedocles, fancied that the blood which they had shed in another state of being was crying against them, and that for thirty thousand years they were to be 'fugitives and vagabonds upon the earth.' The desire of recognizing a lost mother or love or friend in the world below (Phaedo) was a natural feeling which, in that

age as well as in every other, has given distinctness to the hope of immortality. Nor were ethical considerations wanting, partly derived from the necessity of punishing the greater sort of criminals, whom no avenging power of this world could reach. The voice of conscience, too, was heard reminding the good man that he was not altogether innocent. (Republic.) To these indistinct longings and fears an expression was given in the mysteries and Orphic poets: a 'heap of books' (Republic), passing under the names of Musaeus and Orpheus in Plato's time, were filled with notions of an under-world.

16. Yet after all the belief in the individuality of the soul after death had but a feeble hold on the Greek mind. Like the personality of God, the personality of man in a future state was not inseparably bound up with the reality of his existence. For the distinction between the personal and impersonal, and also between the divine and human, was far less marked to the Greek than to ourselves. And as Plato readily passes from the notion of the good to that of God, he also passes almost imperceptibly to himself and his reader from the future life of the individual soul to the eternal being of the absolute soul. There has been a clearer statement and a clearer denial of the belief in modern times than is found in early Greek philosophy, and hence the comparative silence on the whole subject which is often remarked in ancient writers, and particularly in Aristotle. For Plato and Aristotle are not further removed in their teaching about the immortality of the soul than they are in their theory of knowledge.

17. Living in an age when logic was beginning to mould human thought, Plato naturally cast his belief in immortality into a logical form. And when we consider how much the doctrine of ideas was also one of words, it is not surprising that he should have fallen into verbal fallacies: early logic is always mistaking the truth of the form for the truth of the matter. It is easy to see that the alternation of opposites is not the same as the generation of them out of each other; and that the generation of them out of each other, which is the first argument in the Phaedo, is at variance with their mutual exclusion of each other, whether in themselves or in us, which is the last. For even if we admit the distinction which he draws between the opposites and the things which have the opposites, still individuals fall under the latter class; and we have to pass out of the region of human hopes and fears to a conception of an abstract soul which is the impersonation of the ideas. Such a conception, which in Plato himself is but half expressed, is unmeaning to us, and relative only to a particular stage in the history of thought. The doctrine of reminiscence is also a fragment of a former world, which has no place in the philosophy of modern times. But Plato had the wonders of psychology just opening to him, and he had not the explanation of them which is supplied by the analysis of language and the history of the human mind. The question, 'Whence come our

abstract ideas?' he could only answer by an imaginary hypothesis. Nor is it difficult to see that his crowning argument is purely verbal, and is but the expression of an instinctive confidence put into a logical form:—'The soul is immortal because it contains a principle of imperishableness.' Nor does he himself seem at all to be aware that nothing is added to human knowledge by his 'safe and simple answer,' that beauty is the cause of the beautiful; and that he is merely reasserting the Eleatic being 'divided by the Pythagorean numbers,' against the Heracleitean doctrine of perpetual generation. The answer to the 'very serious question' of generation and destruction is really the denial of them. For this he would substitute, as in the Republic, a system of ideas, tested, not by experience, but by their consequences, and not explained by actual causes, but by a higher, that is, a more general notion. Consistency with themselves is the only test which is to be applied to them. (Republic, and Phaedo.)

18. To deal fairly with such arguments, they should be translated as far as possible into their modern equivalents. 'If the ideas of men are eternal, their souls are eternal, and if not the ideas, then not the souls.' Such an argument stands nearly in the same relation to Plato and his age, as the argument from the existence of God to immortality among ourselves. 'If God exists, then the soul exists after death; and if there is no God, there is no existence of the soul after death.' For the ideas are to his mind the reality, the truth, the principle of permanence, as well as of intelligence and order in the world. When Simmias and Cebes say that they are more strongly persuaded of the existence of ideas than they are of the immortality of the soul, they represent fairly enough the order of thought in Greek philosophy. And we might say in the same way that we are more certain of the existence of God than we are of the immortality of the soul, and are led by the belief in the one to a belief in the other. The parallel, as Socrates would say, is not perfect, but agrees in as far as the mind in either case is regarded as dependent on something above and beyond herself. The analogy may even be pressed a step further: 'We are more certain of our ideas of truth and right than we are of the existence of God, and are led on in the order of thought from one to the other.' Or more correctly: 'The existence of right and truth is the existence of God, and can never for a moment be separated from Him.'

19. The main argument of the Phaedo is derived from the existence of eternal ideas of which the soul is a partaker; the other argument of the alternation of opposites is replaced by this. And there have not been wanting philosophers of the idealist school who have imagined that the doctrine of the immortality of the soul is a theory of knowledge, and that in what has preceded Plato is accommodating himself to the popular belief. Such a view can only be elicited from the Phaedo by what may be termed the transcendental method of interpretation, and is

obviously inconsistent with the Gorgias and the Republic. Those who maintain it are immediately compelled to renounce the shadow which they have grasped, as a play of words only. But the truth is, that Plato in his argument for the immortality of the soul has collected many elements of proof or persuasion, ethical and mythological as well as dialectical, which are not easily to be reconciled with one another; and he is as much in earnest about his doctrine of retribution, which is repeated in all his more ethical writings, as about his theory of knowledge. And while we may fairly translate the dialectical into the language of Hegel, and the religious and mythological into the language of Dante or Bunyan, the ethical speaks to us still in the same voice, and appeals to a common feeling.

20. Two arguments of this ethical character occur in the Phaedo. The first may be described as the aspiration of the soul after another state of being. Like the Oriental or Christian mystic, the philosopher is seeking to withdraw from impurities of sense, to leave the world and the things of the world, and to find his higher self. Plato recognizes in these aspirations the foretaste of immortality; as Butler and Addison in modern times have argued, the one from the moral tendencies of mankind, the other from the progress of the soul towards perfection. In using this argument Plato has certainly confused the soul which has left the body, with the soul of the good and wise. (Compare Republic.) Such a confusion was natural, and arose partly out of the antithesis of soul and body. The soul in her own essence, and the soul 'clothed upon' with virtues and graces, were easily interchanged with one another, because on a subject which passes expression the distinctions of language can hardly be maintained.

21. The ethical proof of the immortality of the soul is derived from the necessity of retribution. The wicked would be too well off if their evil deeds came to an end. It is not to be supposed that an Ardiaeus, an Archelaus, an Ismenias could ever have suffered the penalty of their crimes in this world. The manner in which this retribution is accomplished Plato represents under the figures of mythology. Doubtless he felt that it was easier to improve than to invent, and that in religion especially the traditional form was required in order to give verisimilitude to the myth. The myth too is far more probable to that age than to ours, and may fairly be regarded as 'one guess among many' about the nature of the earth, which he cleverly supports by the indications of geology. Not that he insists on the absolute truth of his own particular notions: 'no man of sense will be confident in such matters; but he will be confident that something of the kind is true.' As in other passages (Gorg., Tim., compare Crito), he wins belief for his fictions by the moderation of his statements; he does not, like Dante or Swedenborg, allow himself to be deceived by his own creations.

The Dialogue must be read in the light of the situation. And first of all we are struck by the calmness of the scene. Like the spectators at the time, we cannot pity Socrates; his mien and his language are so noble and fearless. He is the same that he ever was, but milder and gentler, and he has in no degree lost his interest in dialectics; he will not forego the delight of an argument in compliance with the jailer's intimation that he should not heat himself with talking. At such a time he naturally expresses the hope of his life, that he has been a true mystic and not a mere retainer or wand-bearer: and he refers to passages of his personal history. To his old enemies the Comic poets, and to the proceedings on the trial, he alludes playfully; but he vividly remembers the disappointment which he felt in reading the books of Anaxagoras. The return of Xanthippe and his children indicates that the philosopher is not 'made of oak or rock.' Some other traits of his character may be noted; for example, the courteous manner in which he inclines his head to the last objector, or the ironical touch, 'Me already, as the tragic poet would say, the voice of fate calls;' or the depreciation of the arguments with which 'he comforted himself and them;' or his fear of 'misology;' or his references to Homer; or the playful smile with which he 'talks like a book' about greater and less; or the allusion to the possibility of finding another teacher among barbarous races (compare Polit.); or the mysterious reference to another science (mathematics?) of generation and destruction for which he is vainly feeling. There is no change in him; only now he is invested with a sort of sacred character, as the prophet or priest of Apollo the God of the festival, in whose honour he first of all composes a hymn, and then like the swan pours forth his dying lay. Perhaps the extreme elevation of Socrates above his own situation, and the ordinary interests of life (compare his jeu d'esprit about his burial, in which for a moment he puts on the 'Silenus mask'), create in the mind of the reader an impression stronger than could be derived from arguments that such a one has in him 'a principle which does not admit of death.'

The other persons of the Dialogue may be considered under two heads: (1) private friends; (2) the respondents in the argument.

First there is Crito, who has been already introduced to us in the Euthydemus and the Crito; he is the equal in years of Socrates, and stands in quite a different relation to him from his younger disciples. He is a man of the world who is rich and prosperous (compare the jest in the Euthydemus), the best friend of Socrates, who wants to know his commands, in whose presence he talks to his family, and who performs the last duty of closing his eyes. It is observable too that, as in the Euthydemus, Crito shows no aptitude for philosophical discussions. Nor among the friends of Socrates must the jailer be forgotten, who seems to have been introduced by Plato in order to show the impression made by the extraordinary man on the common. The gentle nature of the man is indicated by his weeping at the announcement of his errand

and then turning away, and also by the words of Socrates to his disciples: 'How charming the man is! since I have been in prison he has been always coming to me, and is as good as could be to me.' We are reminded too that he has retained this gentle nature amid scenes of death and violence by the contrasts which he draws between the behaviour of Socrates and of others when about to die.

Another person who takes no part in the philosophical discussion is the excitable Apollodorus, the same who, in the Symposium, of which he is the narrator, is called 'the madman,' and who testifies his grief by the most violent emotions. Phaedo is also present, the 'beloved disciple' as he may be termed, who is described, if not 'leaning on his bosom,' as seated next to Socrates, who is playing with his hair. He too, like Apollodorus, takes no part in the discussion, but he loves above all things to hear and speak of Socrates after his death. The calmness of his behaviour, veiling his face when he can no longer restrain his tears, contrasts with the passionate outcries of the other. At a particular point the argument is described as falling before the attack of Simmias. A sort of despair is introduced in the minds of the company. The effect of this is heightened by the description of Phaedo, who has been the eye-witness of the scene, and by the sympathy of his Phliasian auditors who are beginning to think 'that they too can never trust an argument again.' And the intense interest of the company is communicated not only to the first auditors, but to us who in a distant country read the narrative of their emotions after more than two thousand years have passed away.

The two principal interlocutors are Simmias and Cebes, the disciples of Philolaus the Pythagorean philosopher of Thebes. Simmias is described in the Phaedrus as fonder of an argument than any man living; and Cebes, although finally persuaded by Socrates, is said to be the most incredulous of human beings. It is Cebes who at the commencement of the Dialogue asks why 'suicide is held to be unlawful,' and who first supplies the doctrine of recollection in confirmation of the pre-existence of the soul. It is Cebes who urges that the pre-existence does not necessarily involve the future existence of the soul, as is shown by the illustration of the weaver and his coat. Simmias, on the other hand, raises the question about harmony and the lyre, which is naturally put into the mouth of a Pythagorean disciple. It is Simmias, too, who first remarks on the uncertainty of human knowledge, and only at last concedes to the argument such a qualified approval as is consistent with the feebleness of the human faculties. Cebes is the deeper and more consecutive thinker, Simmias more superficial and rhetorical; they are distinguished in much the same manner as Adeimantus and Glaucon in the Republic.

Other persons, Menexenus, Ctesippus, Lysis, are old friends; Evenus has been already satirized in the Apology; Aeschines and

Epigenes were present at the trial; Euclid and Terpsion will reappear in the Introduction to the Theaetetus, Hermogenes has already appeared in the Cratylus. No inference can fairly be drawn from the absence of Aristippus, nor from the omission of Xenophon, who at the time of Socrates' death was in Asia. The mention of Plato's own absence seems like an expression of sorrow, and may, perhaps, be an indication that the report of the conversation is not to be taken literally.

The place of the Dialogue in the series is doubtful. The doctrine of ideas is certainly carried beyond the Socratic point of view; in no other of the writings of Plato is the theory of them so completely developed. Whether the belief in immortality can be attributed to Socrates or not is uncertain; the silence of the Memorabilia, and of the earlier Dialogues of Plato, is an argument to the contrary. Yet in the Cyropaedia Xenophon has put language into the mouth of the dying Cyrus which recalls the Phaedo, and may have been derived from the teaching of Socrates. It may be fairly urged that the greatest religious interest of mankind could not have been wholly ignored by one who passed his life in fulfilling the commands of an oracle, and who recognized a Divine plan in man and nature. (Xen. Mem.) And the language of the Apology and of the Crito confirms this view.

The Phaedo is not one of the Socratic Dialogues of Plato; nor, on the other hand, can it be assigned to that later stage of the Platonic writings at which the doctrine of ideas appears to be forgotten. It belongs rather to the intermediate period of the Platonic philosophy, which roughly corresponds to the Phaedrus, Gorgias, Republic, Theaetetus. Without pretending to determine the real time of their composition, the Symposium, Meno, Euthyphro, Apology, Phaedo may be conveniently read by us in this order as illustrative of the life of Socrates. Another chain may be formed of the Meno, Phaedrus, Phaedo, in which the immortality of the soul is connected with the doctrine of ideas. In the Meno the theory of ideas is based on the ancient belief in transmigration, which reappears again in the Phaedrus as well as in the Republic and Timaeus, and in all of them is connected with a doctrine of retribution. In the Phaedrus the immortality of the soul is supposed to rest on the conception of the soul as a principle of motion, whereas in the Republic the argument turns on the natural continuance of the soul, which, if not destroyed by her own proper evil, can hardly be destroyed by any other. The soul of man in the Timaeus is derived from the Supreme Creator, and either returns after death to her kindred star, or descends into the lower life of an animal. The Apology expresses the same view as the Phaedo, but with less confidence; there the probability of death being a long sleep is not excluded. The Theaetetus also describes, in a digression, the desire of the soul to fly away and be with God—'and to fly to him is to be like him.' The Symposium may be observed to resemble as well as to differ from the Phaedo. While the first notion of immortality is only in the way of natural procreation or of posthumous fame and glory, the higher revelation of beauty, like the good in the Republic, is the vision of the eternal idea. So deeply rooted in Plato's mind is the belief in immortality; so various are the forms of expression which he employs.

As in several other Dialogues, there is more of system in the Phaedo than appears at first sight. The succession of arguments is based on previous philosophies; beginning with the mysteries and the Heracleitean alternation of opposites, and proceeding to the Pythagorean harmony and transmigration; making a step by the aid of Platonic reminiscence, and a further step by the help of the nous of Anaxagoras; until at last we rest in the conviction that the soul is inseparable from the ideas, and belongs to the world of the invisible and unknown. Then, as in the Gorgias or Republic, the curtain falls, and the veil of mythology descends upon the argument. After the confession of Socrates that he is an interested party, and the acknowledgment that no man of sense will think the details of his narrative true, but that something of the kind is true, we return from speculation to practice. He is himself more confident of immortality than he is of his own arguments; and the confidence which he expresses is less strong than that which his cheerfulness and composure in death inspire in us.

Difficulties of two kinds occur in the Phaedo—one kind to be explained out of contemporary philosophy, the other not admitting of an entire solution. (1) The difficulty which Socrates says that he experienced in explaining generation and corruption; the assumption of hypotheses which proceed from the less general to the more general, and are tested by their consequences; the puzzle about greater and less; the resort to the method of ideas, which to us appear only abstract terms,—these are to be explained out of the position of Socrates and Plato in the history of philosophy. They were living in a twilight between the sensible and the intellectual world, and saw no way of connecting them. They could neither explain the relation of ideas to phenomena, nor their correlation to one another. The very idea of relation or comparison was embarrassing to them. Yet in this intellectual uncertainty they had a conception of a proof from results, and of a moral truth, which remained unshaken amid the questionings of philosophy. (2) The other is a difficulty which is touched upon in the Republic as well as in the Phaedo, and is common to modern and ancient philosophy. Plato is not altogether satisfied with his safe and simple method of ideas. He wants to have proved to him by facts that all things are for the best, and that there is one mind or design which pervades them all. But this 'power of the best' he is unable to explain; and therefore takes refuge in universal ideas. And are not we at this day seeking to discover that which Socrates in a glass darkly foresaw?

Some resemblances to the Greek drama may be noted in all the Dialogues of Plato. The Phaedo is the tragedy of which Socrates is the protagonist and Simmias and Cebes the secondary performers, standing to them in the same relation as to Glaucon and Adeimantus in the Republic. No Dialogue has a greater unity of subject and feeling. Plato has certainly fulfilled the condition of Greek, or rather of all art, which requires that scenes of death and suffering should be clothed in beauty. The gathering of the friends at the commencement of the Dialogue, the dismissal of Xanthippe, whose presence would have been out of place at a philosophical discussion, but who returns again with her children to take a final farewell, the dejection of the audience at the temporary overthrow of the argument, the picture of Socrates playing with the hair of Phaedo, the final scene in which Socrates alone retains his composure—are masterpieces of art. And the chorus at the end might have interpreted the feeling of the play: 'There can no evil happen to a good man in life or death.'

'The art of concealing art' is nowhere more perfect than in those writings of Plato which describe the trial and death of Socrates. Their charm is their simplicity, which gives them verisimilitude; and yet they touch, as if incidentally, and because they were suitable to the occasion, on some of the deepest truths of philosophy. There is nothing in any tragedy, ancient or modern, nothing in poetry or history (with one exception), like the last hours of Socrates in Plato. The master could not be more fitly occupied at such a time than in discoursing of immortality; nor the disciples more divinely consoled. The arguments, taken in the spirit and not in the letter, are our arguments; and Socrates by anticipation may be even thought to refute some 'eccentric notions; current in our own age. For there are philosophers among ourselves who do not seem to understand how much stronger is the power of intelligence, or of the best, than of Atlas, or mechanical force. How far the words attributed to Socrates were actually uttered by him we forbear to ask; for no answer can be given to this question. And it is better to resign ourselves to the feeling of a great work, than to linger among critical uncertainties.

PHAEDO

PERSONS OF THE DIALOGUE: Phaedo, who is the narrator of the dialogue to Echecrates of Phlius. Socrates, Apollodorus, Simmias, Cebes, Crito and an Attendant of the Prison.

SCENE: The Prison of Socrates.

PLACE OF THE NARRATION: Phlius.

ECHECRATES: Were you yourself, Phaedo, in the prison with Socrates on the day when he drank the poison?

PHAEDO: Yes, Echecrates, I was.

ECHECRATES: I should so like to hear about his death. What did he say in his last hours? We were informed that he died by taking poison, but no one knew anything more; for no Phliasian ever goes to Athens now, and it is a long time since any stranger from Athens has found his way hither; so that we had no clear account.

PHAEDO: Did you not hear of the proceedings at the trial?

ECHECRATES: Yes; some one told us about the trial, and we could not understand why, having been condemned, he should have been put to death, not at the time, but long afterwards. What was the reason of this?

PHAEDO: An accident, Echecrates: the stern of the ship which the Athenians send to Delos happened to have been crowned on the day before he was tried.

ECHECRATES: What is this ship?

PHAEDO: It is the ship in which, according to Athenian tradition, Theseus went to Crete when he took with him the fourteen youths, and was the saviour of them and of himself. And they were said to have vowed to Apollo at the time, that if they were saved they would send a yearly mission to Delos. Now this custom still continues, and the whole period of the voyage to and from Delos, beginning when the priest of Apollo crowns the stern of the ship, is a holy season, during which the city is not allowed to be polluted by public executions; and when the vessel is detained by contrary winds, the time spent in going and returning is very considerable. As I was saying, the ship was crowned on the day before the trial, and this was the reason why Socrates lay in prison and was not put to death until long after he was condemned.

ECHECRATES: What was the manner of his death, Phaedo? What was said or done? And which of his friends were with him? Or did the authorities forbid them to be present—so that he had no friends near him when he died?

PHAEDO: No; there were several of them with him.

ECHECRATES: If you have nothing to do, I wish that you would tell me what passed, as exactly as you can.

PHAEDO: I have nothing at all to do, and will try to gratify your wish. To be reminded of Socrates is always the greatest delight to me, whether I speak myself or hear another speak of him.

ECHECRATES: You will have listeners who are of the same mind with you, and I hope that you will be as exact as you can.

PHAEDO: I had a singular feeling at being in his company. For I could hardly believe that I was present at the death of a friend, and therefore I did not pity him, Echecrates; he died so fearlessly, and his words and bearing were so noble and gracious, that to me he appeared blessed. I thought that in going to the other world he could not be without a divine call, and that he would be happy, if any man ever was, when he arrived there, and therefore I did not pity him as might have seemed natural at such an hour. But I had not the pleasure which I usually feel in philosophical discourse (for philosophy was the theme of which we spoke). I was pleased, but in the pleasure there was also a strange admixture of pain; for I reflected that he was soon to die, and this double feeling was shared by us all; we were laughing and weeping by turns, especially the excitable Apollodorus—you know the sort of man?

ECHECRATES: Yes.

PHAEDO: He was quite beside himself; and I and all of us were greatly moved.

ECHECRATES: Who were present?

PHAEDO: Of native Athenians there were, besides Apollodorus, Critobulus and his father Crito, Hermogenes, Epigenes, Aeschines, Antisthenes; likewise Ctesippus of the deme of Paeania, Menexenus, and some others; Plato, if I am not mistaken, was ill.

ECHECRATES: Were there any strangers?

PHAEDO: Yes, there were; Simmias the Theban, and Cebes, and Phaedondes; Euclid and Terpsion, who came from Megara.

ECHECRATES: And was Aristippus there, and Cleombrotus?

PHAEDO: No, they were said to be in Aegina.

ECHECRATES: Any one else?

PHAEDO: I think that these were nearly all.

ECHECRATES: Well, and what did you talk about?

PHAEDO: I will begin at the beginning, and endeavour to repeat the entire conversation. On the previous days we had been in the habit of assembling early in the morning at the court in which the trial took place, and which is not far from the prison. There we used to wait talking with one another until the opening of the doors (for they were not opened very early); then we went in and generally passed the day with Socrates. On the last morning we assembled sooner than usual, having heard on the day before when we quitted the prison in the evening that the sacred ship had come from Delos, and so we arranged to meet very early at the accustomed place. On our arrival the jailer who answered the door, instead of admitting us, came out and told us to stay until he called us. 'For the Eleven,' he said, 'are now with Socrates; they are taking off his chains, and giving orders that he is to die to-day.' He soon returned and said that we might come in. On entering we found Socrates just released from chains, and Xanthippe, whom you know, sitting by him, and holding his child in her arms. When she saw us she uttered a cry and said, as women will: 'O Socrates, this is the last time that either you will converse with your friends, or they with you.' Socrates turned to Crito and said: 'Crito, let some one take her home.' Some of Crito's people accordingly led her away, crying out and beating herself. And when she was gone, Socrates, sitting up on the couch, bent and rubbed his leg, saying, as he was rubbing: How singular is the thing called pleasure, and how curiously related to pain, which might be thought to be the opposite of it; for they are never present to a man at the same instant, and yet he who pursues either is generally compelled to take the other; their bodies are two, but they are joined by a single head. And I cannot help thinking that if Aesop had remembered them, he would have made a fable about God trying to reconcile their strife, and how, when he could not, he fastened their heads together; and this is the reason why when one comes the other follows, as I know by my own experience now, when after the pain in my leg which was caused by the chain pleasure appears to succeed.

Upon this Cebes said: I am glad, Socrates, that you have mentioned the name of Aesop. For it reminds me of a question which has been asked by many, and was asked of me only the day before yesterday by Evenus the poet—he will be sure to ask it again, and therefore if you would like me to have an answer ready for him, you may as well tell me what I should say to him:—he wanted to know why you, who never before wrote a line of poetry, now that you are in prison are turning Aesop's fables into verse, and also composing that hymn in honour of Apollo.

Tell him, Cebes, he replied, what is the truth—that I had no idea of rivalling him or his poems; to do so, as I knew, would be no easy task. But I wanted to see whether I could purge away a scruple which I felt about the meaning of certain dreams. In the course of my life I have often had intimations in dreams 'that I should compose music.' The same dream came to me sometimes in one form, and sometimes in another, but always saying the same or nearly the same words: 'Cultivate and make music,' said the dream. And hitherto I had imagined that this was only intended to exhort and encourage me in the study of philosophy, which has been the pursuit of my life, and is the noblest and best of music. The dream was bidding me do what I was

already doing, in the same way that the competitor in a race is bidden
by the spectators to run when he is already running. But I was not
certain of this, for the dream might have meant music in the popular
sense of the word, and being under sentence of death, and the festival
giving me a respite, I thought that it would be safer for me to satisfy the
scruple, and, in obedience to the dream, to compose a few verses before
I departed. And first I made a hymn in honour of the god of the festival,
and then considering that a poet, if he is really to be a poet, should not
only put together words, but should invent stories, and that I have no
invention, I took some fables of Aesop, which I had ready at hand and
which I knew—they were the first I came upon—and turned them into
verse. Tell this to Evenus, Cebes, and bid him be of good cheer; say
that I would have him come after me if he be a wise man, and not tarry;
and that to-day I am likely to be going, for the Athenians say that I
must.

Simmias said: What a message for such a man! having been a
frequent companion of his I should say that, as far as I know him, he
will never take your advice unless he is obliged.

Why, said Socrates,—is not Evenus a philosopher?

I think that he is, said Simmias.

Then he, or any man who has the spirit of philosophy, will be
willing to die, but he will not take his own life, for that is held to be
unlawful.

Here he changed his position, and put his legs off the couch on to
the ground, and during the rest of the conversation he remained sitting.

Why do you say, enquired Cebes, that a man ought not to take his
own life, but that the philosopher will be ready to follow the dying?

Socrates replied: And have you, Cebes and Simmias, who are the
disciples of Philolaus, never heard him speak of this?

Yes, but his language was obscure, Socrates.

My words, too, are only an echo; but there is no reason why I
should not repeat what I have heard: and indeed, as I am going to
another place, it is very meet for me to be thinking and talking of the
nature of the pilgrimage which I am about to make. What can I do
better in the interval between this and the setting of the sun?

Then tell me, Socrates, why is suicide held to be unlawful? as I
have certainly heard Philolaus, about whom you were just now asking,
affirm when he was staying with us at Thebes: and there are others who
say the same, although I have never understood what was meant by any
of them.

Do not lose heart, replied Socrates, and the day may come when
you will understand. I suppose that you wonder why, when other things
which are evil may be good at certain times and to certain persons,
death is to be the only exception, and why, when a man is better dead,
he is not permitted to be his own benefactor, but must wait for the hand

of another.

Very true, said Cebes, laughing gently and speaking in his native Boeotian.

I admit the appearance of inconsistency in what I am saying; but there may not be any real inconsistency after all. There is a doctrine whispered in secret that man is a prisoner who has no right to open the door and run away; this is a great mystery which I do not quite understand. Yet I too believe that the gods are our guardians, and that we are a possession of theirs. Do you not agree?

Yes, I quite agree, said Cebes.

And if one of your own possessions, an ox or an ass, for example, took the liberty of putting himself out of the way when you had given no intimation of your wish that he should die, would you not be angry with him, and would you not punish him if you could?

Certainly, replied Cebes.

Then, if we look at the matter thus, there may be reason in saying that a man should wait, and not take his own life until God summons him, as he is now summoning me.

Yes, Socrates, said Cebes, there seems to be truth in what you say. And yet how can you reconcile this seemingly true belief that God is our guardian and we his possessions, with the willingness to die which we were just now attributing to the philosopher? That the wisest of men should be willing to leave a service in which they are ruled by the gods who are the best of rulers, is not reasonable; for surely no wise man thinks that when set at liberty he can take better care of himself than the gods take of him. A fool may perhaps think so—he may argue that he had better run away from his master, not considering that his duty is to remain to the end, and not to run away from the good, and that there would be no sense in his running away. The wise man will want to be ever with him who is better than himself. Now this, Socrates, is the reverse of what was just now said; for upon this view the wise man should sorrow and the fool rejoice at passing out of life.

The earnestness of Cebes seemed to please Socrates. Here, said he, turning to us, is a man who is always inquiring, and is not so easily convinced by the first thing which he hears.

And certainly, added Simmias, the objection which he is now making does appear to me to have some force. For what can be the meaning of a truly wise man wanting to fly away and lightly leave a master who is better than himself? And I rather imagine that Cebes is referring to you; he thinks that you are too ready to leave us, and too ready to leave the gods whom you acknowledge to be our good masters.

Yes, replied Socrates; there is reason in what you say. And so you think that I ought to answer your indictment as if I were in a court?

We should like you to do so, said Simmias.

Then I must try to make a more successful defence before you than I did when before the judges. For I am quite ready to admit, Simmias and Cebes, that I ought to be grieved at death, if I were not persuaded in the first place that I am going to other gods who are wise and good (of which I am as certain as I can be of any such matters), and secondly (though I am not so sure of this last) to men departed, better than those whom I leave behind; and therefore I do not grieve as I might have done, for I have good hope that there is yet something remaining for the dead, and as has been said of old, some far better thing for the good than for the evil.

But do you mean to take away your thoughts with you, Socrates? said Simmias. Will you not impart them to us?—for they are a benefit in which we too are entitled to share. Moreover, if you succeed in convincing us, that will be an answer to the charge against yourself.

I will do my best, replied Socrates. But you must first let me hear what Crito wants; he has long been wishing to say something to me.

Only this, Socrates, replied Crito:—the attendant who is to give you the poison has been telling me, and he wants me to tell you, that you are not to talk much, talking, he says, increases heat, and this is apt to interfere with the action of the poison; persons who excite themselves are sometimes obliged to take a second or even a third dose.

Then, said Socrates, let him mind his business and be prepared to give the poison twice or even thrice if necessary; that is all.

I knew quite well what you would say, replied Crito; but I was obliged to satisfy him.

Never mind him, he said.

And now, O my judges, I desire to prove to you that the real philosopher has reason to be of good cheer when he is about to die, and that after death he may hope to obtain the greatest good in the other world. And how this may be, Simmias and Cebes, I will endeavour to explain. For I deem that the true votary of philosophy is likely to be misunderstood by other men; they do not perceive that he is always pursuing death and dying; and if this be so, and he has had the desire of death all his life long, why when his time comes should he repine at that which he has been always pursuing and desiring?

Simmias said laughingly: Though not in a laughing humour, you have made me laugh, Socrates; for I cannot help thinking that the many when they hear your words will say how truly you have described philosophers, and our people at home will likewise say that the life which philosophers desire is in reality death, and that they have found them out to be deserving of the death which they desire.

And they are right, Simmias, in thinking so, with the exception of the words 'they have found them out'; for they have not found out either what is the nature of that death which the true philosopher deserves, or how he deserves or desires death. But enough of them:—

let us discuss the matter among ourselves: Do we believe that there is such a thing as death?

To be sure, replied Simmias.

Is it not the separation of soul and body? And to be dead is the completion of this; when the soul exists in herself, and is released from the body and the body is released from the soul, what is this but death?

Just so, he replied.

There is another question, which will probably throw light on our present inquiry if you and I can agree about it:—Ought the philosopher to care about the pleasures—if they are to be called pleasures—of eating and drinking?

Certainly not, answered Simmias.

And what about the pleasures of love—should he care for them?

By no means.

And will he think much of the other ways of indulging the body, for example, the acquisition of costly raiment, or sandals, or other adornments of the body? Instead of caring about them, does he not rather despise anything more than nature needs? What do you say?

I should say that the true philosopher would despise them.

Would you not say that he is entirely concerned with the soul and not with the body? He would like, as far as he can, to get away from the body and to turn to the soul.

Quite true.

In matters of this sort philosophers, above all other men, may be observed in every sort of way to dissever the soul from the communion of the body.

Very true.

Whereas, Simmias, the rest of the world are of opinion that to him who has no sense of pleasure and no part in bodily pleasure, life is not worth having; and that he who is indifferent about them is as good as dead.

That is also true.

What again shall we say of the actual acquirement of knowledge?—is the body, if invited to share in the enquiry, a hinderer or a helper? I mean to say, have sight and hearing any truth in them? Are they not, as the poets are always telling us, inaccurate witnesses? and yet, if even they are inaccurate and indistinct, what is to be said of the other senses?—for you will allow that they are the best of them?

Certainly, he replied.

Then when does the soul attain truth?—for in attempting to consider anything in company with the body she is obviously deceived.

True.

Then must not true existence be revealed to her in thought, if at all?

Yes.

And thought is best when the mind is gathered into herself and none of these things trouble her—neither sounds nor sights nor pain nor any pleasure,—when she takes leave of the body, and has as little as possible to do with it, when she has no bodily sense or desire, but is aspiring after true being?

Certainly.

And in this the philosopher dishonours the body; his soul runs away from his body and desires to be alone and by herself?

That is true.

Well, but there is another thing, Simmias: Is there or is there not an absolute justice?

Assuredly there is.

And an absolute beauty and absolute good?

Of course.

But did you ever behold any of them with your eyes?

Certainly not.

Or did you ever reach them with any other bodily sense?—and I speak not of these alone, but of absolute greatness, and health, and strength, and of the essence or true nature of everything. Has the reality of them ever been perceived by you through the bodily organs? or rather, is not the nearest approach to the knowledge of their several natures made by him who so orders his intellectual vision as to have the most exact conception of the essence of each thing which he considers?

Certainly.

And he attains to the purest knowledge of them who goes to each with the mind alone, not introducing or intruding in the act of thought sight or any other sense together with reason, but with the very light of the mind in her own clearness searches into the very truth of each; he who has got rid, as far as he can, of eyes and ears and, so to speak, of the whole body, these being in his opinion distracting elements which when they infect the soul hinder her from acquiring truth and knowledge—who, if not he, is likely to attain the knowledge of true being?

What you say has a wonderful truth in it, Socrates, replied Simmias.

And when real philosophers consider all these things, will they not be led to make a reflection which they will express in words something like the following? 'Have we not found,' they will say, 'a path of thought which seems to bring us and our argument to the conclusion, that while we are in the body, and while the soul is infected with the evils of the body, our desire will not be satisfied? and our desire is of the truth. For the body is a source of endless trouble to us by reason of the mere requirement of food; and is liable also to diseases which overtake and impede us in the search after true being: it fills us full of loves, and lusts, and fears, and fancies of all kinds, and endless foolery, and in fact, as men say, takes away from us the power of thinking at all. Whence come wars, and fightings, and factions? whence but from the body and the lusts of the body? wars are occasioned by the love of money, and money has to be acquired for the sake and in the service of the body; and by reason of all these impediments we have no time to give to philosophy; and, last and worst of all, even if we are at leisure and betake ourselves to some speculation, the body is always breaking in upon us, causing turmoil and confusion in our enquiries, and so amazing us that we are prevented from seeing the truth. It has been proved to us by experience that if we would have pure knowledge of anything we must be quit of the body—the soul in herself must behold things in themselves: and then we shall attain the wisdom which we desire, and of which we say that we are lovers, not while we live, but after death; for if while in company with the body, the soul cannot have pure knowledge, one of two things follows—either knowledge is not to be attained at all, or, if at all, after death. For then, and not till then, the soul will be parted from the body and exist in herself alone. In this present life, I reckon that we make the nearest approach to knowledge when we have the least possible intercourse or communion with the body, and are not surfeited with the bodily nature, but keep ourselves pure until the hour when God himself is pleased to release us. And thus having got rid of the foolishness of the body we shall be pure and hold converse with the pure, and know of ourselves the clear light everywhere, which is no other than the light of truth.' For the impure are not permitted to approach the pure. These are the sort of words, Simmias, which the true lovers of knowledge cannot help saying to one another, and thinking. You would agree; would you not?

Undoubtedly, Socrates.

But, O my friend, if this is true, there is great reason to hope that, going whither I go, when I have come to the end of my journey, I shall attain that which has been the pursuit of my life. And therefore I go on my way rejoicing, and not I only, but every other man who believes that his mind has been made ready and that he is in a manner purified.

Certainly, replied Simmias.

And what is purification but the separation of the soul from the body, as I was saying before; the habit of the soul gathering and collecting herself into herself from all sides out of the body; the dwelling in her own place alone, as in another life, so also in this, as far as she can;—the release of the soul from the chains of the body?

Very true, he said.

And this separation and release of the soul from the body is termed death?

To be sure, he said.

And the true philosophers, and they only, are ever seeking to release the soul. Is not the separation and release of the soul from the body their especial study?

That is true.

And, as I was saying at first, there would be a ridiculous contradiction in men studying to live as nearly as they can in a state of death, and yet repining when it comes upon them.

Clearly.

And the true philosophers, Simmias, are always occupied in the practice of dying, wherefore also to them least of all men is death terrible. Look at the matter thus:—if they have been in every way the enemies of the body, and are wanting to be alone with the soul, when this desire of theirs is granted, how inconsistent would they be if they trembled and repined, instead of rejoicing at their departure to that place where, when they arrive, they hope to gain that which in life they desired—and this was wisdom—and at the same time to be rid of the company of their enemy. Many a man has been willing to go to the world below animated by the hope of seeing there an earthly love, or wife, or son, and conversing with them. And will he who is a true lover of wisdom, and is strongly persuaded in like manner that only in the world below he can worthily enjoy her, still repine at death? Will he not depart with joy? Surely he will, O my friend, if he be a true philosopher. For he will have a firm conviction that there and there only, he can find wisdom in her purity. And if this be true, he would be very absurd, as I was saying, if he were afraid of death.

He would, indeed, replied Simmias.

And when you see a man who is repining at the approach of death, is not his reluctance a sufficient proof that he is not a lover of wisdom, but a lover of the body, and probably at the same time a lover of either money or power, or both?

Quite so, he replied.

And is not courage, Simmias, a quality which is specially characteristic of the philosopher?

Certainly.

There is temperance again, which even by the vulgar is supposed to consist in the control and regulation of the passions, and in the sense of superiority to them—is not temperance a virtue belonging to those only who despise the body, and who pass their lives in philosophy?

Most assuredly.

For the courage and temperance of other men, if you will consider them, are really a contradiction.

How so?

Well, he said, you are aware that death is regarded by men in general as a great evil.

Very true, he said.

And do not courageous men face death because they are afraid of yet greater evils?

That is quite true.

Then all but the philosophers are courageous only from fear, and because they are afraid; and yet that a man should be courageous from fear, and because he is a coward, is surely a strange thing.

Very true.

And are not the temperate exactly in the same case? They are temperate because they are intemperate—which might seem to be a contradiction, but is nevertheless the sort of thing which happens with this foolish temperance. For there are pleasures which they are afraid of losing; and in their desire to keep them, they abstain from some pleasures, because they are overcome by others; and although to be conquered by pleasure is called by men intemperance, to them the conquest of pleasure consists in being conquered by pleasure. And that is what I mean by saying that, in a sense, they are made temperate through intemperance.

Such appears to be the case.

Yet the exchange of one fear or pleasure or pain for another fear or pleasure or pain, and of the greater for the less, as if they were coins, is not the exchange of virtue. O my blessed Simmias, is there not one true coin for which all things ought to be exchanged?—and that is wisdom; and only in exchange for this, and in company with this, is anything truly bought or sold, whether courage or temperance or justice. And is not all true virtue the companion of wisdom, no matter what fears or pleasures or other similar goods or evils may or may not attend her? But the virtue which is made up of these goods, when they are severed from wisdom and exchanged with one another, is a shadow of virtue only, nor is there any freedom or health or truth in her; but in the true exchange there is a purging away of all these things, and temperance, and justice, and courage, and wisdom herself are the purgation of them. The founders of the mysteries would appear to have had a real meaning, and were not talking nonsense when they intimated in a figure long ago that he who passes unsanctified and uninitiated into the world below will lie in a slough, but that he who arrives there after initiation and purification will dwell with the gods. For 'many,' as they say in the mysteries, 'are the thyrsus-bearers, but few are the mystics,'—meaning, as I interpret the words, 'the true philosophers.' In the number of whom, during my whole life, I have been seeking, according to my ability, to find a place;—whether I have sought in a right way or not, and whether I have succeeded or not, I shall truly know in a little while, if God will, when I myself arrive in the other world—such is my belief. And therefore I maintain that I am right, Simmias and Cebes, in not grieving or repining at parting from you and my masters in this world, for I believe that I shall equally find good masters and friends in another world. But most men do not believe this saying; if then I succeed in convincing you by my defence better than I did the Athenian judges, it will be well.

Cebes answered: I agree, Socrates, in the greater part of what you say. But in what concerns the soul, men are apt to be incredulous; they fear that when she has left the body her place may be nowhere, and that on the very day of death she may perish and come to an end— immediately on her release from the body, issuing forth dispersed like smoke or air and in her flight vanishing away into nothingness. If she could only be collected into herself after she has obtained release from the evils of which you are speaking, there would be good reason to hope, Socrates, that what you say is true. But surely it requires a great deal of argument and many proofs to show that when the man is dead his soul yet exists, and has any force or intelligence.

True, Cebes, said Socrates; and shall I suggest that we converse a little of the probabilities of these things?

I am sure, said Cebes, that I should greatly like to know your opinion about them.

I reckon, said Socrates, that no one who heard me now, not even if he were one of my old enemies, the Comic poets, could accuse me of idle talking about matters in which I have no concern:—If you please, then, we will proceed with the inquiry.

Suppose we consider the question whether the souls of men after death are or are not in the world below. There comes into my mind an ancient doctrine which affirms that they go from hence into the other world, and returning hither, are born again from the dead. Now if it be true that the living come from the dead, then our souls must exist in the other world, for if not, how could they have been born again? And this would be conclusive, if there were any real evidence that the living are only born from the dead; but if this is not so, then other arguments will have to be adduced.

Very true, replied Cebes.

Then let us consider the whole question, not in relation to man only, but in relation to animals generally, and to plants, and to everything of which there is generation, and the proof will be easier. Are not all things which have opposites generated out of their opposites? I mean such things as good and evil, just and unjust—and there are innumerable other opposites which are generated out of opposites. And I want to show that in all opposites there is of necessity a similar alternation; I mean to say, for example, that anything which becomes greater must become greater after being less.

True.

And that which becomes less must have been once greater and then have become less.

Yes.

And the weaker is generated from the stronger, and the swifter from the slower.

Very true.

And the worse is from the better, and the more just is from the more unjust.

Of course.

And is this true of all opposites? and are we convinced that all of them are generated out of opposites?

Yes.

And in this universal opposition of all things, are there not also two intermediate processes which are ever going on, from one to the other opposite, and back again; where there is a greater and a less there is also an intermediate process of increase and diminution, and that which grows is said to wax, and that which decays to wane?

Yes, he said.

And there are many other processes, such as division and composition, cooling and heating, which equally involve a passage into and out of one another. And this necessarily holds of all opposites, even though not always expressed in words—they are really generated out of one another, and there is a passing or process from one to the other of them?

Very true, he replied.

Well, and is there not an opposite of life, as sleep is the opposite of waking?

True, he said.

And what is it?

Death, he answered.

And these, if they are opposites, are generated the one from the other, and have there their two intermediate processes also?

Of course.

Now, said Socrates, I will analyze one of the two pairs of opposites which I have mentioned to you, and also its intermediate processes, and you shall analyze the other to me. One of them I term sleep, the other waking. The state of sleep is opposed to the state of waking, and out of sleeping waking is generated, and out of waking, sleeping; and the process of generation is in the one case falling asleep, and in the other waking up. Do you agree?

I entirely agree.

Then, suppose that you analyze life and death to me in the same manner. Is not death opposed to life?

Yes.

And they are generated one from the other?

Yes.

What is generated from the living?

The dead.

And what from the dead?

I can only say in answer—the living.

Then the living, whether things or persons, Cebes, are generated from the dead?

That is clear, he replied.

Then the inference is that our souls exist in the world below?

That is true.

And one of the two processes or generations is visible—for surely the act of dying is visible?

Surely, he said.

What then is to be the result? Shall we exclude the opposite process? And shall we suppose nature to walk on one leg only? Must we not rather assign to death some corresponding process of generation?

Certainly, he replied.

And what is that process?

Return to life.

And return to life, if there be such a thing, is the birth of the dead into the world of the living?

Quite true.

Then here is a new way by which we arrive at the conclusion that the living come from the dead, just as the dead come from the living; and this, if true, affords a most certain proof that the souls of the dead exist in some place out of which they come again.

Yes, Socrates, he said; the conclusion seems to flow necessarily out of our previous admissions.

And that these admissions were not unfair, Cebes, he said, may be shown, I think, as follows: If generation were in a straight line only, and there were no compensation or circle in nature, no turn or return of elements into their opposites, then you know that all things would at last have the same form and pass into the same state, and there would be no more generation of them.

What do you mean? he said.

A simple thing enough, which I will illustrate by the case of sleep, he replied. You know that if there were no alternation of sleeping and waking, the tale of the sleeping Endymion would in the end have no meaning, because all other things would be asleep, too, and he would not be distinguishable from the rest. Or if there were composition only, and no division of substances, then the chaos of Anaxagoras would come again. And in like manner, my dear Cebes, if all things which partook of life were to die, and after they were dead remained in the form of death, and did not come to life again, all would at last die, and nothing would be alive—what other result could there be? For if the living spring from any other things, and they too die, must not all things at last be swallowed up in death? (But compare Republic.)

There is no escape, Socrates, said Cebes; and to me your argument seems to be absolutely true.

Yes, he said, Cebes, it is and must be so, in my opinion; and we have not been deluded in making these admissions; but I am confident that there truly is such a thing as living again, and that the living spring from the dead, and that the souls of the dead are in existence, and that the good souls have a better portion than the evil.

Cebes added: Your favorite doctrine, Socrates, that knowledge is simply recollection, if true, also necessarily implies a previous time in which we have learned that which we now recollect. But this would be impossible unless our soul had been in some place before existing in the form of man; here then is another proof of the soul's immortality.

But tell me, Cebes, said Simmias, interposing, what arguments are urged in favour of this doctrine of recollection. I am not very sure at the moment that I remember them.

One excellent proof, said Cebes, is afforded by questions. If you put a question to a person in a right way, he will give a true answer of himself, but how could he do this unless there were knowledge and right reason already in him? And this is most clearly shown when he is taken to a diagram or to anything of that sort. (Compare Meno.)

But if, said Socrates, you are still incredulous, Simmias, I would ask you whether you may not agree with me when you look at the matter in another way;—I mean, if you are still incredulous as to whether knowledge is recollection.

Incredulous, I am not, said Simmias; but I want to have this doctrine of recollection brought to my own recollection, and, from what Cebes has said, I am beginning to recollect and be convinced; but I should still like to hear what you were going to say.

This is what I would say, he replied:—We should agree, if I am not mistaken, that what a man recollects he must have known at some previous time.

Very true.

And what is the nature of this knowledge or recollection? I mean to ask, Whether a person who, having seen or heard or in any way perceived anything, knows not only that, but has a conception of something else which is the subject, not of the same but of some other kind of knowledge, may not be fairly said to recollect that of which he has the conception?

What do you mean?

I mean what I may illustrate by the following instance:—The knowledge of a lyre is not the same as the knowledge of a man?

True.

And yet what is the feeling of lovers when they recognize a lyre, or a garment, or anything else which the beloved has been in the habit of using? Do not they, from knowing the lyre, form in the mind's eye an image of the youth to whom the lyre belongs? And this is recollection. In like manner any one who sees Simmias may remember Cebes; and there are endless examples of the same thing.

Endless, indeed, replied Simmias.

And recollection is most commonly a process of recovering that which has been already forgotten through time and inattention.

Very true, he said.

Well; and may you not also from seeing the picture of a horse or a lyre remember a man? and from the picture of Simmias, you may be led to remember Cebes?

True.

Or you may also be led to the recollection of Simmias himself?

Quite so.

And in all these cases, the recollection may be derived from things either like or unlike?

It may be.

And when the recollection is derived from like things, then another consideration is sure to arise, which is—whether the likeness in any degree falls short or not of that which is recollected?

Very true, he said.

And shall we proceed a step further, and affirm that there is such a thing as equality, not of one piece of wood or stone with another, but that, over and above this, there is absolute equality? Shall we say so?

Say so, yes, replied Simmias, and swear to it, with all the confidence in life.

And do we know the nature of this absolute essence?

To be sure, he said.

And whence did we obtain our knowledge? Did we not see equalities of material things, such as pieces of wood and stones, and gather from them the idea of an equality which is different from them? For you will acknowledge that there is a difference. Or look at the matter in another way:—Do not the same pieces of wood or stone appear at one time equal, and at another time unequal?

That is certain.

But are real equals ever unequal? or is the idea of equality the same as of inequality?

Impossible, Socrates.

Then these (so-called) equals are not the same with the idea of equality?

I should say, clearly not, Socrates.

And yet from these equals, although differing from the idea of equality, you conceived and attained that idea?

Very true, he said.

Which might be like, or might be unlike them?

Yes.

But that makes no difference; whenever from seeing one thing you conceived another, whether like or unlike, there must surely have been an act of recollection?

Very true.

But what would you say of equal portions of wood and stone, or other material equals? and what is the impression produced by them? Are they equals in the same sense in which absolute equality is equal? or do they fall short of this perfect equality in a measure?

Yes, he said, in a very great measure too.

And must we not allow, that when I or any one, looking at any object, observes that the thing which he sees aims at being some other thing, but falls short of, and cannot be, that other thing, but is inferior, he who makes this observation must have had a previous knowledge of that to which the other, although similar, was inferior?

Certainly.

And has not this been our own case in the matter of equals and of absolute equality?

Precisely.

Then we must have known equality previously to the time when we first saw the material equals, and reflected that all these apparent equals strive to attain absolute equality, but fall short of it?

Very true.

And we recognize also that this absolute equality has only been known, and can only be known, through the medium of sight or touch, or of some other of the senses, which are all alike in this respect?

Yes, Socrates, as far as the argument is concerned, one of them is the same as the other.

From the senses then is derived the knowledge that all sensible things aim at an absolute equality of which they fall short?

Yes.

Then before we began to see or hear or perceive in any way, we must have had a knowledge of absolute equality, or we could not have referred to that standard the equals which are derived from the senses?—for to that they all aspire, and of that they fall short.

No other inference can be drawn from the previous statements.

And did we not see and hear and have the use of our other senses as soon as we were born?

Certainly.

Then we must have acquired the knowledge of equality at some previous time?

Yes.

That is to say, before we were born, I suppose?

True.

And if we acquired this knowledge before we were born, and were born having the use of it, then we also knew before we were born and at the instant of birth not only the equal or the greater or the less, but all other ideas; for we are not speaking only of equality, but of beauty, goodness, justice, holiness, and of all which we stamp with the name of essence in the dialectical process, both when we ask and when we answer questions. Of all this we may certainly affirm that we acquired the knowledge before birth?

We may.

But if, after having acquired, we have not forgotten what in each case we acquired, then we must always have come into life having knowledge, and shall always continue to know as long as life lasts—for knowing is the acquiring and retaining knowledge and not forgetting. Is not forgetting, Simmias, just the losing of knowledge?

Quite true, Socrates.

But if the knowledge which we acquired before birth was lost by us at birth, and if afterwards by the use of the senses we recovered what we previously knew, will not the process which we call learning be a recovering of the knowledge which is natural to us, and may not this be rightly termed recollection?

Very true.

So much is clear—that when we perceive something, either by the help of sight, or hearing, or some other sense, from that perception we are able to obtain a notion of some other thing like or unlike which is associated with it but has been forgotten. Whence, as I was saying, one of two alternatives follows:—either we had this knowledge at birth, and continued to know through life; or, after birth, those who are said to learn only remember, and learning is simply recollection.

Yes, that is quite true, Socrates.

And which alternative, Simmias, do you prefer? Had we the knowledge at our birth, or did we recollect the things which we knew previously to our birth?

I cannot decide at the moment.

At any rate you can decide whether he who has knowledge will or will not be able to render an account of his knowledge? What do you say?

Certainly, he will.

But do you think that every man is able to give an account of these very matters about which we are speaking?

Would that they could, Socrates, but I rather fear that to-morrow, at this time, there will no longer be any one alive who is able to give an account of them such as ought to be given.

Then you are not of opinion, Simmias, that all men know these things?

Certainly not.

They are in process of recollecting that which they learned before?

Certainly.

But when did our souls acquire this knowledge?—not since we were born as men?

Certainly not.

And therefore, previously?

Yes.

Then, Simmias, our souls must also have existed without bodies before they were in the form of man, and must have had intelligence.

Unless indeed you suppose, Socrates, that these notions are given us at the very moment of birth; for this is the only time which remains.

Yes, my friend, but if so, when do we lose them? for they are not in us when we are born—that is admitted. Do we lose them at the moment of receiving them, or if not at what other time?

No, Socrates, I perceive that I was unconsciously talking nonsense.

Then may we not say, Simmias, that if, as we are always repeating, there is an absolute beauty, and goodness, and an absolute essence of all things; and if to this, which is now discovered to have existed in our former state, we refer all our sensations, and with this compare them, finding these ideas to be pre-existent and our inborn possession—then our souls must have had a prior existence, but if not, there would be no force in the argument? There is the same proof that these ideas must have existed before we were born, as that our souls existed before we were born; and if not the ideas, then not the souls.

Yes, Socrates; I am convinced that there is precisely the same necessity for the one as for the other; and the argument retreats successfully to the position that the existence of the soul before birth cannot be separated from the existence of the essence of which you speak. For there is nothing which to my mind is so patent as that beauty, goodness, and the other notions of which you were just now speaking, have a most real and absolute existence; and I am satisfied with the proof.

Well, but is Cebes equally satisfied? For I must convince him too.

I think, said Simmias, that Cebes is satisfied: although he is the most incredulous of mortals, yet I believe that he is sufficiently convinced of the existence of the soul before birth. But that after death the soul will continue to exist is not yet proven even to my own satisfaction. I cannot get rid of the feeling of the many to which Cebes was referring—the feeling that when the man dies the soul will be dispersed, and that this may be the extinction of her. For admitting that she may have been born elsewhere, and framed out of other elements, and was in existence before entering the human body, why after having entered in and gone out again may she not herself be destroyed and come to an end?

Very true, Simmias, said Cebes; about half of what was required has been proven; to wit, that our souls existed before we were born:— that the soul will exist after death as well as before birth is the other half of which the proof is still wanting, and has to be supplied; when that is given the demonstration will be complete.

But that proof, Simmias and Cebes, has been already given, said Socrates, if you put the two arguments together—I mean this and the former one, in which we admitted that everything living is born of the dead. For if the soul exists before birth, and in coming to life and being born can be born only from death and dying, must she not after death continue to exist, since she has to be born again?—Surely the proof which you desire has been already furnished. Still I suspect that you and Simmias would be glad to probe the argument further. Like children, you are haunted with a fear that when the soul leaves the body, the wind may really blow her away and scatter her; especially if a man should happen to die in a great storm and not when the sky is calm.

Cebes answered with a smile: Then, Socrates, you must argue us out of our fears—and yet, strictly speaking, they are not our fears, but there is a child within us to whom death is a sort of hobgoblin; him too we must persuade not to be afraid when he is alone in the dark.

Socrates said: Let the voice of the charmer be applied daily until you have charmed away the fear.

And where shall we find a good charmer of our fears, Socrates, when you are gone?

Hellas, he replied, is a large place, Cebes, and has many good men, and there are barbarous races not a few: seek for him among them all, far and wide, sparing neither pains nor money; for there is no better way of spending your money. And you must seek among yourselves too; for you will not find others better able to make the search.

The search, replied Cebes, shall certainly be made. And now, if you please, let us return to the point of the argument at which we digressed.

By all means, replied Socrates; what else should I please?

Very good.

Must we not, said Socrates, ask ourselves what that is which, as we imagine, is liable to be scattered, and about which we fear? and what again is that about which we have no fear? And then we may proceed further to enquire whether that which suffers dispersion is or is not of the nature of soul—our hopes and fears as to our own souls will turn upon the answers to these questions.

Very true, he said.

Now the compound or composite may be supposed to be naturally capable, as of being compounded, so also of being dissolved; but that which is uncompounded, and that only, must be, if anything is, indissoluble.

Yes; I should imagine so, said Cebes.

And the uncompounded may be assumed to be the same and unchanging, whereas the compound is always changing and never the same.

I agree, he said.

Then now let us return to the previous discussion. Is that idea or essence, which in the dialectical process we define as essence or true existence—whether essence of equality, beauty, or anything else—are these essences, I say, liable at times to some degree of change? or are they each of them always what they are, having the same simple self-existent and unchanging forms, not admitting of variation at all, or in any way, or at any time?

They must be always the same, Socrates, replied Cebes.

And what would you say of the many beautiful—whether men or horses or garments or any other things which are named by the same names and may be called equal or beautiful,—are they all unchanging and the same always, or quite the reverse? May they not rather be described as almost always changing and hardly ever the same, either with themselves or with one another?

The latter, replied Cebes; they are always in a state of change.

And these you can touch and see and perceive with the senses, but the unchanging things you can only perceive with the mind—they are invisible and are not seen?

That is very true, he said.

Well, then, added Socrates, let us suppose that there are two sorts of existences—one seen, the other unseen.

Let us suppose them.

The seen is the changing, and the unseen is the unchanging?

That may be also supposed.

And, further, is not one part of us body, another part soul?

To be sure.

And to which class is the body more alike and akin?

Clearly to the seen—no one can doubt that.

And is the soul seen or not seen?

Not by man, Socrates.

And what we mean by 'seen' and 'not seen' is that which is or is not visible to the eye of man?

Yes, to the eye of man.

And is the soul seen or not seen?

Not seen.

Unseen then?

Yes.

Then the soul is more like to the unseen, and the body to the seen?

That follows necessarily, Socrates.

And were we not saying long ago that the soul when using the body as an instrument of perception, that is to say, when using the sense of sight or hearing or some other sense (for the meaning of perceiving through the body is perceiving through the senses)—were we not saying that the soul too is then dragged by the body into the region of the changeable, and wanders and is confused; the world spins round her, and she is like a drunkard, when she touches change?

Very true.

But when returning into herself she reflects, then she passes into the other world, the region of purity, and eternity, and immortality, and unchangeableness, which are her kindred, and with them she ever lives, when she is by herself and is not let or hindered; then she ceases from her erring ways, and being in communion with the unchanging is unchanging. And this state of the soul is called wisdom?

That is well and truly said, Socrates, he replied.

And to which class is the soul more nearly alike and akin, as far as may be inferred from this argument, as well as from the preceding one?

I think, Socrates, that, in the opinion of every one who follows the argument, the soul will be infinitely more like the unchangeable—even the most stupid person will not deny that.

And the body is more like the changing?

Yes.

Yet once more consider the matter in another light: When the soul and the body are united, then nature orders the soul to rule and govern, and the body to obey and serve. Now which of these two functions is akin to the divine? and which to the mortal? Does not the divine appear to you to be that which naturally orders and rules, and the mortal to be that which is subject and servant?

True.

And which does the soul resemble?

The soul resembles the divine, and the body the mortal—there can be no doubt of that, Socrates.

Then reflect, Cebes: of all which has been said is not this the conclusion?—that the soul is in the very likeness of the divine, and immortal, and intellectual, and uniform, and indissoluble, and unchangeable; and that the body is in the very likeness of the human, and mortal, and unintellectual, and multiform, and dissoluble, and changeable. Can this, my dear Cebes, be denied?

It cannot.

But if it be true, then is not the body liable to speedy dissolution? and is not the soul almost or altogether indissoluble?

Certainly.

And do you further observe, that after a man is dead, the body, or visible part of him, which is lying in the visible world, and is called a corpse, and would naturally be dissolved and decomposed and dissipated, is not dissolved or decomposed at once, but may remain for a for some time, nay even for a long time, if the constitution be sound at the time of death, and the season of the year favourable? For the body when shrunk and embalmed, as the manner is in Egypt, may remain almost entire through infinite ages; and even in decay, there are still some portions, such as the bones and ligaments, which are practically indestructible:—Do you agree?

Yes.

And is it likely that the soul, which is invisible, in passing to the place of the true Hades, which like her is invisible, and pure, and noble, and on her way to the good and wise God, whither, if God will, my soul is also soon to go,—that the soul, I repeat, if this be her nature and origin, will be blown away and destroyed immediately on quitting the body, as the many say? That can never be, my dear Simmias and Cebes. The truth rather is, that the soul which is pure at departing and draws after her no bodily taint, having never voluntarily during life had connection with the body, which she is ever avoiding, herself gathered into herself;—and making such abstraction her perpetual study—which means that she has been a true disciple of philosophy; and therefore has in fact been always engaged in the practice of dying? For is not philosophy the practice of death?—

Certainly—

That soul, I say, herself invisible, departs to the invisible world—to the divine and immortal and rational: thither arriving, she is secure of bliss and is released from the error and folly of men, their fears and wild passions and all other human ills, and for ever dwells, as they say of the initiated, in company with the gods (compare Apol.). Is not this true, Cebes?

Yes, said Cebes, beyond a doubt.

But the soul which has been polluted, and is impure at the time of her departure, and is the companion and servant of the body always, and is in love with and fascinated by the body and by the desires and pleasures of the body, until she is led to believe that the truth only exists in a bodily form, which a man may touch and see and taste, and use for the purposes of his lusts,—the soul, I mean, accustomed to hate and fear and avoid the intellectual principle, which to the bodily eye is dark and invisible, and can be attained only by philosophy;—do you suppose that such a soul will depart pure and unalloyed?

Impossible, he replied.

She is held fast by the corporeal, which the continual association and constant care of the body have wrought into her nature.

Very true.

And this corporeal element, my friend, is heavy and weighty and earthy, and is that element of sight by which a soul is depressed and dragged down again into the visible world, because she is afraid of the invisible and of the world below—prowling about tombs and sepulchres, near which, as they tell us, are seen certain ghostly apparitions of souls which have not departed pure, but are cloyed with sight and therefore visible.

(Compare Milton, Comus:—'But when lust, By unchaste looks,

loose gestures, and foul talk, But most by lewd and lavish act of sin, Lets in defilement to the inward parts, The soul grows clotted by contagion, Imbodies, and imbrutes, till she quite lose, The divine property of her first being. Such are those thick and gloomy shadows damp Oft seen in charnel vaults and sepulchres, Lingering, and sitting by a new made grave, As loath to leave the body that it lov'd, And linked itself by carnal sensuality To a degenerate and degraded state.')

That is very likely, Socrates.

Yes, that is very likely, Cebes; and these must be the souls, not of the good, but of the evil, which are compelled to wander about such places in payment of the penalty of their former evil way of life; and they continue to wander until through the craving after the corporeal which never leaves them, they are imprisoned finally in another body. And they may be supposed to find their prisons in the same natures which they have had in their former lives.

What natures do you mean, Socrates?

What I mean is that men who have followed after gluttony, and wantonness, and drunkenness, and have had no thought of avoiding them, would pass into asses and animals of that sort. What do you think?

I think such an opinion to be exceedingly probable.

And those who have chosen the portion of injustice, and tyranny, and violence, will pass into wolves, or into hawks and kites;—whither else can we suppose them to go?

Yes, said Cebes; with such natures, beyond question.

And there is no difficulty, he said, in assigning to all of them places answering to their several natures and propensities?

There is not, he said.

Some are happier than others; and the happiest both in themselves and in the place to which they go are those who have practised the civil and social virtues which are called temperance and justice, and are acquired by habit and attention without philosophy and mind. (Compare Republic.)

Why are they the happiest?

Because they may be expected to pass into some gentle and social kind which is like their own, such as bees or wasps or ants, or back again into the form of man, and just and moderate men may be supposed to spring from them.

Very likely.

No one who has not studied philosophy and who is not entirely pure at the time of his departure is allowed to enter the company of the Gods, but the lover of knowledge only. And this is the reason, Simmias and Cebes, why the true votaries of philosophy abstain from all fleshly lusts, and hold out against them and refuse to give themselves up to them,—not because they fear poverty or the ruin of their families, like the lovers of money, and the world in general; nor like the lovers of power and honour, because they dread the dishonour or disgrace of evil deeds.

No, Socrates, that would not become them, said Cebes.

No indeed, he replied; and therefore they who have any care of their own souls, and do not merely live moulding and fashioning the body, say farewell to all this; they will not walk in the ways of the blind: and when philosophy offers them purification and release from evil, they feel that they ought not to resist her influence, and whither she leads they turn and follow.

What do you mean, Socrates?

I will tell you, he said. The lovers of knowledge are conscious that the soul was simply fastened and glued to the body—until philosophy received her, she could only view real existence through the bars of a prison, not in and through herself; she was wallowing in the mire of every sort of ignorance; and by reason of lust had become the principal accomplice in her own captivity. This was her original state; and then, as I was saying, and as the lovers of knowledge are well aware, philosophy, seeing how terrible was her confinement, of which she was to herself the cause, received and gently comforted her and sought to release her, pointing out that the eye and the ear and the other senses are full of deception, and persuading her to retire from them, and abstain from all but the necessary use of them, and be gathered up and collected into herself, bidding her trust in herself and her own pure apprehension of pure existence, and to mistrust whatever comes to her through other channels and is subject to variation; for such things are visible and tangible, but what she sees in her own nature is intelligible and invisible. And the soul of the true philosopher thinks that she ought not to resist this deliverance, and therefore abstains from pleasures and desires and pains and fears, as far as she is able; reflecting that when a man has great joys or sorrows or fears or desires, he suffers from them, not merely the sort of evil which might be anticipated—as for example, the loss of his health or property which he has sacrificed to his lusts— but an evil greater far, which is the greatest and worst of all evils, and one of which he never thinks.

What is it, Socrates? said Cebes.

The evil is that when the feeling of pleasure or pain is most intense, every soul of man imagines the objects of this intense feeling to be then plainest and truest: but this is not so, they are really the things of sight.

Very true.

And is not this the state in which the soul is most enthralled by the body?

How so?

Why, because each pleasure and pain is a sort of nail which nails and rivets the soul to the body, until she becomes like the body, and believes that to be true which the body affirms to be true; and from agreeing with the body and having the same delights she is obliged to have the same habits and haunts, and is not likely ever to be pure at her departure to the world below, but is always infected by the body; and so she sinks into another body and there germinates and grows, and has therefore no part in the communion of the divine and pure and simple.

Most true, Socrates, answered Cebes.

And this, Cebes, is the reason why the true lovers of knowledge are temperate and brave; and not for the reason which the world gives.

Certainly not.

Certainly not! The soul of a philosopher will reason in quite another way; she will not ask philosophy to release her in order that when released she may deliver herself up again to the thraldom of pleasures and pains, doing a work only to be undone again, weaving instead of unweaving her Penelope's web. But she will calm passion, and follow reason, and dwell in the contemplation of her, beholding the true and divine (which is not matter of opinion), and thence deriving nourishment. Thus she seeks to live while she lives, and after death she hopes to go to her own kindred and to that which is like her, and to be freed from human ills. Never fear, Simmias and Cebes, that a soul which has been thus nurtured and has had these pursuits, will at her departure from the body be scattered and blown away by the winds and be nowhere and nothing.

When Socrates had done speaking, for a considerable time there was silence; he himself appeared to be meditating, as most of us were, on what had been said; only Cebes and Simmias spoke a few words to one another. And Socrates observing them asked what they thought of the argument, and whether there was anything wanting? For, said he, there are many points still open to suspicion and attack, if any one were disposed to sift the matter thoroughly. Should you be considering some other matter I say no more, but if you are still in doubt do not hesitate to say exactly what you think, and let us have anything better which you can suggest; and if you think that I can be of any use, allow me to help you.

Simmias said: I must confess, Socrates, that doubts did arise in our minds, and each of us was urging and inciting the other to put the question which we wanted to have answered and which neither of us liked to ask, fearing that our importunity might be troublesome under present at such a time.

Socrates replied with a smile: O Simmias, what are you saying? I am not very likely to persuade other men that I do not regard my present situation as a misfortune, if I cannot even persuade you that I am no worse off now than at any other time in my life. Will you not allow that I have as much of the spirit of prophecy in me as the swans?

For they, when they perceive that they must die, having sung all their life long, do then sing more lustily than ever, rejoicing in the thought that they are about to go away to the god whose ministers they are. But men, because they are themselves afraid of death, slanderously affirm of the swans that they sing a lament at the last, not considering that no bird sings when cold, or hungry, or in pain, not even the nightingale, nor the swallow, nor yet the hoopoe; which are said indeed to tune a lay of sorrow, although I do not believe this to be true of them any more than of the swans. But because they are sacred to Apollo, they have the gift of prophecy, and anticipate the good things of another world, wherefore they sing and rejoice in that day more than they ever did before. And I too, believing myself to be the consecrated servant of the same God, and the fellow-servant of the swans, and thinking that I have received from my master gifts of prophecy which are not inferior to theirs, would not go out of life less merrily than the swans. Never mind then, if this be your only objection, but speak and ask anything which you like, while the eleven magistrates of Athens allow.

Very good, Socrates, said Simmias; then I will tell you my difficulty, and Cebes will tell you his. I feel myself, (and I daresay that you have the same feeling), how hard or rather impossible is the attainment of any certainty about questions such as these in the present life. And yet I should deem him a coward who did not prove what is said about them to the uttermost, or whose heart failed him before he had examined them on every side. For he should persevere until he has achieved one of two things: either he should discover, or be taught the truth about them; or, if this be impossible, I would have him take the best and most irrefragable of human theories, and let this be the raft upon which he sails through life—not without risk, as I admit, if he cannot find some word of God which will more surely and safely carry him. And now, as you bid me, I will venture to question you, and then I shall not have to reproach myself hereafter with not having said at the time what I think. For when I consider the matter, either alone or with Cebes, the argument does certainly appear to me, Socrates, to be not sufficient.

Socrates answered: I dare say, my friend, that you may be right, but I should like to know in what respect the argument is insufficient.

In this respect, replied Simmias:—Suppose a person to use the same argument about harmony and the lyre—might he not say that harmony is a thing invisible, incorporeal, perfect, divine, existing in the lyre which is harmonized, but that the lyre and the strings are matter and material, composite, earthy, and akin to mortality? And when some one breaks the lyre, or cuts and rends the strings, then he who takes this view would argue as you do, and on the same analogy, that the harmony survives and has not perished—you cannot imagine, he would say, that the lyre without the strings, and the broken strings themselves which are mortal remain, and yet that the harmony, which is of heavenly and immortal nature and kindred, has perished—perished before the mortal. The harmony must still be somewhere, and the wood and strings will decay before anything can happen to that. The thought, Socrates, must have occurred to your own mind that such is our conception of the soul; and that when the body is in a manner strung and held together by the elements of hot and cold, wet and dry, then the soul is the harmony or due proportionate admixture of them. But if so, whenever the strings of the body are unduly loosened or overstrained through disease or other injury, then the soul, though most divine, like other harmonies of music or of works of art, of course perishes at once, although the material remains of the body may last for a considerable time, until they are either decayed or burnt. And if any one maintains that the soul, being the harmony of the elements of the body, is first to perish in that which is called death, how shall we answer him?

Socrates looked fixedly at us as his manner was, and said with a smile: Simmias has reason on his side; and why does not some one of you who is better able than myself answer him? for there is force in his attack upon me. But perhaps, before we answer him, we had better also hear what Cebes has to say that we may gain time for reflection, and when they have both spoken, we may either assent to them, if there is truth in what they say, or if not, we will maintain our position. Please to tell me then, Cebes, he said, what was the difficulty which troubled you?

Cebes said: I will tell you. My feeling is that the argument is where it was, and open to the same objections which were urged before; for I am ready to admit that the existence of the soul before entering into the bodily form has been very ingeniously, and, if I may say so, quite sufficiently proven; but the existence of the soul after death is still, in my judgment, unproven. Now my objection is not the same as that of Simmias; for I am not disposed to deny that the soul is stronger and more lasting than the body, being of opinion that in all such respects the soul very far excels the body. Well, then, says the argument to me, why do you remain unconvinced?—When you see that the weaker continues in existence after the man is dead, will you not admit that the more lasting must also survive during the same period of time? Now I will ask you to consider whether the objection, which, like Simmias, I will express in a figure, is of any weight. The analogy which I will adduce is that of an old weaver, who dies, and after his death somebody says:—He is not dead, he must be alive;—see, there is the coat which he himself wove and wore, and which remains whole and undecayed. And then he proceeds to ask of some one who is incredulous, whether a man lasts longer, or the coat which is in use and wear; and when he is answered that a man lasts far longer, thinks that he has thus certainly demonstrated the survival of the man, who is the more lasting, because the less lasting remains. But that, Simmias, as I would beg you to remark, is a mistake; any one can see that he who talks thus is talking nonsense. For the truth is, that the weaver aforesaid, having woven and worn many such coats, outlived several of them, and was outlived by the last; but a man is not therefore proved to be slighter and weaker than a coat. Now the relation of the body to the soul may be expressed in a similar figure; and any one may very fairly say in like manner that the soul is lasting, and the body weak and short-lived in comparison. He may argue in like manner that every soul wears out many bodies, especially if a man live many years. While he is alive the body deliquesces and decays, and the soul always weaves another garment and repairs the waste. But of course, whenever the soul perishes, she must have on her last garment, and this will survive her; and then at length, when the soul is dead, the body will show its native weakness, and quickly decompose and pass away. I would therefore rather not rely on the argument from superior strength to prove the continued existence of the soul after death. For granting even more than you affirm to be possible, and acknowledging not only that the soul existed before birth, but also that the souls of some exist, and will continue to exist after death, and will be born and die again and again, and that there is a natural strength in the soul which will hold out and be born many times—nevertheless, we may be still inclined to think that she will weary in the labours of successive births, and may at last succumb in one of her deaths and utterly perish; and this death and dissolution of the body which brings destruction to the soul may be unknown to any of us, for no one of us can have had any experience of it: and if so, then I maintain that he who is confident about death has but a foolish confidence, unless he is able to prove that the soul is altogether immortal and imperishable. But if he cannot prove the soul's immortality, he who is about to die will always have reason to fear that when the body is disunited, the soul also may utterly perish.

All of us, as we afterwards remarked to one another, had an unpleasant feeling at hearing what they said. When we had been so firmly convinced before, now to have our faith shaken seemed to introduce a confusion and uncertainty, not only into the previous argument, but into any future one; either we were incapable of forming a judgment, or there were no grounds of belief.

ECHECRATES: There I feel with you—by heaven I do, Phaedo, and when you were speaking, I was beginning to ask myself the same question: What argument can I ever trust again? For what could be more convincing than the argument of Socrates, which has now fallen into discredit? That the soul is a harmony is a doctrine which has always had a wonderful attraction for me, and, when mentioned, came back to me at once, as my own original conviction. And now I must begin again and find another argument which will assure me that when the man is dead the soul survives. Tell me, I implore you, how did Socrates proceed? Did he appear to share the unpleasant feeling which you mention? or did he calmly meet the attack? And did he answer forcibly or feebly? Narrate what passed as exactly as you can.

PHAEDO: Often, Echecrates, I have wondered at Socrates, but never more than on that occasion. That he should be able to answer was nothing, but what astonished me was, first, the gentle and pleasant and approving manner in which he received the words of the young men, and then his quick sense of the wound which had been inflicted by the argument, and the readiness with which he healed it. He might be compared to a general rallying his defeated and broken army, urging them to accompany him and return to the field of argument.

ECHECRATES: What followed?

PHAEDO: You shall hear, for I was close to him on his right hand, seated on a sort of stool, and he on a couch which was a good deal higher. He stroked my head, and pressed the hair upon my neck—he had a way of playing with my hair; and then he said: To-morrow, Phaedo, I suppose that these fair locks of yours will be severed.

Yes, Socrates, I suppose that they will, I replied.

Not so, if you will take my advice.

What shall I do with them? I said.

To-day, he replied, and not to-morrow, if this argument dies and we cannot bring it to life again, you and I will both shave our locks; and if I were you, and the argument got away from me, and I could not hold my ground against Simmias and Cebes, I would myself take an oath, like the Argives, not to wear hair any more until I had renewed the conflict and defeated them.

Yes, I said, but Heracles himself is said not to be a match for two.

Summon me then, he said, and I will be your Iolaus until the sun goes down.

I summon you rather, I rejoined, not as Heracles summoning Iolaus, but as Iolaus might summon Heracles.

That will do as well, he said. But first let us take care that we avoid a danger.

Of what nature? I said.

Lest we become misologists, he replied, no worse thing can happen to a man than this. For as there are misanthropists or haters of men, there are also misologists or haters of ideas, and both spring from the same cause, which is ignorance of the world. Misanthropy arises out of the too great confidence of inexperience;—you trust a man and think him altogether true and sound and faithful, and then in a little while he turns out to be false and knavish; and then another and another, and when this has happened several times to a man, especially when it happens among those whom he deems to be his own most trusted and familiar friends, and he has often quarreled with them, he at last hates all men, and believes that no one has any good in him at all. You must have observed this trait of character?

I have.

And is not the feeling discreditable? Is it not obvious that such an one having to deal with other men, was clearly without any experience of human nature; for experience would have taught him the true state of the case, that few are the good and few the evil, and that the great majority are in the interval between them.

What do you mean? I said.

I mean, he replied, as you might say of the very large and very small, that nothing is more uncommon than a very large or very small man; and this applies generally to all extremes, whether of great and small, or swift and slow, or fair and foul, or black and white: and whether the instances you select be men or dogs or anything else, few are the extremes, but many are in the mean between them. Did you never observe this?

Yes, I said, I have.

And do you not imagine, he said, that if there were a competition in evil, the worst would be found to be very few?

Yes, that is very likely, I said.

Yes, that is very likely, he replied; although in this respect arguments are unlike men—there I was led on by you to say more than I had intended; but the point of comparison was, that when a simple man who has no skill in dialectics believes an argument to be true which he afterwards imagines to be false, whether really false or not, and then another and another, he has no longer any faith left, and great disputers, as you know, come to think at last that they have grown to be the wisest of mankind; for they alone perceive the utter unsoundness and instability of all arguments, or indeed, of all things, which, like the currents in the Euripus, are going up and down in never-ceasing ebb and flow.

That is quite true, I said.

Yes, Phaedo, he replied, and how melancholy, if there be such a thing as truth or certainty or possibility of knowledge—that a man should have lighted upon some argument or other which at first seemed true and then turned out to be false, and instead of blaming himself and his own want of wit, because he is annoyed, should at last be too glad to transfer the blame from himself to arguments in general: and for ever afterwards should hate and revile them, and lose truth and the knowledge of realities.

Yes, indeed, I said; that is very melancholy.

Let us then, in the first place, he said, be careful of allowing or of admitting into our souls the notion that there is no health or soundness in any arguments at all. Rather say that we have not yet attained to soundness in ourselves, and that we must struggle manfully and do our best to gain health of mind—you and all other men having regard to the whole of your future life, and I myself in the prospect of death. For at this moment I am sensible that I have not the temper of a philosopher; like the vulgar, I am only a partisan. Now the partisan, when he is engaged in a dispute, cares nothing about the rights of the question, but is anxious only to convince his hearers of his own assertions. And the difference between him and me at the present moment is merely this— that whereas he seeks to convince his hearers that what he says is true, I am rather seeking to convince myself; to convince my hearers is a secondary matter with me. And do but see how much I gain by the argument. For if what I say is true, then I do well to be persuaded of the truth, but if there be nothing after death, still, during the short time that remains, I shall not distress my friends with lamentations, and my ignorance will not last, but will die with me, and therefore no harm will be done. This is the state of mind, Simmias and Cebes, in which I approach the argument. And I would ask you to be thinking of the truth and not of Socrates: agree with me, if I seem to you to be speaking the truth; or if not, withstand me might and main, that I may not deceive you as well as myself in my enthusiasm, and like the bee, leave my sting in you before I die.

And now let us proceed, he said. And first of all let me be sure that I have in my mind what you were saying. Simmias, if I remember rightly, has fears and misgivings whether the soul, although a fairer and diviner thing than the body, being as she is in the form of harmony, may not perish first. On the other hand, Cebes appeared to grant that the soul was more lasting than the body, but he said that no one could know whether the soul, after having worn out many bodies, might not perish herself and leave her last body behind her; and that this is death, which is the destruction not of the body but of the soul, for in the body the work of destruction is ever going on. Are not these, Simmias and Cebes, the points which we have to consider?

They both agreed to this statement of them.

He proceeded: And did you deny the force of the whole preceding argument, or of a part only?

Of a part only, they replied.

And what did you think, he said, of that part of the argument in which we said that knowledge was recollection, and hence inferred that the soul must have previously existed somewhere else before she was enclosed in the body?

Cebes said that he had been wonderfully impressed by that part of the argument, and that his conviction remained absolutely unshaken. Simmias agreed, and added that he himself could hardly imagine the possibility of his ever thinking differently.

But, rejoined Socrates, you will have to think differently, my Theban friend, if you still maintain that harmony is a compound, and that the soul is a harmony which is made out of strings set in the frame of the body; for you will surely never allow yourself to say that a harmony is prior to the elements which compose it.

Never, Socrates.

But do you not see that this is what you imply when you say that the soul existed before she took the form and body of man, and was made up of elements which as yet had no existence? For harmony is not like the soul, as you suppose; but first the lyre, and the strings, and the sounds exist in a state of discord, and then harmony is made last of all, and perishes first. And how can such a notion of the soul as this agree with the other?

Not at all, replied Simmias.

And yet, he said, there surely ought to be harmony in a discourse of which harmony is the theme.

There ought, replied Simmias.

But there is no harmony, he said, in the two propositions that knowledge is recollection, and that the soul is a harmony. Which of them will you retain?

I think, he replied, that I have a much stronger faith, Socrates, in the first of the two, which has been fully demonstrated to me, than in the latter, which has not been demonstrated at all, but rests only on probable and plausible grounds; and is therefore believed by the many. I know too well that these arguments from probabilities are impostors, and unless great caution is observed in the use of them, they are apt to be deceptive—in geometry, and in other things too. But the doctrine of knowledge and recollection has been proven to me on trustworthy grounds; and the proof was that the soul must have existed before she came into the body, because to her belongs the essence of which the very name implies existence. Having, as I am convinced, rightly accepted this conclusion, and on sufficient grounds, I must, as I suppose, cease to argue or allow others to argue that the soul is a harmony.

Let me put the matter, Simmias, he said, in another point of view: Do you imagine that a harmony or any other composition can be in a state other than that of the elements, out of which it is compounded?

Certainly not.

Or do or suffer anything other than they do or suffer?

He agreed.

Then a harmony does not, properly speaking, lead the parts or elements which make up the harmony, but only follows them.

He assented.

For harmony cannot possibly have any motion, or sound, or other quality which is opposed to its parts.

That would be impossible, he replied.

And does not the nature of every harmony depend upon the

manner in which the elements are harmonized?

I do not understand you, he said.

I mean to say that a harmony admits of degrees, and is more of a harmony, and more completely a harmony, when more truly and fully harmonized, to any extent which is possible; and less of a harmony, and less completely a harmony, when less truly and fully harmonized.

True.

But does the soul admit of degrees? or is one soul in the very least degree more or less, or more or less completely, a soul than another?

Not in the least.

Yet surely of two souls, one is said to have intelligence and virtue, and to be good, and the other to have folly and vice, and to be an evil soul: and this is said truly?

Yes, truly.

But what will those who maintain the soul to be a harmony say of this presence of virtue and vice in the soul?—will they say that here is another harmony, and another discord, and that the virtuous soul is harmonized, and herself being a harmony has another harmony within her, and that the vicious soul is inharmonical and has no harmony within her?

I cannot tell, replied Simmias; but I suppose that something of the sort would be asserted by those who say that the soul is a harmony.

And we have already admitted that no soul is more a soul than another; which is equivalent to admitting that harmony is not more or less harmony, or more or less completely a harmony?

Quite true.

And that which is not more or less a harmony is not more or less harmonized?

True.

And that which is not more or less harmonized cannot have more or less of harmony, but only an equal harmony?

Yes, an equal harmony.

Then one soul not being more or less absolutely a soul than another, is not more or less harmonized?

Exactly.

And therefore has neither more nor less of discord, nor yet of harmony?

She has not.

And having neither more nor less of harmony or of discord, one soul has no more vice or virtue than another, if vice be discord and virtue harmony?

Not at all more.

Or speaking more correctly, Simmias, the soul, if she is a harmony, will never have any vice; because a harmony, being absolutely a harmony, has no part in the inharmonical.

No.

And therefore a soul which is absolutely a soul has no vice?

How can she have, if the previous argument holds?

Then, if all souls are equally by their nature souls, all souls of all living creatures will be equally good?

I agree with you, Socrates, he said.

And can all this be true, think you? he said; for these are the consequences which seem to follow from the assumption that the soul is a harmony?

It cannot be true.

Once more, he said, what ruler is there of the elements of human nature other than the soul, and especially the wise soul? Do you know of any?

Indeed, I do not.

And is the soul in agreement with the affections of the body? or is she at variance with them? For example, when the body is hot and thirsty, does not the soul incline us against drinking? and when the body is hungry, against eating? And this is only one instance out of ten thousand of the opposition of the soul to the things of the body.

Very true.

But we have already acknowledged that the soul, being a harmony, can never utter a note at variance with the tensions and relaxations and vibrations and other affections of the strings out of which she is composed; she can only follow, she cannot lead them?

It must be so, he replied.

And yet do we not now discover the soul to be doing the exact opposite—leading the elements of which she is believed to be composed; almost always opposing and coercing them in all sorts of ways throughout life, sometimes more violently with the pains of medicine and gymnastic; then again more gently; now threatening, now admonishing the desires, passions, fears, as if talking to a thing which is not herself, as Homer in the Odyssey represents Odysseus doing in the words—

'He beat his breast, and thus reproached his heart:
Endure, my heart; far worse hast thou endured!'

Do you think that Homer wrote this under the idea that the soul is a harmony capable of being led by the affections of the body, and not rather of a nature which should lead and master them—herself a far diviner thing than any harmony?

Yes, Socrates, I quite think so.

Then, my friend, we can never be right in saying that the soul is a harmony, for we should contradict the divine Homer, and contradict ourselves.

True, he said.

Thus much, said Socrates, of Harmonia, your Theban goddess, who has graciously yielded to us; but what shall I say, Cebes, to her husband Cadmus, and how shall I make peace with him?

I think that you will discover a way of propitiating him, said Cebes; I am sure that you have put the argument with Harmonia in a manner that I could never have expected. For when Simmias was mentioning his difficulty, I quite imagined that no answer could be given to him, and therefore I was surprised at finding that his argument could not sustain the first onset of yours, and not impossibly the other, whom you call Cadmus, may share a similar fate.

Nay, my good friend, said Socrates, let us not boast, lest some evil eye should put to flight the word which I am about to speak. That, however, may be left in the hands of those above, while I draw near in Homeric fashion, and try the mettle of your words. Here lies the point:—You want to have it proven to you that the soul is imperishable and immortal, and the philosopher who is confident in death appears to you to have but a vain and foolish confidence, if he believes that he will fare better in the world below than one who has led another sort of life, unless he can prove this; and you say that the demonstration of the strength and divinity of the soul, and of her existence prior to our becoming men, does not necessarily imply her immortality. Admitting the soul to be long-lived, and to have known and done much in a former state, still she is not on that account immortal; and her entrance into the human form may be a sort of disease which is the beginning of dissolution, and may at last, after the toils of life are over, end in that which is called death. And whether the soul enters into the body once only or many times, does not, as you say, make any difference in the fears of individuals. For any man, who is not devoid of sense, must fear, if he has no knowledge and can give no account of the soul's immortality. This, or something like this, I suspect to be your notion, Cebes; and I designedly recur to it in order that nothing may escape us, and that you may, if you wish, add or subtract anything.

But, said Cebes, as far as I see at present, I have nothing to add or subtract: I mean what you say that I mean.

Socrates paused awhile, and seemed to be absorbed in reflection. At length he said: You are raising a tremendous question, Cebes, involving the whole nature of generation and corruption, about which, if you like, I will give you my own experience; and if anything which I say is likely to avail towards the solution of your difficulty you may make use of it.

I should very much like, said Cebes, to hear what you have to say.

Then I will tell you, said Socrates. When I was young, Cebes, I had a prodigious desire to know that department of philosophy which is called the investigation of nature; to know the causes of things, and why a thing is and is created or destroyed appeared to me to be a lofty profession; and I was always agitating myself with the consideration of questions such as these:—Is the growth of animals the result of some decay which the hot and cold principle contracts, as some have said? Is the blood the element with which we think, or the air, or the fire? or perhaps nothing of the kind—but the brain may be the originating power of the perceptions of hearing and sight and smell, and memory and opinion may come from them, and science may be based on memory and opinion when they have attained fixity. And then I went on to examine the corruption of them, and then to the things of heaven and earth, and at last I concluded myself to be utterly and absolutely incapable of these enquiries, as I will satisfactorily prove to you. For I was fascinated by them to such a degree that my eyes grew blind to things which I had seemed to myself, and also to others, to know quite well; I forgot what I had before thought self-evident truths; e.g. such a fact as that the growth of man is the result of eating and drinking; for when by the digestion of food flesh is added to flesh and bone to bone, and whenever there is an aggregation of congenial elements, the lesser bulk becomes larger and the small man great. Was not that a reasonable notion?

Yes, said Cebes, I think so.

Well; but let me tell you something more. There was a time when I thought that I understood the meaning of greater and less pretty well; and when I saw a great man standing by a little one, I fancied that one was taller than the other by a head; or one horse would appear to be greater than another horse: and still more clearly did I seem to perceive that ten is two more than eight, and that two cubits are more than one, because two is the double of one.

And what is now your notion of such matters? said Cebes.

I should be far enough from imagining, he replied, that I knew the cause of any of them, by heaven I should; for I cannot satisfy myself that, when one is added to one, the one to which the addition is made becomes two, or that the two units added together make two by reason of the addition. I cannot understand how, when separated from the other, each of them was one and not two, and now, when they are brought together, the mere juxtaposition or meeting of them should be the cause of their becoming two: neither can I understand how the division of one is the way to make two; for then a different cause would produce the same effect,—as in the former instance the addition and juxtaposition of one to one was the cause of two, in this the separation and subtraction of one from the other would be the cause. Nor am I any longer satisfied that I understand the reason why one or anything else is either generated or destroyed or is at all, but I have in my mind some confused notion of a new method, and can never admit the other.

Then I heard some one reading, as he said, from a book of

Anaxagoras, that mind was the disposer and cause of all, and I was delighted at this notion, which appeared quite admirable, and I said to myself: If mind is the disposer, mind will dispose all for the best, and put each particular in the best place; and I argued that if any one desired to find out the cause of the generation or destruction or existence of anything, he must find out what state of being or doing or suffering was best for that thing, and therefore a man had only to consider the best for himself and others, and then he would also know the worse, since the same science comprehended both. And I rejoiced to think that I had found in Anaxagoras a teacher of the causes of existence such as I desired, and I imagined that he would tell me first whether the earth is flat or round; and whichever was true, he would proceed to explain the cause and the necessity of this being so, and then he would teach me the nature of the best and show that this was best; and if he said that the earth was in the centre, he would further explain that this position was the best, and I should be satisfied with the explanation given, and not want any other sort of cause. And I thought that I would then go on and ask him about the sun and moon and stars, and that he would explain to me their comparative swiftness, and their returnings and various states, active and passive, and how all of them were for the best. For I could not imagine that when he spoke of mind as the disposer of them, he would give any other account of their being as they are, except that this was best; and I thought that when he had explained to me in detail the cause of each and the cause of all, he would go on to explain to me what was best for each and what was good for all. These hopes I would not have sold for a large sum of money, and I seized the books and read them as fast as I could in my eagerness to know the better and the worse.

What expectations I had formed, and how grievously was I disappointed! As I proceeded, I found my philosopher altogether forsaking mind or any other principle of order, but having recourse to air, and ether, and water, and other eccentricities. I might compare him to a person who began by maintaining generally that mind is the cause of the actions of Socrates, but who, when he endeavoured to explain the causes of my several actions in detail, went on to show that I sit here because my body is made up of bones and muscles; and the bones, as he would say, are hard and have joints which divide them, and the muscles are elastic, and they cover the bones, which have also a covering or environment of flesh and skin which contains them; and as the bones are lifted at their joints by the contraction or relaxation of the muscles, I am able to bend my limbs, and this is why I am sitting here in a curved posture—that is what he would say, and he would have a similar explanation of my talking to you, which he would attribute to sound, and air, and hearing, and he would assign ten thousand other causes of the same sort, forgetting to mention the true cause, which is, that the Athenians have thought fit to condemn me, and accordingly I have thought it better and more right to remain here and undergo my sentence; for I am inclined to think that these muscles and bones of mine would have gone off long ago to Megara or Boeotia—by the dog they would, if they had been moved only by their own idea of what was best, and if I had not chosen the better and nobler part, instead of playing truant and running away, of enduring any punishment which the state inflicts. There is surely a strange confusion of causes and conditions in all this. It may be said, indeed, that without bones and muscles and the other parts of the body I cannot execute my purposes. But to say that I do as I do because of them, and that this is the way in which mind acts, and not from the choice of the best, is a very careless and idle mode of speaking. I wonder that they cannot distinguish the cause from the condition, which the many, feeling about in the dark, are always mistaking and misnaming. And thus one man makes a vortex all round and steadies the earth by the heaven; another gives the air as a support to the earth, which is a sort of broad trough. Any power which in arranging them as they are arranges them for the best never enters into their minds; and instead of finding any superior strength in it, they rather expect to discover another Atlas of the world who is stronger and more everlasting and more containing than the good;—of the obligatory and containing power of the good they think nothing; and yet this is the principle which I would fain learn if any one would teach me. But as I have failed either to discover myself, or to learn of any one else, the nature of the best, I will exhibit to you, if you like, what I have found to be the second best mode of enquiring into the cause.

I should very much like to hear, he replied.

Socrates proceeded:—I thought that as I had failed in the contemplation of true existence, I ought to be careful that I did not lose the eye of my soul; as people may injure their bodily eye by observing and gazing on the sun during an eclipse, unless they take the precaution of only looking at the image reflected in the water, or in some similar medium. So in my own case, I was afraid that my soul might be blinded altogether if I looked at things with my eyes or tried to apprehend them by the help of the senses. And I thought that I had better have recourse to the world of mind and seek there the truth of existence. I dare say that the simile is not perfect—for I am very far from admitting that he who contemplates existences through the medium of thought, sees them only 'through a glass darkly,' any more than he who considers them in action and operation. However, this was the method which I adopted: I first assumed some principle which I judged to be the strongest, and then I affirmed as true whatever seemed to agree with this, whether relating to the cause or to anything else; and that which disagreed I regarded as untrue. But I should like to explain my meaning more clearly, as I do not think that you as yet understand me.

No indeed, replied Cebes, not very well.

There is nothing new, he said, in what I am about to tell you; but only what I have been always and everywhere repeating in the previous discussion and on other occasions: I want to show you the nature of that cause which has occupied my thoughts. I shall have to go back to those familiar words which are in the mouth of every one, and first of all assume that there is an absolute beauty and goodness and greatness, and the like; grant me this, and I hope to be able to show you the nature of the cause, and to prove the immortality of the soul.

Cebes said: You may proceed at once with the proof, for I grant you this.

Well, he said, then I should like to know whether you agree with me in the next step; for I cannot help thinking, if there be anything beautiful other than absolute beauty should there be such, that it can be beautiful only in as far as it partakes of absolute beauty—and I should say the same of everything. Do you agree in this notion of the cause?

Yes, he said, I agree.

He proceeded: I know nothing and can understand nothing of any other of those wise causes which are alleged; and if a person says to me that the bloom of colour, or form, or any such thing is a source of beauty, I leave all that, which is only confusing to me, and simply and singly, and perhaps foolishly, hold and am assured in my own mind that nothing makes a thing beautiful but the presence and participation of beauty in whatever way or manner obtained; for as to the manner I am uncertain, but I stoutly contend that by beauty all beautiful things become beautiful. This appears to me to be the safest answer which I can give, either to myself or to another, and to this I cling, in the persuasion that this principle will never be overthrown, and that to myself or to any one who asks the question, I may safely reply, That by beauty beautiful things become beautiful. Do you not agree with me?

I do.

And that by greatness only great things become great and greater greater, and by smallness the less become less?

True.

Then if a person were to remark that A is taller by a head than B, and B less by a head than A, you would refuse to admit his statement, and would stoutly contend that what you mean is only that the greater is greater by, and by reason of, greatness, and the less is less only by, and by reason of, smallness; and thus you would avoid the danger of saying that the greater is greater and the less less by the measure of the head, which is the same in both, and would also avoid the monstrous absurdity of supposing that the greater man is greater by reason of the head, which is small. You would be afraid to draw such an inference, would you not?

Indeed, I should, said Cebes, laughing.

In like manner you would be afraid to say that ten exceeded eight by, and by reason of, two; but would say by, and by reason of, number; or you would say that two cubits exceed one cubit not by a half, but by magnitude?-for there is the same liability to error in all these cases.

Very true, he said.

Again, would you not be cautious of affirming that the addition of one to one, or the division of one, is the cause of two? And you would loudly asseverate that you know of no way in which anything comes into existence except by participation in its own proper essence, and consequently, as far as you know, the only cause of two is the participation in duality—this is the way to make two, and the participation in one is the way to make one. You would say: I will let alone puzzles of division and addition—wiser heads than mine may answer them; inexperienced as I am, and ready to start, as the proverb says, at my own shadow, I cannot afford to give up the sure ground of a principle. And if any one assails you there, you would not mind him, or answer him, until you had seen whether the consequences which follow agree with one another or not, and when you are further required to give an explanation of this principle, you would go on to assume a higher principle, and a higher, until you found a resting-place in the best of the higher; but you would not confuse the principle and the consequences in your reasoning, like the Eristics—at least if you wanted to discover real existence. Not that this confusion signifies to them, who never care or think about the matter at all, for they have the wit to be well pleased with themselves however great may be the turmoil of their ideas. But you, if you are a philosopher, will certainly do as I say.

What you say is most true, said Simmias and Cebes, both speaking at once.

ECHECRATES: Yes, Phaedo; and I do not wonder at their assenting. Any one who has the least sense will acknowledge the wonderful clearness of Socrates' reasoning.

PHAEDO: Certainly, Echecrates; and such was the feeling of the whole company at the time.

ECHECRATES: Yes, and equally of ourselves, who were not of the company, and are now listening to your recital. But what followed?

PHAEDO: After all this had been admitted, and they had that ideas exist, and that other things participate in them and derive their names from them, Socrates, if I remember rightly, said:—

This is your way of speaking; and yet when you say that Simmias is greater than Socrates and less than Phaedo, do you not predicate of Simmias both greatness and smallness?

Yes, I do.

But still you allow that Simmias does not really exceed Socrates, as the words may seem to imply, because he is Simmias, but by reason of the size which he has; just as Simmias does not exceed Socrates because he is Simmias, any more than because Socrates is Socrates, but because he has smallness when compared with the greatness of Simmias?

True.

And if Phaedo exceeds him in size, this is not because Phaedo is Phaedo, but because Phaedo has greatness relatively to Simmias, who is comparatively smaller?

That is true.

And therefore Simmias is said to be great, and is also said to be small, because he is in a mean between them, exceeding the smallness of the one by his greatness, and allowing the greatness of the other to exceed his smallness. He added, laughing, I am speaking like a book, but I believe that what I am saying is true.

Simmias assented.

I speak as I do because I want you to agree with me in thinking, not only that absolute greatness will never be great and also small, but that greatness in us or in the concrete will never admit the small or admit of being exceeded: instead of this, one of two things will happen, either the greater will fly or retire before the opposite, which is the less, or at the approach of the less has already ceased to exist; but will not, if allowing or admitting of smallness, be changed by that; even as I, having received and admitted smallness when compared with Simmias, remain just as I was, and am the same small person. And as the idea of greatness cannot condescend ever to be or become small, in like manner the smallness in us cannot be or become great; nor can any other opposite which remains the same ever be or become its own opposite, but either passes away or perishes in the change.

That, replied Cebes, is quite my notion.

Hereupon one of the company, though I do not exactly remember which of them, said: In heaven's name, is not this the direct contrary of what was admitted before—that out of the greater came the less and out of the less the greater, and that opposites were simply generated from opposites; but now this principle seems to be utterly denied.

Socrates inclined his head to the speaker and listened. I like your courage, he said, in reminding us of this. But you do not observe that there is a difference in the two cases. For then we were speaking of opposites in the concrete, and now of the essential opposite which, as is affirmed, neither in us nor in nature can ever be at variance with itself: then, my friend, we were speaking of things in which opposites are inherent and which are called after them, but now about the opposites which are inherent in them and which give their name to them; and these essential opposites will never, as we maintain, admit of generation into or out of one another. At the same time, turning to Cebes, he said: Are you at all disconcerted, Cebes, at our friend's objection?

No, I do not feel so, said Cebes; and yet I cannot deny that I am often disturbed by objections.

Then we are agreed after all, said Socrates, that the opposite will never in any case be opposed to itself?

To that we are quite agreed, he replied.

Yet once more let me ask you to consider the question from another point of view, and see whether you agree with me:—There is a thing which you term heat, and another thing which you term cold?

Certainly.

But are they the same as fire and snow?

Most assuredly not.

Heat is a thing different from fire, and cold is not the same with snow?

Yes.

And yet you will surely admit, that when snow, as was before said, is under the influence of heat, they will not remain snow and heat; but at the advance of the heat, the snow will either retire or perish?

Very true, he replied.

And the fire too at the advance of the cold will either retire or perish; and when the fire is under the influence of the cold, they will not remain as before, fire and cold.

That is true, he said.

And in some cases the name of the idea is not only attached to the idea in an eternal connection, but anything else which, not being the idea, exists only in the form of the idea, may also lay claim to it. I will try to make this clearer by an example:—The odd number is always called by the name of odd?

Very true.

But is this the only thing which is called odd? Are there not other things which have their own name, and yet are called odd, because, although not the same as oddness, they are never without oddness?— that is what I mean to ask—whether numbers such as the number three are not of the class of odd. And there are many other examples: would you not say, for example, that three may be called by its proper name, and also be called odd, which is not the same with three? and this may be said not only of three but also of five, and of every alternate number—each of them without being oddness is odd, and in the same way two and four, and the other series of alternate numbers, has every number even, without being evenness. Do you agree?

Of course.

Then now mark the point at which I am aiming:—not only do essential opposites exclude one another, but also concrete things, which, although not in themselves opposed, contain opposites; these, I say, likewise reject the idea which is opposed to that which is contained in them, and when it approaches them they either perish or withdraw. For example; Will not the number three endure annihilation or anything sooner than be converted into an even number, while remaining three?

Very true, said Cebes.

And yet, he said, the number two is certainly not opposed to the number three?

It is not.

Then not only do opposite ideas repel the advance of one another, but also there are other natures which repel the approach of opposites.

Very true, he said.

Suppose, he said, that we endeavour, if possible, to determine what these are.

By all means.

Are they not, Cebes, such as compel the things of which they have possession, not only to take their own form, but also the form of some opposite?

What do you mean?

I mean, as I was just now saying, and as I am sure that you know, that those things which are possessed by the number three must not only be three in number, but must also be odd.

Quite true.

And on this oddness, of which the number three has the impress, the opposite idea will never intrude?

No.

And this impress was given by the odd principle?

Yes.

And to the odd is opposed the even?

True.

Then the idea of the even number will never arrive at three?

No.

Then three has no part in the even?

None.

Then the triad or number three is uneven?

Very true.

To return then to my distinction of natures which are not opposed, and yet do not admit opposites—as, in the instance given, three, although not opposed to the even, does not any the more admit of the even, but always brings the opposite into play on the other side; or as two does not receive the odd, or fire the cold—from these examples (and there are many more of them) perhaps you may be able to arrive at the general conclusion, that not only opposites will not receive opposites, but also that nothing which brings the opposite will admit the opposite of that which it brings, in that to which it is brought. And here let me recapitulate—for there is no harm in repetition. The number five will not admit the nature of the even, any more than ten, which is the double of five, will admit the nature of the odd. The double has another opposite, and is not strictly opposed to the odd, but nevertheless rejects the odd altogether. Nor again will parts in the ratio 3:2, nor any fraction in which there is a half, nor again in which there is a third, admit the notion of the whole, although they are not opposed to the whole: You will agree?

Yes, he said, I entirely agree and go along with you in that.

And now, he said, let us begin again; and do not you answer my question in the words in which I ask it: let me have not the old safe answer of which I spoke at first, but another equally safe, of which the truth will be inferred by you from what has been just said. I mean that if any one asks you 'what that is, of which the inherence makes the body hot,' you will reply not heat (this is what I call the safe and stupid answer), but fire, a far superior answer, which we are now in a condition to give. Or if any one asks you 'why a body is diseased,' you will not say from disease, but from fever; and instead of saying that oddness is the cause of odd numbers, you will say that the monad is the cause of them: and so of things in general, as I dare say that you will understand sufficiently without my adducing any further examples.

Yes, he said, I quite understand you.

Tell me, then, what is that of which the inherence will render the body alive?

The soul, he replied.

And is this always the case?

Yes, he said, of course.

Then whatever the soul possesses, to that she comes bearing life?

Yes, certainly.

And is there any opposite to life?

There is, he said.

And what is that?

Death.

Then the soul, as has been acknowledged, will never receive the opposite of what she brings.

Impossible, replied Cebes.

And now, he said, what did we just now call that principle which repels the even?

The odd.

And that principle which repels the musical, or the just?

The unmusical, he said, and the unjust.

And what do we call the principle which does not admit of death?

The immortal, he said.

And does the soul admit of death?

No.

Then the soul is immortal?

Yes, he said.

And may we say that this has been proven?

Yes, abundantly proven, Socrates, he replied.

Supposing that the odd were imperishable, must not three be imperishable?

Of course.

And if that which is cold were imperishable, when the warm principle came attacking the snow, must not the snow have retired whole and unmelted—for it could never have perished, nor could it have remained and admitted the heat?

True, he said.

Again, if the uncooling or warm principle were imperishable, the fire when assailed by cold would not have perished or have been extinguished, but would have gone away unaffected?

Certainly, he said.

And the same may be said of the immortal: if the immortal is also imperishable, the soul when attacked by death cannot perish; for the preceding argument shows that the soul will not admit of death, or ever be dead, any more than three or the odd number will admit of the even, or fire or the heat in the fire, of the cold. Yet a person may say: 'But although the odd will not become even at the approach of the even, why may not the odd perish and the even take the place of the odd?' Now to him who makes this objection, we cannot answer that the odd principle is imperishable; for this has not been acknowledged, but if this had been acknowledged, there would have been no difficulty in contending that at the approach of the even the odd principle and the number three took their departure; and the same argument would have held good of fire and heat and any other thing.

Very true.

And the same may be said of the immortal: if the immortal is also imperishable, then the soul will be imperishable as well as immortal; but if not, some other proof of her imperishableness will have to be given.

No other proof is needed, he said; for if the immortal, being eternal, is liable to perish, then nothing is imperishable.

Yes, replied Socrates, and yet all men will agree that God, and the essential form of life, and the immortal in general, will never perish.

Yes, all men, he said—that is true; and what is more, gods, if I am not mistaken, as well as men.

Seeing then that the immortal is indestructible, must not the soul, if she is immortal, be also imperishable?

Most certainly.

Then when death attacks a man, the mortal portion of him may be supposed to die, but the immortal retires at the approach of death and is preserved safe and sound?

True.

Then, Cebes, beyond question, the soul is immortal and imperishable, and our souls will truly exist in another world!

I am convinced, Socrates, said Cebes, and have nothing more to object; but if my friend Simmias, or any one else, has any further objection to make, he had better speak out, and not keep silence, since I do not know to what other season he can defer the discussion, if there is anything which he wants to say or to have said.

But I have nothing more to say, replied Simmias; nor can I see any reason for doubt after what has been said. But I still feel and cannot help feeling uncertain in my own mind, when I think of the greatness of the subject and the feebleness of man.

Yes, Simmias, replied Socrates, that is well said: and I may add that first principles, even if they appear certain, should be carefully considered; and when they are satisfactorily ascertained, then, with a sort of hesitating confidence in human reason, you may, I think, follow the course of the argument; and if that be plain and clear, there will be no need for any further enquiry.

Very true.

But then, O my friends, he said, if the soul is really immortal, what care should be taken of her, not only in respect of the portion of time which is called life, but of eternity! And the danger of neglecting her from this point of view does indeed appear to be awful. If death had only been the end of all, the wicked would have had a good bargain in dying, for they would have been happily quit not only of their body, but of their own evil together with their souls. But now, inasmuch as the soul is manifestly immortal, there is no release or salvation from evil except the attainment of the highest virtue and wisdom. For the soul when on her progress to the world below takes nothing with her but nurture and education; and these are said greatly to benefit or greatly to injure the departed, at the very beginning of his journey thither.

For after death, as they say, the genius of each individual, to whom he belonged in life, leads him to a certain place in which the dead are gathered together, whence after judgment has been given they pass into the world below, following the guide, who is appointed to conduct them from this world to the other: and when they have there received their due and remained their time, another guide brings them back again after many revolutions of ages. Now this way to the other world is not, as Aeschylus says in the Telephus, a single and straight path—if that were so no guide would be needed, for no one could miss it; but there are many partings of the road, and windings, as I infer from the rites and sacrifices which are offered to the gods below in places where three ways meet on earth. The wise and orderly soul follows in the straight path and is conscious of her surroundings; but the soul which desires the body, and which, as I was relating before, has long been fluttering about the lifeless frame and the world of sight, is after many struggles and many sufferings hardly and with violence carried away by her attendant genius, and when she arrives at the place where the other souls are gathered, if she be impure and have done impure deeds, whether foul murders or other crimes which are the brothers of these, and the works of brothers in crime—from that soul every one flees and turns away; no one will be her companion, no one her guide, but alone she wanders in extremity of evil until certain times are fulfilled, and when they are fulfilled, she is borne irresistibly to her own fitting habitation; as every pure and just soul which has passed through life in the company and under the guidance of the gods has also her own proper home.

Now the earth has divers wonderful regions, and is indeed in nature and extent very unlike the notions of geographers, as I believe on the authority of one who shall be nameless.

What do you mean, Socrates? said Simmias. I have myself heard many descriptions of the earth, but I do not know, and I should very much like to know, in which of these you put faith.

And I, Simmias, replied Socrates, if I had the art of Glaucus would tell you; although I know not that the art of Glaucus could prove the truth of my tale, which I myself should never be able to prove, and even if I could, I fear, Simmias, that my life would come to an end before the argument was completed. I may describe to you, however, the form and regions of the earth according to my conception of them.

That, said Simmias, will be enough.

Well, then, he said, my conviction is, that the earth is a round body in the centre of the heavens, and therefore has no need of air or any similar force to be a support, but is kept there and hindered from falling or inclining any way by the equability of the surrounding heaven and by her own equipoise. For that which, being in equipoise, is in the centre of that which is equably diffused, will not incline any way in any degree, but will always remain in the same state and not deviate. And this is my first notion.

Which is surely a correct one, said Simmias.

Also I believe that the earth is very vast, and that we who dwell in the region extending from the river Phasis to the Pillars of Heracles inhabit a small portion only about the sea, like ants or frogs about a marsh, and that there are other inhabitants of many other like places; for everywhere on the face of the earth there are hollows of various forms and sizes, into which the water and the mist and the lower air collect. But the true earth is pure and situated in the pure heaven—there are the stars also; and it is the heaven which is commonly spoken of by us as the ether, and of which our own earth is the sediment gathering in the hollows beneath. But we who live in these hollows are deceived into the notion that we are dwelling above on the surface of the earth; which is just as if a creature who was at the bottom of the sea were to fancy that he was on the surface of the water, and that the sea was the heaven through which he saw the sun and the other stars, he having never come to the surface by reason of his feebleness and sluggishness, and having never lifted up his head and seen, nor ever heard from one who had seen, how much purer and fairer the world above is than his own. And such is exactly our case: for we are dwelling in a hollow of the earth, and fancy that we are on the surface; and the air we call the heaven, in which we imagine that the stars move. But the fact is, that owing to our feebleness and sluggishness we are prevented from reaching the surface of the air: for if any man could arrive at the exterior limit, or take the wings of a bird and come to the top, then like a fish who puts his head out of the water and sees this world, he would see a world beyond; and, if the nature of man could sustain the sight, he would acknowledge that this other world was the place of the true heaven and the true light and the true earth. For our earth, and the stones, and the entire region which surrounds us, are spoilt and corroded, as in the sea all things are corroded by the brine, neither is there any noble or perfect growth, but caverns only, and sand, and an endless slough of mud: and even the shore is not to be compared to the fairer sights of this world. And still less is this our world to be compared with the other. Of that upper earth which is under the heaven, I can tell you a charming tale, Simmias, which is well worth hearing.

And we, Socrates, replied Simmias, shall be charmed to listen to you.

The tale, my friend, he said, is as follows:—In the first place, the earth, when looked at from above, is in appearance streaked like one of those balls which have leather coverings in twelve pieces, and is decked with various colours, of which the colours used by painters on earth are in a manner samples. But there the whole earth is made up of them, and they are brighter far and clearer than ours; there is a purple of wonderful lustre, also the radiance of gold, and the white which is in the earth is whiter than any chalk or snow. Of these and other colours the earth is made up, and they are more in number and fairer than the eye of man has ever seen; the very hollows (of which I was speaking) filled with air and water have a colour of their own, and are seen like light gleaming amid the diversity of the other colours, so that the whole presents a single and continuous appearance of variety in unity. And in this fair region everything that grows—trees, and flowers, and fruits— are in a like degree fairer than any here; and there are hills, having stones in them in a like degree smoother, and more transparent, and fairer in colour than our highly-valued emeralds and sardonyxes and jaspers, and other gems, which are but minute fragments of them: for there all the stones are like our precious stones, and fairer still (compare Republic). The reason is, that they are pure, and not, like our precious stones, infected or corroded by the corrupt briny elements which coagulate among us, and which breed foulness and disease both in earth and stones, as well as in animals and plants. They are the jewels of the upper earth, which also shines with gold and silver and the like, and they are set in the light of day and are large and abundant and in all places, making the earth a sight to gladden the beholder's eye. And there are animals and men, some in a middle region, others dwelling about the air as we dwell about the sea; others in islands which the air flows round, near the continent: and in a word, the air is used by them as the water and the sea are by us, and the ether is to them what the air is to us. Moreover, the temperament of their seasons is such that they have no disease, and live much longer than we do, and have sight and hearing and smell, and all the other senses, in far greater perfection, in the same proportion that air is purer than water or the ether than air. Also they have temples and sacred places in which the gods really dwell, and they hear their voices and receive their answers, and are conscious of them and hold converse with them, and they see the sun, moon, and stars as they truly are, and their other blessedness is of a piece with this.

Such is the nature of the whole earth, and of the things which are around the earth; and there are divers regions in the hollows on the face of the globe everywhere, some of them deeper and more extended than that which we inhabit, others deeper but with a narrower opening than ours, and some are shallower and also wider. All have numerous perforations, and there are passages broad and narrow in the interior of the earth, connecting them with one another; and there flows out of and into them, as into basins, a vast tide of water, and huge subterranean streams of perennial rivers, and springs hot and cold, and a great fire, and great rivers of fire, and streams of liquid mud, thin or thick (like the rivers of mud in Sicily, and the lava streams which follow them), and the regions about which they happen to flow are filled up with them. And there is a swinging or see-saw in the interior of the earth which moves all this up and down, and is due to the following cause:— There is a chasm which is the vastest of them all, and pierces right through the whole earth; this is that chasm which Homer describes in the words,—'Far off, where is the inmost depth beneath the earth;' and which he in other places, and many other poets, have called Tartarus. And the see-saw is caused by the streams flowing into and out of this chasm, and they each have the nature of the soil through which they flow. And the reason why the streams are always flowing in and out, is that the watery element has no bed or bottom, but is swinging and surging up and down, and the surrounding wind and air do the same; they follow the water up and down, hither and thither, over the earth— just as in the act of respiration the air is always in process of inhalation and exhalation;—and the wind swinging with the water in and out produces fearful and irresistible blasts: when the waters retire with a rush into the lower parts of the earth, as they are called, they flow through the earth in those regions, and fill them up like water raised by a pump, and then when they leave those regions and rush back hither, they again fill the hollows here, and when these are filled, flow through subterranean channels and find their way to their several places, forming seas, and lakes, and rivers, and springs. Thence they again enter the earth, some of them making a long circuit into many lands, others going to a few places and not so distant; and again fall into Tartarus, some at a point a good deal lower than that at which they rose, and others not much lower, but all in some degree lower than the point from which they came. And some burst forth again on the opposite side, and some on the same side, and some wind round the earth with one or many folds like the coils of a serpent, and descend as far as they can, but always return and fall into the chasm. The rivers flowing in either direction can descend only to the centre and no further, for opposite to the rivers is a precipice.

Now these rivers are many, and mighty, and diverse, and there are four principal ones, of which the greatest and outermost is that called Oceanus, which flows round the earth in a circle; and in the opposite direction flows Acheron, which passes under the earth through desert places into the Acherusian lake: this is the lake to the shores of which the souls of the many go when they are dead, and after waiting an appointed time, which is to some a longer and to some a shorter time, they are sent back to be born again as animals. The third river passes out between the two, and near the place of outlet pours into a vast region of fire, and forms a lake larger than the Mediterranean Sea, boiling with water and mud; and proceeding muddy and turbid, and winding about the earth, comes, among other places, to the extremities of the Acherusian Lake, but mingles not with the waters of the lake, and after making many coils about the earth plunges into Tartarus at a deeper level. This is that Pyriphlegethon, as the stream is called, which throws up jets of fire in different parts of the earth. The fourth river goes out on the opposite side, and falls first of all into a wild and savage region, which is all of a dark-blue colour, like lapis lazuli; and this is that river which is called the Stygian river, and falls into and forms the Lake Styx, and after falling into the lake and receiving strange powers in the waters, passes under the earth, winding round in the opposite direction, and comes near the Acherusian lake from the opposite side to Pyriphlegethon. And the water of this river too mingles with no other, but flows round in a circle and falls into Tartarus over against Pyriphlegethon; and the name of the river, as the poets say, is Cocytus.

Such is the nature of the other world; and when the dead arrive at the place to which the genius of each severally guides them, first of all, they have sentence passed upon them, as they have lived well and piously or not. And those who appear to have lived neither well nor ill, go to the river Acheron, and embarking in any vessels which they may find, are carried in them to the lake, and there they dwell and are purified of their evil deeds, and having suffered the penalty of the wrongs which they have done to others, they are absolved, and receive the rewards of their good deeds, each of them according to his deserts. But those who appear to be incurable by reason of the greatness of their crimes—who have committed many and terrible deeds of sacrilege, murders foul and violent, or the like—such are hurled into Tartarus which is their suitable destiny, and they never come out. Those again who have committed crimes, which, although great, are not irremediable—who in a moment of anger, for example, have done violence to a father or a mother, and have repented for the remainder of their lives, or, who have taken the life of another under the like extenuating circumstances—these are plunged into Tartarus, the pains of which they are compelled to undergo for a year, but at the end of the year the wave casts them forth—mere homicides by way of Cocytus, parricides and matricides by Pyriphlegethon—and they are borne to the Acherusian lake, and there they lift up their voices and call upon the victims whom they have slain or wronged, to have pity on them, and to be kind to them, and let them come out into the lake. And if they prevail, then they come forth and cease from their troubles; but if not, they are carried back again into Tartarus and from thence into the rivers unceasingly, until they obtain mercy from those whom they have wronged: for that is the sentence inflicted upon them by their judges. Those too who have been pre-eminent for holiness of life are released from this earthly prison, and go to their pure home which is above, and dwell in the purer earth; and of these, such as have duly purified themselves with philosophy live henceforth altogether without the body, in mansions fairer still which may not be described, and of which the time would fail me to tell.

Wherefore, Simmias, seeing all these things, what ought not we to do that we may obtain virtue and wisdom in this life? Fair is the prize, and the hope great!

A man of sense ought not to say, nor will I be very confident, that the description which I have given of the soul and her mansions is exactly true. But I do say that, inasmuch as the soul is shown to be immortal, he may venture to think, not improperly or unworthily, that something of the kind is true. The venture is a glorious one, and he ought to comfort himself with words like these, which is the reason why I lengthen out the tale. Wherefore, I say, let a man be of good cheer about his soul, who having cast away the pleasures and ornaments of the body as alien to him and working harm rather than good, has sought after the pleasures of knowledge; and has arrayed the soul, not in some foreign attire, but in her own proper jewels, temperance, and justice, and courage, and nobility, and truth—in these adorned she is ready to go on her journey to the world below, when her hour comes. You, Simmias and Cebes, and all other men, will depart at some time or other. Me already, as the tragic poet would say, the voice of fate calls. Soon I must drink the poison; and I think that I had better repair to the bath first, in order that the women may not have the trouble of washing my body after I am dead.

When he had done speaking, Crito said: And have you any commands for us, Socrates—anything to say about your children, or any other matter in which we can serve you?

Nothing particular, Crito, he replied: only, as I have always told you, take care of yourselves; that is a service which you may be ever rendering to me and mine and to all of us, whether you promise to do so or not. But if you have no thought for yourselves, and care not to walk according to the rule which I have prescribed for you, not now for the first time, however much you may profess or promise at the moment, it will be of no avail.

We will do our best, said Crito: And in what way shall we bury you?

In any way that you like; but you must get hold of me, and take care that I do not run away from you. Then he turned to us, and added with a smile:—I cannot make Crito believe that I am the same Socrates who have been talking and conducting the argument; he fancies that I am the other Socrates whom he will soon see, a dead body—and he asks, How shall he bury me? And though I have spoken many words in the endeavour to show that when I have drunk the poison I shall leave you and go to the joys of the blessed,—these words of mine, with which I was comforting you and myself, have had, as I perceive, no effect upon Crito. And therefore I want you to be surety for me to him now, as at the trial he was surety to the judges for me: but let the promise be of another sort; for he was surety for me to the judges that I would remain, and you must be my surety to him that I shall not remain, but go away and depart; and then he will suffer less at my death, and not be grieved when he sees my body being burned or buried. I would not have him sorrow at my hard lot, or say at the burial, Thus we lay out Socrates, or, Thus we follow him to the grave or bury him; for false words are not only evil in themselves, but they infect the soul with evil. Be of good cheer, then, my dear Crito, and say that you are burying my body only, and do with that whatever is usual, and what you think best.

When he had spoken these words, he arose and went into a chamber to bathe; Crito followed him and told us to wait. So we remained behind, talking and thinking of the subject of discourse, and also of the greatness of our sorrow; he was like a father of whom we were being bereaved, and we were about to pass the rest of our lives as orphans. When he had taken the bath his children were brought to him—(he had two young sons and an elder one); and the women of his family also came, and he talked to them and gave them a few directions in the presence of Crito; then he dismissed them and returned to us.

Now the hour of sunset was near, for a good deal of time had passed while he was within. When he came out, he sat down with us again after his bath, but not much was said. Soon the jailer, who was the servant of the Eleven, entered and stood by him, saying:—To you, Socrates, whom I know to be the noblest and gentlest and best of all who ever came to this place, I will not impute the angry feelings of other men, who rage and swear at me, when, in obedience to the authorities, I bid them drink the poison—indeed, I am sure that you will not be angry with me; for others, as you are aware, and not I, are to blame. And so fare you well, and try to bear lightly what must needs be—you know my errand. Then bursting into tears he turned away and went out.

Socrates looked at him and said: I return your good wishes, and will do as you bid. Then turning to us, he said, How charming the man is: since I have been in prison he has always been coming to see me, and at times he would talk to me, and was as good to me as could be, and now see how generously he sorrows on my account. We must do as he says, Crito; and therefore let the cup be brought, if the poison is prepared: if not, let the attendant prepare some.

Yet, said Crito, the sun is still upon the hill-tops, and I know that many a one has taken the draught late, and after the announcement has been made to him, he has eaten and drunk, and enjoyed the society of his beloved; do not hurry—there is time enough.

Socrates said: Yes, Crito, and they of whom you speak are right in so acting, for they think that they will be gainers by the delay; but I am right in not following their example, for I do not think that I should gain anything by drinking the poison a little later; I should only be ridiculous in my own eyes for sparing and saving a life which is already forfeit. Please then to do as I say, and not to refuse me.

Crito made a sign to the servant, who was standing by; and he went out, and having been absent for some time, returned with the jailer carrying the cup of poison. Socrates said: You, my good friend, who are experienced in these matters, shall give me directions how I am to proceed. The man answered: You have only to walk about until your legs are heavy, and then to lie down, and the poison will act. At the same time he handed the cup to Socrates, who in the easiest and gentlest manner, without the least fear or change of colour or feature, looking at the man with all his eyes, Echecrates, as his manner was, took the cup and said: What do you say about making a libation out of this cup to any god? May I, or not? The man answered: We only prepare, Socrates, just so much as we deem enough. I understand, he said: but I may and must ask the gods to prosper my journey from this to the other world—even so—and so be it according to my prayer. Then raising the cup to his lips, quite readily and cheerfully he drank off the poison. And hitherto most of us had been able to control our sorrow; but now when we saw him drinking, and saw too that he had finished the draught, we could no longer forbear, and in spite of myself my own tears were flowing fast; so that I covered my face and wept, not for him, but at the thought of my own calamity in having to part from such a friend. Nor was I the first; for Crito, when he found himself unable to restrain his tears, had got up, and I followed; and at that moment, Apollodorus, who had been weeping all the time, broke out in a loud and passionate cry which made cowards of us all. Socrates alone retained his calmness: What is this strange outcry? he said. I sent away the women mainly in order that they might not misbehave in this way, for I have been told that a man should die in peace. Be quiet, then, and have patience. When we heard his words we were ashamed, and refrained our tears; and he walked about until, as he said, his legs began to fail, and then he lay on his back, according to the directions, and the man who gave him the poison now and then looked at his feet and legs; and after a while he pressed his foot hard, and asked him if he could feel; and he said, No; and then his leg, and so upwards and upwards, and showed us that he was cold and stiff. And he felt them himself, and said: When the poison reaches the heart, that will be the end. He was beginning to grow cold about the groin, when he uncovered his face, for he had covered himself up, and said—they were his last words—he said: Crito, I owe a cock to Asclepius; will you remember to pay the debt? The debt shall be paid, said Crito; is there anything else? There was no answer to this question; but in a minute or two a movement was heard, and the attendants uncovered him; his eyes were set, and Crito closed his eyes and mouth.

Such was the end, Echecrates, of our friend; concerning whom I may truly say, that of all the men of his time whom I have known, he was the wisest and justest and best.

THE END